ZERO NIGHT

THE UNTOLD STORY OF WORLD WAR TWO'S MOST DARING GREAT ESCAPE

MARK FELTON

ICON

First published in the UK in 2014 by
Icon Books Ltd, Omnibus Business Centre,
39–41 North Road, London N7 9DP
info@iconbooks.com
www.iconbooks.com

This edition published in the UK in 2015 by Icon Books Ltd

Sold in the UK, Europe and Asia
by Faber & Faber Ltd, Bloomsbury House,
74–77 Great Russell Street,
London WC1B 3DA or their agents

Distributed in the UK, Europe and Asia
by TBS Ltd, TBS Distribution Centre, Colchester Road,
Frating Green, Colchester CO7 7DW

Distributed in Australia and New Zealand
by Allen & Unwin Pty Ltd,
PO Box 8500, 83 Alexander Street,
Crows Nest, NSW 2065

Distributed in South Africa by
Jonathan Ball, Office B4, The District,
41 Sir Lowry Road, Woodstock 7925

Distributed in India by Penguin Books India,
7th Floor, Infinity Tower – C, DLF Cyber City,
Gurgaon 122002, Haryana

ISBN: 978-184831-847-2

Typeset in Adobe Text by Marie Doherty
Printed and bound in the UK by Clays Ltd, St Ives plc

Contents

List of illustrations   vii
About the author   ix
Acknowledgements   xiii
A note on the text   xv
Prologue   xvii

1   Barbed Wire Horizon   1
2   Trial and Error   17
3   The Wire   29
4   Short Circuit   43
5   Diversions   55
6   'Big X'   69
7   Operation Timber   81
8   Practice Makes Perfect   91
9   The Road Less Travelled   107
10   Pack Up Your Troubles   123
11   Fifteen Yards to Freedom   133
12   Zero Night   147
13   'Another British Evacuation'   163
14   A Walk in the Woods   171
15   '*Hände hoch*!'   187
16   The Bitter Road   199
17   Three Blind Mice   213
18   Comet Line   227
19   The Last Frontier   243

Epilogue   255
Maps   263
Bibliography   267
Notes   271
Index   291

List of Illustrations

1. Tom Stallard with fellow Durham Light Infantry officers.
2. POW officers including Rupert Fuller, Maurice Few and Albert Arkwright.
3. Jock Hamilton-Baillie with fellow prisoners.
4. Jock Hamilton-Baillie's identity card from Colditz.
5. MI9 sketch map of Oflag VI-B.
6. Maurice Few's hand-drawn map of Oflag VI-B.
7. One of the ingenious scaling contraptions used in the escape.
8. A further view of the escape contraptions the day after the escape.
9. Andrée De Jongh.
10. Andrée De Jongh and her father Frédéric.
11. Baron Jean Greindl (aka 'Nemo').
12. Jean-François Nothomb (aka 'Franco').
13. Elvire De Greef with her children.
14. Albert Johnson.
15. Rupert Fuller, Henry Coombe-Tennant and Albert Arkwright.
16. Andrée De Jongh, Micheline Ugeux and Elvire De Greef meeting RAF officers whom they helped to escape.

About the author

Mark Felton has written over a dozen books on prisoners of war, Japanese war crimes and Nazi war criminals, and writes regularly for magazines such as *Military History Monthly* and *World War II*. He is the author of *Today is a Good Day to Fight*, an acclaimed history of the American West, *Japan's Gestapo* (named 'Best Book of 2009' by *The Japan Times*), and *The Sea Devils: Operation Struggle and the Last Great Raid of World War Two* (July 2015). After a decade spent working in Shanghai, Dr Felton now lives in Colchester. He is married with one son.

To Fang Fang,
with love

Acknowledgements

I should like to acknowledge the kind assistance of many individuals who have contributed so much of their time, knowledge and in many cases their memories to this project to tell the stories of the Warburg Wire Job escapers. This book could not have been written without them. They are: Major Michael Bond (Tom Stallard's godson); Ben Hamilton-Baillie (Lieutenant Jock Hamilton-Baillie's son); Colonel Richard Cousens, OBE (son of Major Johnnie Cousens); Kenneth Jacob (son of Warburg POW Captain Kenneth Jacob); Kevin Storey, BEM, Durham Light Infantry Museum Curator; Liz Bregazzi, County Archivist, Durham County Record Office; Joanne Penny, Service Personnel and Veterans Agency; Jo-Anne Watts, Liaison Librarian, University Library, Keele University; Sally Richards and Shahera Begum, Imperial War Museum, London; Major Chris Lawton, MBE, Officer-in-Command, The Rifles Office, Durham; Anne Beckwith-Smith; Major Colin Hepburn, Regimental Secretary, The Royal Tank Regiment; Emily Dezurick-Badran, Cambridge University Library; Amanda Tomè, Archivist, Harriet Irving Library, University of New Brunswick; Philip Chinnery, Historian, Ex-Prisoners of War Association; Steven Tagg, Doncaster Museum and Art Gallery; Nina Janz, Bundesarchiv, Abteilung Militärarchiv, Freiburg; Matthew Homyk and Patricia Kahney; and Shirley Felton. A great many thanks to Andrew Lownie, my fantastic agent, whose enthusiasm and encouragement are deeply appreciated, and to my editor Duncan Heath and the excellent team at Icon Books.

Finally, I want to thank my wonderfully accomplished wife Fang Fang for her support, encouragement, advice and love.

A note on the text

Most of the dialogue sequences in this book come directly from the veterans themselves, from written sources, diaries or spoken interviews. I have changed the tense to make it more immediate. Occasionally, where only basic descriptions of what happened exist, I have created small sections of dialogue, attempting to remain true to the characters and to their manners of speech.

Prologue

A shilling coin jangled insistently inside an empty tin can, followed by someone whispering 'Get out, Doug!' in an urgent hiss. Muttering a stream of oaths under his breath, Doug Crawford quickly reversed out of the narrow tunnel, its wet clay walls lit by a single guttering carbide lamp near the tunnel face.

'Doug, hurry up, the Jerries are on their way!' hissed Captain David Fielding, sitting on the wooden floor of the deserted 'silence hut' next to the camp library. The tunnel was almost finished and Crawford had been working on the vertical shaft below the exit hole when the alarm was given. Somehow, the Germans had found out about the tunnel and were racing towards them across the huge camp, hoping to capture the diggers and their escape hole.[1]

Several other members of the digging team crouched by the tunnel entrance, their faces masks of apprehension. By the window one man was 'stooging', acting as a lookout. Beyond the hut several other stooges kept watch for Germans, using prearranged signals. 'They're coming', hissed the stooge by the window. 'Maybe three minutes!' Fielding frantically pulled the long piece of string attached to the rudimentary tin can alarm, his heart racing and his guts in nervous tumult. He yelled down the dark shaft: 'I'm sorry Doug, it's every man for himself!'[2] Seconds later the digging team dispersed into the compound, striding off in different directions to confuse the Germans.

Emerging from the tunnel entrance into the room like a mole coming up for air, Captain Crawford presented a dreadful sight. Dressed incongruously in long white underpants tucked into long socks, a balaclava helmet and a long-sleeved woollen singlet, he was covered in mud from head to toe. But there would be no time to clean up – he had to get out of the hut and back to his accommodation before the German guards arrived, or face a lengthy spell in solitary confinement for his trouble.

A great pile of wet dirt lay on the hut floor, feverishly excavated with homemade tools, tin cups and bare hands. They had been doing what the prisoners called a 'blitz' – a fast breakout limited to a small handful of escapers.

Alexander 'Doug' Crawford of the Royal Australian Artillery caused quite a stir as he and Fielding attempted to stroll nonchalantly through Oflag VI-B after the rest of the diggers had scattered from the silence hut. He looked like he was on his way home from a long day at the coalface, and expected instant arrest. Two Germans came running towards him, and to his horror he saw that one of them was Hauptmann Rademacher, the camp security officer, with a shorter private puffing along behind him, a rifle slung over his shoulder. Crawford tensed, expecting to be staring down the barrel of a Luger in the next few seconds. But, incredibly, the Germans just jogged past on their way to the hut containing the tunnel, not even glancing at the Australian. The prisoners often joked that their captors were single-minded in the extreme, and Crawford's lucky escape seemed to confirm this view. Not keen to push his luck any further, Crawford ducked into the nearest accommodation hut to try to make himself more presentable before slipping back to his own billet.

It was the second 'blitz' tunnel that Crawford, Fielding and their small team had lost to the Germans in the past few weeks. Their first effort had almost reached the perimeter fence. 'The air in the thing was foul', recalled Crawford. 'It was twenty inches base, twenty inches upright, and oval in shape, because we were digging in clay.' When the Germans discovered Crawford's first tunnel 'they filled it in, from the edge of the building out to the wire'. The second effort was an attempt to quickly dig into the loosely filled-in old tunnel, the last thing the Germans expected. It was a perfectly good escape route, so they had decided not to waste it. Crawford and Fielding were under pressure. 'The Escape Committee have agreed that if we get one man out they will give us all a high priority on a future escape',[3] Fielding had told Crawford the night before they began.

Being involved in a big escape attempt was what drove men like Crawford to keep making small and often reckless 'blitz' attempts. It demonstrated to the camp's 'X' Committee, the organisation that controlled all escapes, that they had determination, resourcefulness and, above all, guts. And Crawford, like many men in the camp, was absolutely desperate to be free. It was the dream of such men to earn a place on 'the big show', a mass escape.

Beneath huts and shower blocks throughout Oflag VI-B during the spring of 1942 dozens of tunnels slowly snaked towards the huge perimeter fences, dug by British and Australian officers who had already honed their escaping skills in other camps, young men who for the most part had nothing to do except try to escape. But plans usually came to naught, months of strenuous effort were wasted and successful escapes were practically non-existent. But what Doug Crawford didn't yet realise was that his most recent failed tunnel had earned him a place on an extraordinary new team of men who were dedicated to making the war's first great escape.

Doug was about to become an 'Olympian'.

CHAPTER ONE

Barbed Wire Horizon

However efficient you were, there had to be
that additional and elusive element of luck that
was to favour the very few who 'made it'.

Captain Maurice Few, Royal Sussex Regiment

Columns of dense black smoke puffed into the cold sky as the locomotive, a Nazi eagle embossed on its boiler, hauled a line of cattle cars into Warburg's pretty little station. Lining the platform were dozens of German soldiers bundled up in field-grey greatcoats and side caps, their gloved hands grasping Mauser rifles. Military policemen pulled at the leads of barking Alsatians whose breath plumed in the chilly October air. The wooden cattle car doors were flung back on their runners, the prisoners blinking at the light.

To guttural shouts of '*Aus, Tommis, aus, aus*!' and the occasional rifle butt or pushing hand, the British and Australian prisoners jumped down onto the platform with their kitbags and started to line up. Many were extremely thin, their eyes hollowed by months of near-starvation rations. For almost an hour they stood around smoking, blowing on their freezing hands or stamping their feet while their bad-tempered guards counted and recounted them. Then they were herded into ragged ranks by their sentries, who more than once smashed a rifle butt into the face or head of an obstinate prisoner, and a stiff-backed Wehrmacht officer, clipboard under his arm, bellowed out the order '*Marsch*!' The 3,000-man column of Army and RAF prisoners began to march its way towards the new camp through the flat north German countryside.

*

An hour later the column of prisoners wearily approached the tall wooden gates of Oflag VI-B. Their hearts sank as they viewed the vast enclosure that stretched before them across the treeless plain. Conversation almost ceased – the only sound was thousands of boots pounding the road to prison.

It was late 1941 and most of the British had been prisoners since the Battle of France seventeen months before. They were members of units that had been given the unenviable task of providing a rearguard around the Dunkirk perimeter so that the rest of the ill-fated British Expeditionary Force could get back to England. They had resigned themselves to capture but had fought on, outnumbered and outgunned, until overrun by German tanks and infantry in dozens of short and very bloody engagements. They were men like Major Albert Arkwright of the Royal Scots Fusiliers, a 35-year-old regular soldier with receding blond hair and piercing blue eyes whose life had been saved by his batman taking most of the blast of a German stick grenade that was flung at them on 24 May 1940. Arkwright's batman trudged along behind his officer on the road to Oflag VI-B, his face heavily scarred from the reconstructive surgery that German doctors had performed on his ghastly wounds.

Close by was the handsome, fair-haired Major Tom Stallard, second-in-command of the 1st Battalion, Durham Light Infantry, who had watched his battalion being filleted by German panzers on the Lys river, unable to stop the armoured onslaught as they had been bereft of anti-tank weapons. Those who survived the panzers had attempted to escape across a bridge but had mostly been mown down by German machine guns, shot in the back as they fled.

Born in Bath on 13 May 1904, Stallard was of medium height with a slim, runner's build, and at 37 was already a highly

2

experienced combat officer. After Sherborne and Sandhurst he had been commissioned into the Durhams in 1924. Following security duties in Northern Ireland in 1925–27 he had served in Egypt, where he became an accomplished polo player, before moving on to the infamous Northwest Frontier of India in 1929. Here he saw sporadic action against tribesmen in Waziristan on the Afghan border during the Relief of Datta Khel and the clearing of Islamic fundamentalist fighters from the border town of Makeen (both in present-day Pakistan). In 1937 Stallard, by now battalion adjutant, had witnessed first-hand the brutal Japanese assault on Shanghai when his battalion had been rushed to China to help protect the city's International Settlement. The British troops had been forced to stand by while Japanese forces cold-bloodedly murdered Chinese civilians just a few yards away. Britain was not at war with Japan at the time and the Durhams' sole duty was to protect the British section of the city from Japanese molestation.

Stallard did not take kindly to prison camp life – he was too active, mentally and physically, to accept its dull routine, frustrations and complete lack of objective. Instead, he decided that escaping would be his goal – his one and only aim, to the point where it would become an all-encompassing obsession.[1]

Majors Arkwright and Stallard were already fast friends, having planned escapes together in their previous camp, Oflag VII-C at Laufen. Stallard possessed the quiet authority of a true leader and was one of the most determined escape artists in German captivity. Arkwright had only the highest praise for him, remarking that 'his flair for organisation, resourcefulness, and active mind made him in every sense an ideal leader'.[2] Others described Stallard as 'magnetic', and he was all of those things and more. Stallard's unique ability was to be able to concentrate every faculty he possessed on the single objective of escape. Most of the prisoners were happy to spend an hour or two a day on some long-term tunnelling project even though the chance of success was remote in the extreme. As long as the possibility of success remained they were content, and could spend the rest of their time attending lectures, reading books or listening to music. Stallard was not like this. He attacked his subject with unfaltering devotion and single-mindedness.[3]

Other prisoners marching into Warburg camp were men from the 51st Highland Division, sacrificed in Normandy by Churchill in a futile effort to keep the French Army fighting after Dunkirk. One among them had already made five escapes, and his later contribution to the first 'great escape' from Oflag VI-B was to prove inspirational. Of average height, with brown hair and often seen wearing an impish grin, 23-year-old Lieutenant Jock Hamilton-Baillie was known by his friends simply as 'HB' or alternatively 'The Camp Brain', the latter sobriquet being particularly apt. His last escape had taken him literally to within a stone's throw of Switzerland after he had broken out of a German castle and walked to the Alps. Such failure would have broken the spirits of lesser men, but what HB lacked in luck he more than made up for in pluck and determination. The German commandant at Laufen had been so impressed by HB's daring that instead of punishing him when he was recaptured, he had thrown a dinner in his honour.[4]

Many others, including a large contingent of Australians, had been captured following the German invasion of Crete in 1941 – another monumental foul-up that had necessitated the evacuation by sea of an entire British army. The Australians had had a terrible time of it since capture. They had spent six long weeks in a bug-ridden compound in Salonika, then endured a nightmare cattle-truck journey up into Germany and two months in a repulsive camp at Lübeck before a transfer to Warburg. They had not received any Red Cross food or clothing and a number were suffering from the deficiency disease beriberi, or were underweight. The Senior British Officer (SBO), with the approval of all the other prisoners, would insist that the Australian contingent receive two Red Cross parcels per week instead of the usual one for a one-month period to try to build them up.[5]

Prominent among the antipodean escapers was 28-year-old Captain Doug Crawford, a tall, well-built Australian Rules footballer with a predictably dry sense of humour and a smart military moustache. Other Aussies who were later to play an important role in the Warburg Wire Job included 29-year-old Lieutenant Jack Champ, an inveterate escaper with a cheeky grin, and Captain Rex Baxter, a tall, rangy officer from Melbourne. Baxter had been captured in hospital in Athens in 1941 when the city had been overrun while he was recuperating from a bomb splinter wound.[6]

Marching proudly with a straight back and an appropriately grim expression at the head of the column of POWs was the most senior British officer in German captivity, Major General Victor Fortune, former commander of the 51st Highland Division. Captivity had come hard to a man of Fortune's age, rank and disposition.

Flanking the column every twenty yards was a German soldier, a rifle slung over his right shoulder, leather equipment jangling as he trudged along, eyes darting suspiciously from prisoner to prisoner. The POWs could see the looming guard towers and perimeter fences as they drew level with the main gate, the muzzles of machine guns in the towers covering the lines upon lines of wooden single-storey accommodation huts that stretched off into the distance. Fastened to the fence at regular intervals was a neatly painted white sign, its black lettering chillingly announcing in both German and English:

HALT! LAGERGRENZE!
Bei Überschreiten Des Drahtes
Wird Geschossen

STOP! CAMP BOUNDARY!
P.W. Trying To Cross The Wire
Will Be Shot At!

Before the POWs entered the main camp they marched past a smaller compound close by. What they saw here took away any remaining illusions they may have harboured concerning their enemy. Three filthy-looking men in tan-coloured uniforms lay prostrate on the smaller camp's parade square as several German soldiers mercilessly beat them with pickaxe handles amid much shouting and cursing. 'What on earth?' muttered an astonished Major Stallard, walking at the head of a group of officers from the Durhams. 'Russians, sir', replied a younger officer. 'Looks like the Jerries are using them for heavy labour', added another. British prisoners cursed the Germans up and down the column as they passed the brutal little scene, but they could do nothing for the Soviet soldiers.

Just as Stallard and his group passed through the gates into their own camp a pistol shot cracked out from behind them, making them jump. 'Christ almighty, they've just shot one of the Russians!' shouted an RAF pilot several paces back. A large German NCO holstered his Walther pistol while shouting orders, the body of the Soviet prisoner lying at his feet in an ever-widening pool of blood. He turned and stared challengingly at the passing British, who stared back with equal hatred. Some shook their heads in quiet despair. The response of their Wehrmacht guards was predictable, yelling '*Raus! Raus!*' or '*Schnell!*' as they hurried the British prisoners into the camp as fast as possible, pushing them along with their rifle butts.

An hour later and almost 3,000 prisoners were arranged in neat ranks on the camp's main sports ground facing a small wooden dais. After much counting and more shouting by their guards, the POWs had been given a short speech of welcome from the commandant, Oberst (Colonel) Stürtzkopf. Tall, immaculately turned out, with highly polished leather jackboots, service cap worn at a slightly rakish angle, Stürtzkopf looked every inch the upright Prussian officer. The prisoners would soon learn that their estimation of the man was accurate – he was tough but fair. The man standing next to him, however, was cut from different cloth entirely. Hauptmann (Captain) Rademacher was chief security officer, responsible for preventing escapes and punishing infractions against camp rules. Aged about 50, with grey hair and rather handsome Teutonic features, he was unashamedly theatrical, gesturing wildly as he spoke. The prisoners soon discovered that the man was unhinged. He would often pull his Luger out and wave it around while yelling at them, occasionally loosing off a shot or two into the air. He also owned a beautiful sword that he would wear when he wanted to create an impression.[7] This was unsheathed and brandished with vigour when Rademacher's emotions got the better of him, which was often.

Rademacher was most infamous for his 'bastard' searches, cruel and unnecessary treatment that focused on the prisoners' few personal belongings. Accompanied by two of his henchmen, Rademacher would march into any hut and at first apologise for the inconvenience to the startled prisoners. His personality would soon change. If less contraband was found than he expected, his rage would grow deeper. He would stamp back and forth across the wooden floor, ordering the guards to find the radio and tunnel that he knew must exist, waving his pistol and/or sword about to emphasise his superiority in front of the silent British prisoners.[8]

At the height of his rage Rademacher would order the POWs' belongings to be thrown out of the windows and door, regardless of the weather outside. Soon a tangled mess of blankets, clothing, and personal effects would pile up. Tins of milk and jam from the Red Cross would be tipped over the hut floor and then walked in. Rademacher would often squeeze toothpaste all over the prisoners' bunks. As the prisoners who arrived at Oflag VI-B soon discovered, they could do nothing about Rademacher or his 'bastard' searches – to complain or intervene would have meant instant punishment.[9]

*

Stürtzkopf had the POWs subdivided into five 'battalions', as the Germans termed them, each of roughly 600 men and given its own section of the camp and its own German security officer, though a British POW was also appointed to each battalion as senior officer.

The prisoners had come from four POW camps that the Germans suddenly emptied to create the vast Oflag VI-B at Warburg. Among the thousands of men was a hardcore of escape artists who had already made life very difficult for the Germans in their first camps – men like Stallard, Arkwright and Hamilton-Baillie – and it seemed to many of the POWs that the intention of the Germans in sending them to Warburg was to place all of their bad eggs into one well-guarded basket.

The hardcore escapers were busy quietly comparing notes as they waited on parade, eyes taking in everything, scanning their surroundings for opportunities, kicking the dusty soil with their boots. Tom Stallard chatted with Major Arkwright. 'I say, Tom', said Arkwright, 'what's that for, do you reckon?', indicating with his eyes a long wooden hut set in its own little compound just outside the main gate, strands of barbed wire hammered across its narrow, high windows. 'Cooler', said Stallard, using the POW colloquialism for the solitary confinement punishment block. 'Jolly large', said Arkwright.

'I think they might be expecting plenty of trade', replied Stallard with a grin.

Although it was Oberst Stürtzkopf's primary responsibility to keep the prisoners firmly under lock and key in one of the biggest camps in Germany, he was also a realist. He knew that it was every soldier's duty to attempt to escape, and no matter the camp, escape attempts would occur. It was the German staff's job to minimise the number of attempts and their success rate, and to punish those who were caught.

The camp seemed to stretch for ever, enclosing almost three-quarters of a mile of dusty plain between Paderborn and Kassel in north-western Germany. The perimeter fence was twelve feet high and doubled, meaning that there were two parallel fences with a barbed wire-filled void in between to make climbing it impossible. Floodlights illuminated the fence at night, and sentries patrolled its length or stared down from a dozen wooden watchtowers that were equipped with machine guns and searchlights. A road ran from one end of the camp to the other, passing through heavily guarded gates at each end.

Stallard and his cohorts' eyes soaked up every aspect of the camp's layout and security. But only when they were dismissed from the parade and assigned to their huts did the absolute necessity of escape become clear. The accommodation at Warburg was like nothing they had seen before.

'They must be joking', said Arkwright, as he and fifteen of his colleagues were herded into one of the rooms inside the 29 large huts the Germans had allocated for prisoner accommodation. In other camps only six to eight POWs shared a room. Double bunks lined the walls, straw-filled palliasses giving off an unpleasantly musty smell. Rodent droppings lay beneath the bunks. The windows were grimy, the rooms smelly and the huts generally in a poor condition and extremely draughty.

At Warburg each hut was divided into ten large and four smaller rooms. The large rooms, which measured about twenty feet by twelve feet, each accommodated between twelve and sixteen officers. A few acetylene lamps dimly lit the rooms, for the huts were without electricity.[10] For several months the Germans would lock the prisoners into these stygian sheds from dusk till dawn.

The prisoners soon discovered that Warburg was almost unfit for human habitation. Mice and rats scampered around underneath the bunks at night, or ran across the sleeping forms of the prisoners, leaving their droppings everywhere. The vermin in turn carried fleas that added to the lice that already infested the prisoners' uniforms and sleeping quarters. The British had never experienced such conditions as prisoners, and the medical officers daily expected a serious outbreak of disease. They were not disappointed, as diphtheria soon made an appearance.

Tom Stallard viewed his accommodation with barely concealed revulsion. 'I don't know about you chaps, but I intend to get the hell out of here as soon as I can', he announced, his lip curling in disgust. 'I wouldn't lodge my dog in a place like this.' Added to the prisoners' misery was inadequate heating that made the huts freezing cold during the harsh German winter, cold enough that cases of bronchitis were reported to add to those of diphtheria. There were also no indoor latrines, just stinking earthen ones that required constant emptying.

The British soon worked out why the accommodation was so bad. Lieutenant Colonel H.R. Swinburn, an early and influential member of 'X', the camp Escape Committee, discovered that the camp 'was only a makeshift affair which was supposed to make do for a few months until such time as the war ended in the Germans' favour'.[11] Some officers deluded themselves into believing that so many POWs had been gathered together so that they could be repatriated to Britain. With Hitler's armies stalled outside Moscow by winter 1941, this eventuality looked increasingly unlikely.

To the further horror of the prisoners, the Germans continued to deliberately starve them. Already lean after months of captivity, the prisoners started losing weight by the stone rather than the pound. Meals in October 1941 consisted of hot vegetable soup only once a day with a meagre issue of bread, margarine and jam, amounting to only about 1,000 calories. Fortunately Red Cross parcels were available in large quantities; without these the prisoners would have started dying of starvation.

Sickness spread quickly among the POWs, packed like sardines inside their filthy huts. The Germans provided an infirmary with 84 beds and this was filled to capacity between October and December 1941, 'a bad sign', commented an MI9 intelligence report, 'considering that no sick prisoners of war had been brought into the camp when it opened up'.[12]

*

Meetings between the major escape leaders and a large number of willing volunteers had begun in their vermin-infested accommodation shortly after arrival. Groups were coalescing around certain charismatic and experienced escapers, and the mixing together of four camps' worth of prisoners meant that there was an abundance of talent, many providing fresh ideas and impetus to solving the perennial problem of 'getting out'. The seven-man 'X' Committee had been formed under the leadership of Brigadier H.C.H. Eden (codename 'Big X'), tasked with formally approving each escape plan to prevent any overlapping with other groups and vetoing the more reckless or suicidal ones.

'The soil around here is just about perfect for tunnelling',[13] announced Jock Hamilton-Baillie to a close group of his fellow diggers at one such meeting shortly after arrival. Hamilton-Baillie would be one of the camp's most prominent 'Toasters',[14] POW codename for potential escapers. 'We'll also have little trouble scraping together enough timber to line the tunnel with all these wooden huts to pilfer', he added. 'The Jerries have also dropped the ball by placing some of the huts so close to the wire.' In some places the huts were less than five feet from the perimeter.

'I think that Hager will prove to be a thorn in our side, HB', said Captain M.E. Few, a handsome officer in the mould of a young John F. Kennedy. Although the camp security officer Rademacher was widely despised, there were several other candidates among the German staff for 'most hated jailer'. A strong contender was Leutnant (Second Lieutenant) Hager, a former schoolmaster, one of the battalion commanders, who treated the POWs under him harshly.

Hager seemed to personify everything that the prisoners hated about their captors. Major Arkwright reckoned that the German sentries detested the martinet Hager almost as much as the prisoners did, as he was regularly observed bawling at them on the slightest pretext.[15] Hager became a figure of fear and loathing, a strutting jackbooted Nazi clutching a notebook containing the names, photographs and descriptions of 'problem' prisoners in one gloved hand. His cold eyes and stony expression at the twice-daily roll calls commanded silence; his relentless inspections of the huts in a never-ending hunt for illicit escape equipment were sources of constant stress for the prisoners. Discovery meant a stint in the cooler, where conditions were even more spartan than in the regular camp, and where a man was left alone with his thoughts for days on end on a diet of bread and water.

On 15 January 1942 the Germans suddenly moved General Fortune, Brigadier Eden and 200 of the most senior officers to Oflag IX-A, and Colonel G.W. Kennedy was detailed to take over as Senior British Officer. The leadership of the 'X' Committee was decimated by the sudden move. Eden handed over his role as 'Big X' to a much more junior officer, the respected Major Ken Wylie. The effect of having younger men in charge of escape planning was to inject some much-needed drive and determination into the entire enterprise and the fostering of closer cooperation between the Escape Committee and seasoned escapologists like Major Stallard and Hamilton-Baillie.

At the same time as the senior officers were moved out, morale began to steadily improve as the Germans made efforts to tackle conditions inside the camp. At the end of December 1941 ten new brick accommodation buildings had been completed, easing some of the overcrowding, and by the end of January 1942 the Germans, fearing the outbreak of diseases like typhus, exterminated the fleas and vermin that had plagued the prisoners since their arrival. Food gradually improved too, both in quality and quantity, but the dining halls remained very overcrowded. The sanitary conditions still left much to be desired and the heating and lighting were as inadequate as ever.

The Germans did create an excellent 4,000-volume library, three netball pitches and a cinder football ground so that the POWs could burn off some energy, stave off boredom and divert their attention from escaping. But the changed conditions actually had the opposite effect. With minds and bodies somewhat rejuvenated, the number of little escape attempts by small groups of plucky young officers increased exponentially. A veritable rabbit warren of tunnels soon appeared beneath Oflag VI-B, dug with furious speed by small groups of determined escapers.

*

The tunnels that were dug by the prisoners ranged from very professional operations with electric lights to quite small affairs. Good carpenters and joiners were needed as well as tunnellers to line the tunnels with timber and create concealed entrances. Although dirty, dark and often dangerous work, some of the tunnellers actually enjoyed the process. 'Time spent on the face was not a terrible chore because the pleasure of being completely on one's own, except for one's mate who you handed mud and stones to, in a camp full of thousands of people was unusual',[16] wrote 26-year-old Welsh Guards Captain Hamish Forbes. A tall, elegant man from an aristocratic Scottish family, Forbes would become an inveterate tunnel man at Warburg, as well as involving himself in several other types of escape. The only downside to tunnelling, as far as Forbes was concerned, was too long spent on damp earth, which led to stomach aches and the occasional low-grade infection.[17]

Major Arkwright, Hamilton-Baillie and over 30 other officers had started a major tunnel during the winter of 1941–42. They had broken ground a month after arrival, digging down below one of the accommodation huts located just fifteen yards from the perimeter fence. For nearly five arduous months this tight-knit group worked in shifts, carefully removing the spoil and installing wooden props in the tunnel shaft until it was almost twenty yards long. Getting rid of the dirt led to some ingenious ideas. One was pouches that were worn inside the trousers, pinned at one end. Tunnellers would walk out onto the sports fields, covertly release the pins allowing the earth to run down their legs and over the ground, and then tramp it into the surface of the field. Tons of spoil was also hidden in the roof spaces of huts, particularly the camp theatre. But nature, rather than the Germans, conspired against the tunnellers when late one night in March 1942 the heaviest rainstorm the prisoners had yet seen deluged the camp. The soil that was so easy to dig out became the tunnel's Achilles' heel, soaking up so much rainwater that the tunnel collapsed under its weight.

The frustration felt by the teams was palpable – months of intensive labour completely wasted in the space of a couple of hours. 'Tunnels at that time were rather a sore subject',[18] commented Arkwright with commendable understatement. On the night of the collapse the commander of that evening's digging party was 28-year-old Squadron Leader 'Dim' Strong, a Wellington bomber pilot who had been shot down off the coast of Denmark in September 1941. Once he and his men had dug themselves back out of their ruined, waterlogged tunnel and discovered grinning and armed German soldiers at the entrance, the appropriately named Strong, in a moment of impotent fury, had advanced on the German guards 'with clenched fist and flashing eyes' and received ten days in the cooler for his trouble. Hager had Strong's record card marked 'especially obstinate and arrogant' and he was removed from the camp shortly afterwards. He was part of a group of 50 officers that the Germans deemed 'hard cases and troublemakers'[19] and these men were sent to Stalag Luft III at Sagan in Poland, the future site of the 'Great Escape' in 1944.

Dim Strong's reaction was not unexpected from men who had been starved, forced to live in squalor and then witnessed their hard labour ruined because of the vagaries of the German weather. Smaller tunnelling efforts launched around the same time also invariably failed. 'The German technique in discovering them is, frankly, getting better than our ingenuity at keeping them hidden', said Arkwright at an escape meeting called after the loss of the main tunnel.

'I think the main problem is the number of people we can actually get out of them before Jerry intervenes', said Hamilton-Baillie. 'Really none of the tunnels have been fully successful. A few people, one or two, get out of some, but they break them too close to the wire and are seen quite soon.'[20] The men waiting inside the tunnel would then be captured, and months of work lost. The psychological blow was incalculable to men who had stared with increasing desperation at the barbed wire fences penning them like animals inside the camp. Several were already showing signs of cracking up, becoming what the prisoners termed 'wire happy'. One had nearly been shot dead for climbing into the perimeter wire in a probable suicide attempt.[21]

'"Deep Field" certainly complicates matters', said Stallard, referring to the new German method of capturing tunnellers. Oberst Stürtzkopf had realised that finding a tunnel entrance was extremely difficult, for the prisoners had become adept at concealment. But finding the exit would be straightforward, as the tunnel would break the surface beyond the wire at the moment of escape and prisoners would start emerging and running off. The Germans therefore created a twenty-man unit that was ordered to patrol at night about 50 yards beyond the wire. Once the guards in the towers had pinpointed the tunnel exit, 'Deep Field', as the prisoners christened the German snatch squad, would rapidly descend on the escape point and gather up most of the prisoners. 'We began to realise that the German command were frightened of large escapes, and a lot later we found out that the critical number was twenty', said HB. 'Anything over twenty who got out, it went to the Nazi hierarchy who investigated why this had been allowed and made trouble for the commandant.'[22] Only much later did the tight-knit group of escapers realise that 'Deep Field' presented them with a marvellous opportunity.

'I think we'd better give tunnels a rest for a while', said Stallard bitterly, to the agreement of many of his co-conspirators, with the exception of Hamilton-Baillie, who refused to be dissuaded even when working on other, non-subterranean projects.

Stallard continued: 'I can't go on with this business if I'm going to see tunnel after tunnel discovered. It's a futile waste of time and resources.'

'So we dismissed tunnels', said Arkwright, 'and went on to the second method, which gave us two alternatives: to pass through the entrance gate disguised or concealed in such a way as to hood-wink the sentry, or to cut a hole in the wire fence and make our own exit.'[23] As Arkwright and his team were to discover, finding an alternative to tunnelling was to prove one of the greatest challenges of their captivity. But from the depths of their collective despera-tion would emerge a brilliant idea, a conception so fresh that not even the far-sighted German administration had any contingency against it.

CHAPTER TWO

Trial and Error

*Warburg, an overcrowded hutted camp with nonexistent
sanitation, all mud in winter, all dust and smell in summer.*

Captain Dick Tomes, Royal Warwickshire Regiment

Walking slowly towards the main gate, the German
Unteroffizier (corporal) occasionally turned back and
shouted '*Raus, raus!*' at the group of men following him. Twelve
others dutifully picked up the pace at the corporal's command, eleven workers dressed in slightly shabby civilian clothes
and another armed sentry bringing up the rear. Before them
Oflag VI-B's main gate loomed. In fact it was two gates – an inner
double gate controlled by an armed sentry that adjoined the camp's
inner perimeter fence, then a gap, followed by the main outer gate,
also guarded, creating a rectangular-shaped wire box between the
two portals. A wooden guard tower with machine gun overlooked
the inner gate and beyond it were the guardroom and the punishment cell block.[1]

'Halt!' bellowed the corporal, and his ragtag party stopped
before the inner gate. 'Eleven French orderlies leaving the camp',
he said to the gate guard.

'Pass?' asked the sentry, holding out his hand for the necessary
documentation.

The corporal reached inside his greatcoat pocket and produced
the paperwork.

'Carry on', said the guard, unlocking the wood and wire gate.

The little party trudged through the two sets of gates and started to walk up the main road outside the camp. They had gone perhaps 50 yards when the sentry, bothered by something on the pass, shouted for them to come back.

'What's the problem?' asked the escort corporal.

'Your papers are not in order', said the guard. 'They are missing the duty officer's signature. I can't let you leave.'

'But it will make me late delivering these men', said the corporal, gesturing to the work party behind him.

'I can't help that', said the sentry. 'Leutnant Hager was only down here yesterday and he gave us all a talk about correct documentation. He made it clear that any slackness would earn a soldier a transfer to the Eastern Front.'

'That's Hager', replied the corporal, grimacing. 'All right, I'll have to take them back in and get the duty officer to sign me off.' He turned to the work party. 'About turn ... *Marsch*!' And they shuffled back into the camp. Once out of sight of the main gate the corporal stopped, removed his side cap and turned to the French orderlies.

'Too damned close for comfort, chaps', he said in perfect English.

'I don't know, we thought you handled it beautifully, Stevens', said one of the Frenchmen, who beneath the costume was RAF Squadron Leader 'Bush' Kennedy. The rest of the party agreed with Kennedy's comment.

'Let's get out of these togs before Jerry catches on', said the other German guard, Flying Officer 'Prince' Palmer, unbuttoning his greatcoat.

Kennedy, Palmer and the others had just made a unique escape attempt. But the man who had led them was also unique.

*

Tom Stallard's would not be the only large-scale escape that was put before the Committee. The general disillusionment with tunnelling had forced some officers to become more creative in their escape attempts.[2] Bluff was a well-tested method.

The man who played the German corporal so well was not British at all. Twenty-two-year-old Pilot Officer Peter Stevens had transferred into Oflag VI-B with another RAF officer following a failed escape from Lübeck. He was already an expert evader: the British police had been actively seeking him long before his game of cat-and-mouse with the Wehrmacht. Born Georg Hein in Hannover in 1919 to a wealthy Jewish family, he had been sent to school in England. When war broke out in 1939 all Germans resident in England were supposed to register as 'enemy aliens' and be interned, but, not prepared to accept this fate, Hein assumed the identity of a deceased school friend, Peter Stevens, and enlisted in the RAF. He trained as a bomber pilot and was commissioned in November 1940, despite the fact that he was then the subject of a police manhunt. On his 23rd combat mission over Germany, Stevens had been shot down.

Arriving at Warburg on 12 October 1941, Stevens discovered that he was something of a celebrity. Any officer who had managed to remain free for even a couple of days was lauded by the other prisoners, several of whom pumped him for information about the outside. Every prisoner who escaped and was recaptured underwent a quick interrogation from his own camp Intelligence Officer. 'I' would pass on any relevant information to the Escape Committee for use in future operations.[3]

Promoted to Flying Officer in November, Stevens took part in the audacious bluff that almost succeeded in getting over a dozen men out of Warburg without digging a tunnel or cutting the wire. They would simply walk out of the main gate.

If unmasked by the Germans, Stevens would have been immediately handed over to the dreaded Gestapo and undoubtedly executed as both a traitor and a Jew, so he was playing for much higher stakes than any other prisoner in Warburg.

Camp tailors Dominic Bruce and Peter Tunstall had taken a pair of RAF greatcoats, recut them and then dyed them Wehrmacht field-grey. Stevens and his escape partner 'Prince' Palmer also wore fake black leather belts with silver buckles and leather equipment. They were both armed with imitation Mauser rifles that had been cleverly carved out of solid blocks of wood and then painted. The eleven French orderlies were of course suitably disguised British officers.

*

The camp Escape Committee insisted that the audacious bluff be tried again after a suitable cooling-off period. The uniforms and weapons had been carefully hidden and the Germans were none the wiser. In such a big camp, Germans were coming and going all the time, new guards transferring in as replacements while others left or returned from leave or hospital. Stevens volunteered enthusiastically when given the chance to lead the escape again. The advantage of having a native German in on an escape was incalculable, and in the case of a bluff, language was the most important factor.

On 8 December 1941 Stevens, dressed once more as the German Unteroffizier, marched another party of 'French' orderlies up to the main gate, this time with two fake German privates as escorts. But the fresh guard on the gate became suspicious because he didn't recognise any of the soldiers. Although that was not unusual in itself, he decided to follow his instincts. 'Show me your paybooks', said the guard in an aggressive tone. 'All of you.'

Not having fake paybooks, only a forged gate pass, Stevens, thinking on his feet, quickly replied: 'We've left them in our quarters. Shall we go back and get them?'

'I think you'd better', ordered the guard, eyeing the little group suspiciously. So Stevens, bellowing orders in German, marched the prisoners back into the main camp, but as they tramped through an interior gate the guard decided to fetch some help in identifying Stevens and his two 'German' companions. Perhaps he had noticed that something was not quite right about the uniforms or the weapons. Either way, he followed protocol and raised the alarm, at which point Stevens and his party scattered like hunted rabbits. Unfortunately, Royal Navy pilot Lieutenant C.H. Filmer and Squadron Leader 'Bush' Kennedy were quickly snatched by guards and sent to the cooler.[4] The rest escaped punishment after disappearing into the camp and ditching their disguises but it would be some time before such a bluff, dubbed 'The Coolest Escape of the War',[5] could be attempted again.

Stevens would later play an important part in Stallard's Wire Job scheme, using his language skills to assist the camp's forgery department in the production of identity documents. He also became an accomplished scrounger, chatting to guards and bribing them for vital equipment needed by the escape organisation, such as cameras, film and woodworking tools.

'Escape season' was at an end for 1941, save for the slow tunnelling efforts that continued all year round. The weather was freezing, with deep snowfall. On New Year's Eve the RAF battalion celebrated the coming year with a raucous party fuelled by illicit homemade hooch. The temperature was −25°C and the water pipes froze, forcing the prisoners to collect water for washing in buckets from the one still-functioning tap in the camp. The huts actually shrank during the winter, the thin wooden walls contracting in the cold so that the prisoners could see out between the boards.[6] A bitter wind howled across the open Warburg Plain, making life even more uncomfortable for the prisoners who wandered around bundled up in every item of clothing they owned. In fact, the winter of 1941–42 was the coldest seen in Germany for 40 years.[7]

The New Year brought Hauptmann Rademacher's suspicions to the fore. On 4 March he ordered two recently uncovered tunnels to be blown up with dynamite – the explosions were so great that windows in the nearby huts imploded.[8] Throughout March

Allied air raids increased, with nearby German towns the targets. On the 10th, 12th, 14th and 17th there were night raids, during which the Germans would hastily extinguish the camp's lights as an air raid siren wailed mournfully. The prisoners would lie in their huts listening to the drone of aero engines passing high above them, and if they looked out of their windows in certain directions they could see a glow against the horizon as the bombs did their work. It raised morale, but it also made the Germans more aggressive and unpredictable. On 17 March, just before the fourth air raid, Rademacher claimed that there was a tunnel in Hut 29. He ordered all 150 prisoners out and the rooms dug up. Nothing was found, but the officers had to endure considerable discomfort.

*

9 April 1942 had been a cold day, winter's grip still lingering on the north German plain. Now, the weak sun was starting to fade from the horizon. Stallard, Dick Page, a strongly built officer, and James McDonnell, a fluent German speaker, pretended to hoe and weed a vegetable patch close to the wire. They wore nondescript outfits and blended in well with the usual bustle of activity as prisoners attempted to grow extra food or loitered about outside their huts watching. Stallard and his companions were waiting for a particular event to take place. Close by, watchers had the two nearest guard towers under intense observation. Stallard was watching a POW outside one of the huts, waiting for the signal that the German guards in the towers were both looking away from his position.[9]

Suddenly, the signal was made. Dropping his hoe, Stallard muttered to his two companions and the three men rapidly crossed the path that ran around the inside of the perimeter, stepped over the 'line of death' – a trip wire parallel to the inner fence – and pressed up against the fence itself. No warning shouts followed their movement, and no shots.

A few days before, Stallard had made an interesting discovery.

Looking at the fence, he had noticed how the top section leaned into the camp to prevent anyone climbing it. But this arrangement actually made it impossible for the guards in the adjacent towers to see into the space below the overhang. If someone stood or lay against the inner fence they would be invisible to the guards. Stallard had quickly formulated a plan – he and two companions would dash to cover under the overhang, cut through the inner fence, crawl through the barbed wire coils between the two fences, cut another hole in the outer fence, and then stroll off looking like German civilians going about their usual agricultural tasks outside the perimeter. The escape would have to be launched in broad daylight because during clear days Rademacher did not place any sentries on foot along the perimeter, only sentries in the towers and on the gates. The biggest dangers would be crossing the 'line of death' and dashing to the wire, and walking away from the camp on the other side in full view of the guards.

So far, the plan was working like clockwork. But timing was all-important. They had left the attempt until dusk so that they would be less conspicuous as they walked away, but this meant that it would not be long before the German ground sentries came on duty. A prisoner close by reported to Stallard that the sentries were parading by the German guardroom and were preparing to take up their posts.[10]

Page worked quickly with his homemade wire-cutters and clipped a hole in the inner fence big enough for the three of them to crawl through. Then the three escapers wriggled slowly and carefully through the barbed wire coils, pausing to unhitch each other's clothing if they became snagged. Page then cut another hole in the outer fence. Tugging on homemade cloth caps and pulling out small satchels filled with rations, Page, Stallard and McDonnell struggled through the hole, stood up and began to saunter away through the open fields that surrounded the camp. McDonnell's job, fortunately not required, was to answer any questions from the guard towers in perfect German, to convince them that they were simply locals going about their lawful business.

As Stallard and his companions walked away they all felt an itching between their shoulder blades where they expected a bullet at any minute. But their ruse had been completely successful. The guards had not challenged them, or indeed shown any interest in them at all. Stallard's team was on the run for ten days before recapture, an amazing achievement in itself.[11]

*

Stallard's successful escape was met by considerable German anger. On 10 April Rademacher held the whole camp on a very long parade. It was still unseasonably cold and Rademacher was enjoying himself, watching the prisoners shivering and stamping their feet in the frigid wind. Leutnant Hager refused to dismiss his parade, sending two prisoners to the cooler for impertinence. A sentry walked over to 32-year-old Wing Commander Douglas Bader and casually smashed his rifle butt into the fighter ace's toes. He was extremely surprised when instead of screaming in agony Bader just smiled. Having two false legs could occasionally prove to be an advantage. In response, Hager had Bader sent to the cooler as well.[12]

German efforts to stymie British escapes continued to bring them some successes. On 17 April a tunnel in Hut 21 was discovered. Bader, back on parade, caused a small incident when he upbraided Hager for failing to salute him, a Wing Commander being a considerably higher rank than a mere Second Lieutenant. At a meeting before Oberst Stürtzkopf, Hager was forced to apologise. It was curious that Bader could be hauled off repeatedly to the cooler, yet the Germans were also sticklers for correct military procedure.[13]

*

With the arrival of spring the last snows melted and the air began to warm. This meant one thing for the British – 'escape season' had arrived. Some escapes were completely spur-of-the-moment, and one in particular worked very well. On 13 May 1942, Tom Stallard's 38th birthday, Captain Maurice Few of the Royal Sussex Regiment was loitering around his battalion's parade square just before morning *Appell* (roll call) when a German civilian tractor towing a small trailer entered the camp on some routine maintenance task. German and French labourers often came into the camp – as evidenced by Stevens' attempt to bluff his way out with a dozen fake French forced labourers – many becoming invaluable sources of information for the prisoners. This morning, several prisoners quickly diverted the guards' attention for a few vital seconds while Captain Few hopped into the trailer and secreted himself beneath a large spare wheel and some tools. The tractor was then driven along the road to the main gate and waved through by the guard after a cursory examination.

After about 30 minutes the tractor came to a jerking halt. Few could hear German voices and the sound of train whistles and gingerly popped his head up for a quick peek around. He was outside Warburg station. But, his heart sinking, he also realised that it was impossible to get out of the trailer as German soldiers and civilians were everywhere. Still dressed in his British Army battledress, Few would have been apprehended within seconds of emerging. Cursing his bad luck, he settled back down beneath the wheel and waited.

After a while the tractor driver returned, started the engine and drove away. After another 30 bone-shaking minutes Few heard the tractor slow down, and then the horribly familiar sound of the camp's wooden gates being opened and the driver joking with the sentries. Once it was safe, Few exited the trailer again and disappeared into the nearest hut. But his absence from morning roll call had been noted.

Major Wylie and the Escape Committee agreed that Few should not hand himself over to his battalion security officer, Leutnant Hager, for punishment, but rather that he should become a 'ghost', hiding out in the camp and giving the illusion that his escape had been a success. It would annoy the Germans and lead to large numbers of troops being tied up in scouring the surrounding countryside, train stations and roads looking for him. Hager discovered Few's presence only at the end of August 1942, when Oflag VI-B was being closed down.[14]

*

Few's brief 'escape', Stevens' two failures to bluff his way out, the tunnel failures of the previous few months, and Stallard's own failure convinced the hardened escapers not that getting out of the camp was impossible, but that the methods contrived so far were fundamentally flawed. Bluffing one's way out of the main gate was extremely difficult – there were only so many 'Stevenses' in the camp, men whose grasp of German was sufficiently good to pass the time of day with suspicious gate guards. 'None of us spoke a word of German', said Arkwright of his own close group, 'nor were we possessed of any histrionic ability, and to fool the sentry seemed beyond our powers.'[15] Tunnelling, though continuing at a fevered pace, particularly by officers like Hamilton-Baillie, had been abandoned by some prisoners as too long-winded and too easily prone to discovery, and Captain Few's recent escape was more by luck than design. Stallard's attempt to cut through the wire had worked, but the numbers who could escape like this were extremely limited and it could be done only during daylight when there were no foot sentries walking the perimeter.

On 18 May four British officers, Bruce, Hamilton, Willis and Douglas Bader, were involved in another attempt to simply cut through the perimeter wire using Stallard's method. But they were brought up short when they were spotted by a German sentry, who fired a warning shot at them. Other guards were swiftly upon the scene and all four men were arrested and sent to solitary confinement by Rademacher.

The next night a heavy air raid occurred, followed by another on the 24th against Münster. Two days after that, a tunnel in Hut 20 was discovered; months of hard work down the drain.[16]

Stallard, Arkwright, HB and the senior escaping staff were all frustrated, confounded by the Germans at every turn and increasingly depressed. The overriding emotion they felt was the urge to be free men again.[17] It was an almost consuming desire to be far away from the camp; from wooden walls, semi-starvation, barbed wire, rats and searchlights; from routine, crushing boredom and sudden attacks of homesickness; from an overwhelming feeling of personal redundancy that could be assuaged only by often reckless attempts at escape. The camp was their cage, their barbed wire horizon.

But from the depths of this new and depressing low emerged a fresh and revolutionary idea so simple that they were to kick themselves for not having thought of it sooner.

CHAPTER THREE

The Wire

We can lay our plans, perfect our scheme, and manufacture the necessary apparatus with the minimum of risk of detection.

Major Tom Stallard, Durham Light Infantry

The slim Major Tom Stallard, his fair hair neatly parted and brushed back from his thoughtful face, stood up and cast a commanding eye over the assembled officers. A German had once described Stallard as 'a fine Nordic type'. He was certainly as brave and daring as any Viking chieftain. One of the chief attributes that made him such a formidable leader was his ability to quickly seize the essentials of a plan, assess the acceptable risks involved and determine the organisation. Wearing his khaki service-dress tunic, he smiled, placing his hands behind his back. A captive he may have been, but Stallard never gave off a dejected or defeated air – in fact he looked as though he had just stepped into the officers' mess for a swift whisky and soda at the end of a normal day's regimental duty, instead of into a rather down-at-heel wooden hut in the middle of Germany.

Stallard had called a small and secret meeting of some of the best escape artists at Oflag VI-B with the express purpose of revealing to them his highly unorthodox new plan, before presenting it to the 'X' Committee. For several days before, Stallard had approached various officers whom he knew personally or by reputation, and invited them to join a scheme that he was working up. Stallard, already a legend at Oflag VI-B for his long list of unsuccessful escape attempts at previous camps, had a certain aura about him that soon gained him plenty of adherents. The officers of all ranks and services gathered in one of the accommodation huts, chattering like excited schoolboys looking forward to a field trip with a popular teacher. Stallard stood and brought them to order with a raised hand.

It was night-time and Germans only rarely entered the main camp after dark. Prisoners were no longer routinely locked inside their huts at night; so, as long as careful precautions were taken, the meeting should not attract undue attention as long they kept their activities quiet, low-key and short. Stallard, as a precaution, had posted a handful of trusted lookouts who would warn of any sudden appearance by a German.

'Gentlemen, orthodox thinking has long been that there are three ways of getting out of a prison camp', said Stallard, pausing for effect. 'Under the wire, through the wire, and out the main gate by the employment of a ruse.' A murmur rippled through his small audience. 'One thing I think we can all agree on is that in this camp the first method, tunnelling, is not working at all. The Germans have learned how to find tunnels as fast as we have learned how to dig them.'

'Personally, Tom, I've had my fill of tunnels', piped up Major Albert Arkwright. 'There's nothing new about them.'[1]

'I agree, Arkwright', said Stallard, 'we've tried going under the wire so many times that I think we ought to consider doing something else instead.'

'You mean another attempt to bluff our way through the main gate?' asked a dark-haired captain from the Welsh Guards seated at the back.

'Actually, no', said Stallard. 'I also think that we can discard any notions of cutting through the wire. As most of you know, in April I succeeded in doing so, but the number of men who can be got out in this fashion is too small.' When Stallard spoke he had the habit of slightly tilting his head back and raising his chin, which gave the effect of him looking down his nose at his audience. But although this appeared a rather supercilious mannerism, Stallard never condescended to others and those who knew him did not think him snobbish or superior.[2] His sense of humour and his selflessness towards his fellow prisoners was well known and admired.

'No, Arkwright, what I have in mind is something quite different. In the past, if we were very lucky, we managed to get out, what, one, two, or three chaps before the Huns intervened. Well, I've had enough of half measures – in fact you could say I'm sick and tired of failure.' A fierce look entered Stallard's piercing eyes, a hard, flinty expression that spoke of a burning obsession that was barely under control.

'Most of us have been in the bag since Dunkirk and this place has to be one of the lowest low points since then. Gentlemen, I intend put on a show the like of which the Huns have never seen before. They won't know what hit them', said Stallard, smacking a fist into his open hand for effect. 'And I'm not talking about taking out one, two or three, no ... I'm talking about one, two or three hundred!'

Loud gasps of shock, excitement and disbelief ran through Stallard's audience. No one had ever heard of such an ambitious idea before. 'That's right, chaps, hundreds of men free at a single stroke', said Stallard, seeming to grow an extra couple of inches as he spoke. 'It's never been done before, but I believe that it can be done here, in this dreadful place – a show to make the Germans' heads spin.'

'But how, Tom?' asked Arkwright excitedly. 'How on earth can such a thing be accomplished, especially without tunnelling?'

'The answer, gentlemen, is right before our very eyes every miserable day that we spend in this Nazi Butlin's', said Stallard. The officers exchanged puzzled glances or simply stared blankly at Stallard. 'The wire, gentlemen, the wire.'

'But I thought you said that getting a large number of chaps through the wire was impossible, old boy', pointed out Captain Skelly Ginn, a well-known constructor of tools and gadgets used in numerous escapes, adjusting his black eye patch as he spoke.

'Indeed it is, Skelly', said Stallard, a mischievous look passing over his face like a cloud. 'Indeed it is. But like the birds, we will sprout wings and fly out!'

'By Jove, Stallard, are you putting us on?' blurted out RAF Squadron Leader Morrice, his pipe clenched between his teeth.

'Absolutely not, Morrice. We may not "fly out" in the literal sense, but you "Brylcreem Boys" will be integral to this show', said Stallard jovially, sparking off some good-natured banter between the Army officers and their RAF counterparts. In fact, relations between the Army and the RAF in Oflag VI-B were never particularly good, and would become increasingly rancorous during the planning of the great escape.[3]

'What about the colonials?' said tunnel expert Doug Crawford.

'It will be a nice change for you to have your head above ground, Crawford', replied Stallard, alluding to Captain Crawford's many tunnel blitz escapades over the past year. 'Some of the chaps thought you were trying to escape back to Australia.' Crawford nodded vigorously in agreement.

'They don't call us "diggers" for nothing, mate', said Crawford, to widespread laughter.

'Seriously, chaps, I mean what I say. The wire is our way out', said Stallard. Several officers laughed nervously, perhaps worried that their chief escape artist was showing the first symptoms of going 'wire happy'.

'Don't worry', said Stallard, reading their puzzled expressions. 'I'm not quite ready for the basket-weaving course just yet. Now, some of you chaps may remember Jumbo's scheme to go *over* the wire.'

Major 'Jumbo' Macleod, of the Queen's Own Cameron

Highlanders, sat on the Escape Committee and was never short of ideas, but he had hatched what was, at the time, taken as a rather eccentric notion to 'vault' the wire.

'But Tom, Jumbo's scheme was vetoed on the grounds of practicality', said Arkwright, sitting with his arms folded in the front row.

'True', said Stallard. 'But I for one happen to think that the theory was sound. We just needed to find some way to overcome the wire quickly. That was where Jumbo's scheme fell down.'

For the next half hour Stallard and his audience discussed 'the wire' – the symbol of their captivity, the fences that formed the horizons of their captive existence and the limits of their self-contained little world. Stallard outlined his basic plan – to cross the wire somehow – and asked for suggestions and ideas. They saw the fences every day, yet until this moment perhaps most of them had never considered them to be an aid to escape rather than an impediment.

As the discussion continued behind the shuttered hut windows, outside a searchlight from one of the guard towers swept balefully across the silent camp like an all-seeing eye. As the light completed its sweep it fell briefly upon the huge perimeter fences, light dew twinkling as it dripped from the barbed wire.

*

The prisoners feared the wire, and with good reason. It was not just symbolic of their incarceration; it was also symbolic of death. Get too close and the wire would be the last thing one saw on this earth. Most prisoners stayed away from it as if it carried some deadly disease.

As Stallard knew all too well from his earlier escape attempt, at Oflag VI-B there was not one but two perimeter fences enclosing the muddy camp. Each was eight feet high and they were placed six feet apart. The fence poles were larch logs set in concrete foundations at precise intervals of five yards. The fences themselves consisted of strands of barbed wire at intervals of a foot from ground level to the top of the fence. Between the poles were vertical strands of barbed wire, creating a very strong mesh effect.[4]

The six-foot void between the two fences was filled with a four-foot-high tangled mass of coiled barbed wire, so even if a prisoner managed to cut a hole in the first fence, he would have little chance, without a serious amount of time, to tunnel his way through this viciously sharp tangle. The time issue had prevented Stallard from taking out more than two companions when he had cut the wire in April.

Every 25 yards there was a lamp-post that clearly illuminated the fences at night, and at the top of the fence facing into the camp was a wire apron about a foot tall that leaned in to prevent scaling attempts – not that anyone had yet attempted to climb it. Finally, a trip wire, a single strand two feet six inches high, ran parallel to the inner fence about two yards in from it.[5] If a prisoner stepped over this 'line of death', a sentry could legally shoot him if he ignored the guard's order to halt.

The perimeter fence did not form a perfect rectangle around the camp but instead had several additional angles to encompass extra groups of buildings. At each corner along its length was an eighteen-foot-tall wooden guard tower fitted with a powerful searchlight and a field telephone linked to the German guardhouse. This meant that a guard in a tower could quickly muster help in the event of an escape. Six feet above the perimeter fence were more wires – these carried electricity to the searchlights, telephones and the floodlights.[6]

Each guard tower contained a sentry at all times of the day and night manning a 7.92mm MG34 light machine gun, a very fast-firing belt-fed weapon that could hammer out 900 rounds per minute. Each sentry also carried a rifle. Soldiers armed with 7.92mm Mauser 98K five-shot bolt-action rifles guarded the two entrance gates at either end of the metalled road that ran from one side of the camp to the other.[7]

The German garrison lived in their own compound attached to the main camp. During the hours of darkness, additional sentries were posted outside the perimeter wire whose job was to patrol up and down in the intervals between the guard towers. There was also what the prisoners termed the 'Deep Field', the twenty-man squad of guards who roved around all night well beyond the perimeter. Their job was to fall upon any tunnel that broke the surface outside the wire and sweep up the prisoners as they emerged from the hole. All of this added up to a formidable security apparatus, just as the Germans had designed it. The threat of force was implicit. Cross the 'line of death' and one was fair game for the dozens of heavily armed guards in the towers and on foot around the perimeter.

Since Jumbo Macleod had first suggested going over the wire in January 1942 a lot had changed in the camp from a security standpoint. Stallard was not the only officer who was watching the perimeter. Lieutenant Jock Hamilton-Baillie – 'HB' – had noticed a glaring mistake committed by the Germans that he had passed on with some glee to Stallard. The placing of 'Deep Field' outside the camp perimeter actually hindered effective security. 'If we can get beyond the wire by some means they can't open fire with machine guns and rifles in the dark because they'd be shooting at their own people who are patrolling outside', said HB to Stallard one afternoon as they strolled by the wire. 'I think that we can make definite use of that.'[8]

Macleod may have been the first to consider going over the wire, but 'Big X' and the Escape Committee had rejected it as too impractical and ill-thought-out. Major Arkwright and his best friends, Captains Henry Coombe-Tennant, a Welsh Guards officer and nephew of former prime minister Arthur Balfour, and Rupert Fuller, a Territorial Army officer and peacetime schoolteacher, had been racking their own brains for an alternative to the infernal job of tunnelling when the wire had begun to pique their interest as well.

Instead of cutting through the wire, suggested Fuller, echoing Macleod's idea, why not simply go over it? It was, after all, just a fence, albeit a big and well-defended one, and fences could be climbed. 'Yes, it has some advantages', said Arkwright. 'In the first place I don't think it's been tried before and therefore would be the last thing the Jerries would expect us to do.'[9] But try as they might, Arkwright, Coombe-Tennant and Fuller could not find a solution as to how to cross not one, but two widely separated fences without getting shot in the process.

*

Stallard called another nocturnal meeting a few days later, after he had asked various officers to consider some of the challenges created by his own plan. HB was an early adherent and set about roughing out a design for an apparatus that could be used to scale the fence. By the time of this next meeting HB was well prepared and even more enthusiastic than usual.

Concluding the meeting, during which great progress had been made in preparing the presentation of the plan for the Escape Committee, Stallard said: 'We can lay our plans, perfect our scheme, and manufacture the necessary apparatus with the minimum of risk of detection. It's a scheme which, with proper forethought and due caution, is almost bound to bring us at least to the starting-point. The Huns won't suspect a thing. They will, after all, still be looking for tunnels so I propose that we also continue digging as a backup to the wire job. The Huns will become suspicious if we suddenly cease all escape operations.' Stallard turned to Hamilton-Baillie, who was perched on the edge of his seat with a thoughtful expression on his face. 'Now HB', said Stallard, 'I'd like you to tell us all about the climbing contraption that you've invented.'

'I can do more than that, sir', said HB, grinning from ear to ear. 'I've taken the liberty of knocking up a scale model.' He reached behind his chair and picked up an object that was neatly covered with a grey blanket. HB placed it on the table in the middle of the room and, with a flourish worthy of a stage magician, whipped the blanket away. The assembled officers, murmurs of excitement passing between them, crowded in closer for a better look at HB's furtive labours.

Twenty-three-year-old HB had been born in Carlisle and educated at Clifton and the Royal Military Academy, Woolwich. After the outbreak of war prevented him from going up to Cambridge, HB had been commissioned into the Royal Engineers, where he was one of the brightest young officers. Sent over to France in September 1939, HB's unit was transferred to General Fortune's doomed 51st Highland Division. They had withdrawn with the French Tenth Army to Saint-Valery-en-Caux on the Normandy coast. HB's engineering skills were put to work trying to repair the wrecked port facilities to allow the British division's rescue by the Royal Navy. While employed building anti-tank defences in the town HB was wounded in the legs by shrapnel. Shortly afterwards Saint-Valery-en-Caux surrendered to Erwin Rommel's 7th Panzer Division, and HB found himself unwillingly 'in the bag'.

Because of the wounds to his legs, HB, though an integral part of the escape team for the wire job, would not be going himself.[10] His input would be brilliant nonetheless.

The model consisted of an exact replica of a section of the camp perimeter fences carefully constructed out of wood, papier-mâché and bits of old wire. The detail was extraordinary.

'Right', said HB, rubbing his hands together with glee. 'Here we have the two parallel fences, barbed wire between and electrical power lines above. The problem is how do we get from Point A', indicating with his finger the line of death, 'to Point B', moving to the outside of the perimeter, 'without first going to jail. The answer is', he said, reaching inside his tunic pocket, 'this!' HB pulled out a miniature ladder with a long board clamped to its front.

Warming to his subject, HB continued. 'Now, each wooden

ladder section will be eleven feet long with seven rungs. The top rung protrudes laterally eight inches each side of the two stays of the ladder', said HB, pointing to the miniature ladder that he held in his hand. 'At the top of the ladder on the underneath side two chocks of wood will project about six inches from, and at right angles to, the stays; these will be firmly attached, and their object is to act as claws and fasten on to the top horizontal wire of the fence.'[11] HB hooked the first ladder into place on the model fence.

'Do you think the wires will hold the weight of the ladder and the chaps on it?' asked Captain David Walker, Stallard's second-in-command for the fence job. Thirty-one-year-old Walker had joined The Black Watch, one of Scotland's most distinguished infantry regiments, and served in India and the Sudan, then in Canada as aide-de-camp to the Governor General, Lord Tweedsmuir (the novelist John Buchan). He had married a Canadian, Willa, in July 1939 before returning to the UK to train recruits. Walker had been captured alongside Hamilton-Baillie and the other members of the doomed 51st Highland Division at Saint-Valery.

'I've thought of that, sir. Even if the wire gives way, the claws on the bottom of the ladder will simply sink into the next strand of horizontal wire.[12]

'Now, once the ladder is in place we have a bridge consisting of two pieces of sturdy duckboard nailed together, about eight feet long, and quite heavy as it has to support the weight of the men as they climb across', explained HB, pointing to his miniaturised version. 'The bridge has two runners protruding from each end. One end of the bridge locks in place with the standing ladder, thus. To launch the bridge, one chap goes up the ladder – a second man holds the ladder tight – he pushes the bridge which has long handles on the back to counterbalance it until these notches engage with a bit of wood across the top of the ladder, these two ropes come taut which makes a rigid joint between the ladder and the bridge',[13] said HB, pointing out two pieces of string on the model.

'The bridge has a duckboard top until the far side, then there is a gap and a bar, which I call a "trapeze bar". So you climb the ladder, run across the bridge, grab the trapeze bar, and "hey presto!" swing down and run away.'[14] HB explained that the trapeze bar could be made from a hockey stick handle nailed to the ends of the runners.

'First-class, HB, absolutely first-class', said Stallard, thumping him on the back. Many other officers voiced a similar opinion.

'I can't take all the credit, chaps; this was rather a team effort.' HB had worked in secret with Captain Steve Russell of The Black Watch and Lieutenant George Cruickshank, Gordon Highlanders, to perfect the apparatus, but his had been the original idea.

And what an idea – more than one officer was intrigued as to where HB, who was primarily concerned with tunnels at his previous camp and at Warburg, had gained the inspiration for such an amazing contraption. When he was at Clifton College, HB had been very interested in medieval siege structures, particularly the design and construction of assault ladders to scale castle walls. His studies had provided him with the inspiration for the Warburg scaling apparatus, a brilliant synthesis between historical engineering and the modern challenge of the POW camp.[15]

'How many men to raise this contraption?' Arkwright asked.

'Four', replied HB. 'Two at each end will be needed to carry it from the hut to the wire. The two chaps at the front will quickly raise the ladder and engage the claws in the top strand of wire. We envision that they would then stand on either side of the ladder to steady it. The two at the rear would then swing into action. One grabs the bridge handles and then mounts the ladder, pushing the bridge ahead of him and locking it into place as I've described. His teammate assists as necessary.'

'Although what I've described seems quite straightforward', said HB, his brow furrowing, 'there are a few problems. Firstly, there is the weight of the bridge. It will require quite strenuous effort to heave it into place. Another problem is the light and tele-phone wires running above the perimeter fence; care will have to be taken to avoid snagging the bridge on them in the dark. Also, when the last three men are crossing, with one man on the trapeze bar and two others on the bridge, their weight will inevitably over-balance the entire set-up as no one will be on the ladder. We are working on solutions.'[16]

'One other thing, sir', said HB to Stallard. 'Something like this', pointing at the model apparatus, 'is going to require a lot of wood, nails and rope. I can give you a rough estimate, but the final calcula-tions are dependent on how many men you want to get out.'

'How many could you safely get over one of these contraptions in, say, a minute?' asked Stallard.

'I should say no more than ten, sir', replied HB. 'And then only with considerable training and strong teamwork.'

'I'm planning to take out 250', stated Stallard bluntly. The other officers gasped.

'Why sir, that's 25 contraptions!' said a startled HB. 'Good lord ... I'm going to need to make some calculations and get back to you. I won't say it's impossible at this stage, but you know how keen the Jerries are on keeping us away from wood.' The Germans were well aware of British efforts to scrounge wood for shoring up tun-nels, and took measures to severely limit the stocks available inside the camp for fuel, cooking and general maintenance. Stallard's requirement would be far in excess of the normal demands of a fair-sized tunnel, but as with everything else associated with the operation, the word 'impossible' was not in common usage.

Once the hubbub had died down after Stallard's bombshell, Major Arkwright spoke. 'I think I speak for all of us when I say that this scheme could very well work, Tom. I should add that it's the most daring scheme any of us have ever heard, but if HB's superb demonstration is anything to go by, it's by no means pie-in-the-sky. I know that I've grown heartily sick of enterprises where the risk of detection in the early stages is so high, and where two months' work might be brought to nothing by a false move or a stroke of bad luck.'[17] The assembled officers voiced their agreement as one. The wire job, unlike a tunnel, would give the escapers a great deal of freedom to choose when to mount it.

'I'm gratified by your support, gentlemen', said Stallard, 'but let's not jump the gun. Although we are almost ready to present our little scheme before "Big X" and his Committee, we know that one of the first things they will want to consider are the risks involved. I'm not going to soft-soap you – Jumbo's original scheme was turned down precisely because of those risks. Though HB's team has come up with a work of genius concerning the climbing apparatus, and many of you other chaps have made some sterling suggestions, this job of ours is damned dangerous.' Stallard was not overstating the point. Unlike being inside the relative protection of a tunnel, the escapers would have to clamber over a perimeter fence guarded by armed sentries who had orders to shoot to kill any prisoner who attempted to escape. 'We still face some serious problems that have to be solved', continued Stallard. 'Firstly, we have to find some way to distract the guards from the areas of the fence that we intend to climb. I'm going to ask Johnnie Cousens to take on that job.'

'It will be my pleasure, Tom', said Major Cousens.

Cousens, born in Edinburgh in 1906, had been a long-time friend and colleague of Stallard's since he had joined the same Durhams battalion in 1927, and Stallard had attended his wedding in June 1937. Like Stallard, Cousens had been educated at Sandhurst and was devoted to sport, particularly riding and fishing.[18] Keen horsemen both, they had played polo for the regiment in Egypt and Cousens also rode point-to-point.[19] 'I've already started working up a couple of ideas', added Cousens.

'From now on, Johnnie, you will be "OC Diversions" as it's going to be up to you to control the escape on the night we decide upon', said Stallard, who knew he could trust his friend implicitly. Cousens nodded solemnly.

'Secondly, there's the problem of lighting – the bally fence is lit up like the proverbial Christmas tree at night and that simply won't do. Ideally, we need to find some way to knock out the lights, at least on the stretch of wire that we are going to assault. This was the major stumbling block last time a scheme like this went before "Big X". Lastly, we need to work out if we can scrounge enough material for the ladders. As you know, I favour a really big show, the bigger and bolder the better. We can really only try something like this once, unlike tunnelling, so I say we get out as many warm bodies as possible.'

Stallard stood once again before them, his eyes burning with almost evangelical fervour. 'Imagine 250 of us loose in the German countryside. The Huns will be absolutely knocked for six. Even if only a handful make it home, we'll cause such a stink they'll not forget this camp in a hurry. Thousands of troops will be tied up hunting us down and the diversion of men and resources will be enormous.' Stallard laughed.

'I dare say this little scheme of ours might prove to be the greatest escape of the whole war!'

CHAPTER FOUR

Short Circuit

I take off my hat to those who switched off the lights,
not only for their amazing ingenuity but also because
the fact that they were to carry out this part of the
operation automatically excluded them from taking
a place among those who were hoping to escape.

Major Albert Arkwright, Royal Scots Fusiliers

'Good Lord!' exclaimed Captain Ken Searle, quickly taking hold of his emotions before a guard noticed his astonishment. 'I don't believe it!' he muttered under his breath, tearing his eyes away with great difficulty from the electrical wiring that ran along the top of the camp's perimeter fence. If there was ever a single Eureka moment in planning the first great escape, this was that moment.

Searle, good-looking, dark brown hair neatly parted on the left and brushed back from his serious face, a Ronald Colman moustache making him look a little older than his 27 years, had been taking his usual 'daily constitutional' round the perimeter path that the prisoners had dubbed 'The Circuit'.

The sky was lead-grey, threatening yet more rain. Unusually, today Searle had the path almost to himself, largely because it was slick with the notorious Warburg mud. Searle, an officer in the Royal Army Ordnance Corps (RAOC), was bored and had been amusing himself by tracing the visible portions of the various wiring circuits for the perimeter's floodlights, the guards' searchlights, and the sentry-box telephones.[1]

The RAOC serviced and maintained all of the army's weapons, equipment and vehicles, and highly trained technicians like Captain Searle were worth their weight in gold in the covert world of POW camp escapology.

As Searle expected, all the raised sentry boxes along the perimeter, what the prisoners called 'Goon boxes', shared one common telephone line that led directly back to the main German guardroom located outside the perimeter in the north-east corner of the camp. The phone wires were carried on the same poles as the perimeter floodlights that were positioned about every 25 yards along the full length of the fence. Though not particularly bright, these floodlights were powerful enough to make any direct attempt on the wire at night virtually suicidal.[2]

Searle sauntered along inside No. 4 Battalion's area of the camp, puffing disinterestedly at his pipe and casting furtive glances at the fence through narrowed eyes. The mental exercise was as stimulating as his walk. The guard in the nearest Goon tower paid him little heed. Searle noticed that the electric cables that supplied power to the floodlights, as well as power to the sentry's searchlight in each guard tower, were also suspended from the same floodlighting poles. Electrically, the combined floodlights and searchlights circuit, what Searle later labelled the 'security ring main', was entirely separate from the 'accommodation ring main', which supplied power only for lighting certain huts. This simple arrangement permitted the German guardroom to turn off the hut lighting whenever there was an air raid warning, while leaving their perimeter floodlighting and searchlights fully operational, thereby not compromising their ability to maintain perimeter defences and deter escape attempts.

Searle continued on his stroll, unsurprised to find this arrangement. But then, quite suddenly, he noticed something that was, as he later stated, 'incredibly inept'[3]. Such was his astonishment that for several seconds Searle stood completely still, his pipe threatening to tumble from his open mouth. From the security ring main on one of the floodlighting poles came a major unfused spur line right across all the perimeter defences and straight into the wooden hut that housed the cobbler's workshop and the camp tailor's machines, as well as the barber's shop.

The cobbler's hut was a long, thin, single-storey wooden building in the bottom right-hand corner of No. 4 Battalion's area, just north of the main road that bisected the camp, and parallel to the fence. The Germans viewed the workshop as a kindness, helping the prisoners to keep their uniforms and boots repaired and also giving them the chance for regular haircuts. A small group of British prisoners who in peacetime had practised these trades worked in the hut during the daytime before returning at night to their own accommodation, separate from the officers. Altogether, there were 400 British 'other ranks' prisoners, mostly privates and corporals, in Warburg, acting as batmen to the more senior officers, cooks and mess staff, cleaners, gardeners, repairmen and tradesmen. Many were expert scroungers, due to the nature of their jobs. Many were also possessed of sufficient German to follow the often quite revealing chatter of sentries escorting other ranks' working parties outside the camp. These working parties were usually taken to Warburg village each day, or out to neighbouring farms, thereby frequently acquiring valuable local information.[4]

The cobbler's hut was on the 'British' side of the fence, across the wire from the German quarters. Searle realised the importance of his discovery at once. In the cobbler's hut was an extension of the security ring main that supplied power to the perimeter floodlights and searchlights along the northern side of the camp, and there was clearly no fuse on that extension. Searle suddenly came to his senses. A German sentry in a tower was watching him with growing interest. 'Careful, don't stare', Searle thought to himself. 'Surely I must be mistaken – somewhere I must have missed a cable swapover.' Turning round, Searle nonchalantly strolled back the way he had come, slowly relighting his pipe while scanning the wiring. 'Go through the whole set-up again', he thought, 'every wire – every junction – just keep walking.'[5] The German sentry lost interest and resumed staring into the compound.

'Yes, it's all still as I thought – still the same!' Searle's inner voice silently screamed. 'Yes? ... Yes!! ... YES!!' said the voice, 'no doubt about it – no more uncertainty – that incredible mis-wiring is a fact! – a genuinely re-verifiable FACT!!'[6]

The significance of Searle's chance discovery was not lost on him for a second. He would have to tell someone, and fast. Not being fused, an electrical spur like that offered the prisoners direct access to the main electrical control panel in the German guard-room, or wherever, and that made it possible for the prisoners virtually to control the local perimeter lights at will from within the camp.

Searle, his heart pounding in his chest, walked slowly back to his hut in No. 1 Battalion's area, fighting the urge to break into a run, determined on a course of action. He must present this explosive new information to 'Big X' and the Escape Committee tonight.

*

That evening after supper, Searle met in secret with the Warburg Escape Committee. Its members sat on wooden chairs and benches in one of the huts, smoking and making notes on odd pieces of scrap paper. Once Searle had somewhat excitedly divulged his information before Major Wylie – 'Big X' – he fielded the inevitable questions with the comfortable assurance of an expert in his field.

'Are you sure that this is as simple as it sounds?' asked Wylie, leaning back in his chair. 'I mean, no one here doubts your expert-ise in matters electrical, Searle, but what I find hard to believe is that our jailers could have made such an obvious error.'

'I checked it several times, sir, and the pattern of the wiring doesn't leave any other conclusion. As for making an error, I'd say it was more of a colossal blunder', said Searle, smiling broadly. 'Perhaps we credit our captors with too much Teutonic intelligence, because whomever put in the spur line to the cobbler's hut either didn't know his business, or he didn't care.' Searle thought a friendly hand must have been at work with the installation, which had been done quite evidently under the supervision of guards with no knowledge of electrical circuits. Later, it was suspected that the electrician might have been a civilian forced worker from occupied Europe. There were a number of Poles held for such labour in the neighbourhood.[7]

Searle fielded questions from the Committee patiently, explaining, in layman's terms, the electrical theory and the different ring mains, currents, fuses and so on. 'I'd like to add that our control could be imposed quite unobtrusively at any time we choose', said Searle, a comment that generated a sharp intake of breath from several committee members.

'You mean to say that we can control the perimeter lights?' asked Major Robert Melsome, the camp Intelligence Officer.

'In a nutshell, yes', said Searle. 'The cobbler's workshop is on our side of the wire and would be quite easily accessible at almost any time after dark. From within I believe that I can short the perimeter lights, and most importantly I can do it in such a way that the Jerries will never guess that we are doing it. It will look like a technical malfunction rather than deliberate sabotage.'

'The hut is locked at night so you're going to need a copy of the German guard's key', said Melsome with a slightly mischievous grin. 'It shouldn't pose too much of a problem if handled carefully.'

'Right, gentlemen, any more questions for Searle?' asked Wylie. No one spoke, so Wylie turned back to Searle. 'Can you give us a minute, old chap?' Searle went into another room in the hut where he waited anxiously while the Escape Committee debated his findings, smoking his pipe and pacing up and down the dusty floor. Then the door was opened and Lieutenant Bert

Graham, 1st Lothians and Border Yeomanry, the junior member of the Committee, called him back.

'Well, Searle, the Committee's had a chance to discuss what you've told us and we think that the best way to settle any doubts is for you to lay on a demonstration', said Wylie. 'Could such a demonstration be arranged in such a manner that there is absolutely no risk whatsoever of disclosing your quite remarkable discovery to the Germans?'

'I think so, sir', replied an elated Searle. 'On the old principle that two heads are usually better than one, I'd like to ask for some help.'

'Whom do you have in mind?'

'Ron Moulson', said Searle. 'He's fellow RAOC and a first-class electrics man.' Searle's friend Captain Moulson looked more like a professor than an army officer, with black-framed round glasses, but like Searle he possessed a skill set that very few officers at Warburg had, and Searle needed him.

'What say you?' Wylie asked Melsome.

'Moulson's a stout fellow', said Melsome. 'But I don't want anyone else after him let in on the scheme at this stage. If everything plays out, this revelation will be a dream come true for our escape efforts.'

'Right, Searle, you are cleared to proceed with the demonstration. It's going to be your show, including obtaining the key to the hut', said Wylie. 'Keep us informed of your progress and when the demonstration will be made. In the meantime, anything you require, just ask.'

*

Stealing a key from an armed German sentry in daylight was the first order of business for Searle and Moulson, who was delighted to be let in on the scheme and began detailed planning immediately. Whenever the cobbler's workshop was open for business, an armed German was posted just inside the door, the hut key dangling

tantalisingly from a hook on his black leather belt. It was imperative that the German not realise that the key was missing even for
a second, or the entire scheme would be stillborn. To be caught
stealing from a sentry would have guaranteed the culprit a long stay
in the cooler, not to mention drawn the German security officer's
attention to the question of why a prisoner wanted to steal the key
to that particular hut.

Searle and Moulson were electrical engineers, not pickpockets,
but after some debate they thrashed out a simple plan involving one
of the British orderlies working in the camp. The orderly would
organise a distraction for a few seconds, time enough for Searle to
lift the key from the guard and quickly press it into a tin of 'wax',
leaving an impression of both sides. The 'wax' was really melted
German *ersatz* soap mixed with Red Cross margarine.

On the day of the theft the cobbler's workshop was crowded
with officers waiting to have boots mended, clothes repaired or
their hair trimmed. They were a jolly crowd, laughing and joking
with one another while the German sentry stood by the open door,
a bored expression fixed on his face, fingers hooked into his belt.
The soldier-artisans hammered, stitched and cut, a cacophony of
whirring machine parts and buzzing hair clippers intermingling
with the drone of conversation. It was not an altogether unpleasant
place to hang about in, a hive of activity and purpose.

Searle and Moulson joined the throng, holding pairs of boots
that needed mending, sidling up behind the guard. Searle's batman
ducked in front of the guard. He glanced back at Searle, who gave
the briefest nod of his head. The batman had already arranged a
little distraction with another soldier. They started to argue, raising their voices and pushing each other. The sentry immediately
rushed forward to separate them, and in the resulting scrum as the
POWs pressed forward shouting and whistling, Searle relieved the
German of his key, passing it quickly to Moulson. Turning away,
Moulson, working fast, pressed the long iron key into the 'wax',

taking an impression of both sides, then passed the key back to Searle, who replaced it on the German's belt just as order in the hut was restored. The two engineers, having just committed the first criminal act of their lives, swiftly left the hut, hands still shaking from the adrenalin.

Within a day, Searle and Moulson had in their possession a duplicate key cleverly recut by one of the camp's amateur locksmiths from a substitute key obtained from some unknown and very secret source. The two engineers were now ready to demonstrate their theory.

*

Searle and Moulson would keep the demonstration very simple. They planned to short out the northern perimeter lighting for just five minutes, so that they could confirm precisely which circuits were securely out of action, and then to clear the electrical fault quickly and, most importantly, well before the Germans had any chance of discovering what had gone wrong with their lights. Searle and Moulson also aimed to remove every shred of evidence that might lead any German electricians sent to check the line to suspect that such an inexplicable short-circuit could conceivably have been engineered by their British prisoners.

The two officers set about designing a simple hand-made electrical device to short the mains with. It comprised a pair of arcing horns specially designed so that they could be firmly attached to the two incoming power cables at the main switch feeding the various machine tools in the cobbler's workshop.[8] The arcing horns looked rather like a large capital Y split vertically down its middle stem and then reassembled with an appropriate insulation gap between the two halves.

This arrangement made it easy for Searle and Moulson to short across the two incoming cables by means of a simple heavy-current shorting bar mounted like a T-piece across the end of a long wooden insulating handle. 'Most importantly', said Searle when he explained his design to the Escape Committee a few days later, 'this arcing horn configuration provides us with a reassuring safeguard against the possibility of other significant wiring errors elsewhere in the German portion of the installation.'

'What is it made from?' asked 'Big X'.

'The metal comes from the German loudspeakers that some of the chaps pinched a few months back', replied Moulson, grinning with pleasure. The metal used in the arcing horn had to be a good conductor of electricity. Fortunately, Searle and Moulson had been involved in building ventilation fans for escape tunnels for many months. Quantities of thin insulated wire had been required to make the fans' electrical windings, but such material was almost impossible to source inside the camp. However, one night a small team of prisoners had surreptitiously removed the camp's public address loudspeakers, used to disseminate Nazi propaganda. Excellent copper wire had been scavenged from them. When a German telecommunications team had arrived at the camp to replace the missing loudspeakers, driving a service truck packed with much useful componentry, a group of RAF officers had quickly and unobtrusively rifled it after setting a diversion. This theft resulted in Searle and Moulson obtaining some aluminium rodding that was absolutely ideal for the cobbler's hut job.

'Our principal uncertainty is the likely magnitude of the short-circuit current we can expect', Captain Moulson told the Committee, some of whom were viewing the demonstration like a particularly complex science class. 'If something goes wrong, and we have to open the circuit at full fault current, we want to be sure that we can safely extinguish any resulting electrical arcing before it does any tell-tale damage to the hut or to the local wiring.'

'You mean that you don't want to burn the place down!' said Wylie.

'Whatever happens', said Searle, 'we have to be absolutely

certain that we safely preserve our electrical secret, even if a mishap occurs during the demonstration.' The members of the Escape Committee nodded vigorously. 'In our opinion', Searle continued, holding up the arcing horns he had made, 'these provide the degree of electrical safeguard necessary to preserve the secret, notwithstanding the utterly unpredictable circumstances of the test.'

It was agreed that Searle and Moulson would mount their demonstration the following night.

*

It was now late May, and the air was mild and settled when Searle and Moulson mounted their assault on the cobbler's hut. They wore khaki battledress, black balaclava helmets and gym shoes. Both men had blackened their faces and hands with soot from the stove in their room. They flitted between the darkened huts, working their way as quietly and quickly as they dared towards the cobbler's workshop, both carrying small haversacks on their backs. The perimeter floodlights burned brightly, and the searchlights mounted in the guard towers swung back and forth across the rows of huts. German sentries walked slowly along the perimeter fence or stood chatting to comrades, an occasional laugh or part of a conversation drifting across the still air. Throughout the camp the prisoners slept in their bunks, oblivious to Searle and Moulson's secret mission.

If the two Englishmen were caught interfering with the lights they could expect no mercy from the Germans. Such activity was firmly within the category of 'sabotage', and Searle and Moulson could expect arrest by the Gestapo, heavy interrogation and a likely death by firing squad or transfer to a concentration camp.

Sweating, the two men sprinted up to the cobbler's hut door and pressed their backs against the wood as a searchlight beam illuminated the open ground they had just covered. Panting, their ears straining for any out-of-place noise, the men waited until their heartbeats slowed before Searle reached into his pocket and took out the duplicate key. The door lock gave with a loud metallic click and the door opened smoothly, both men diving into the blackened hut, shutting and locking the door behind them. Searle reached into his haversack and took out a small torch. 'Cover the windows', he whispered to Moulson, who stooped and took out several squares of thick blackout cloth from their backpacks.

Once the windows had been covered, Searle switched on his torch. The main German barracks was only a few dozen yards from the hut on the other side of the wire. They could not afford a single mistake. Scattered throughout the camp was a group of 'watchers', POWs who had volunteered to surreptitiously watch the perimeter and guard towers and record the effects of Searle's demonstration.

The two officers worked quickly. The circuit was shorted and the north of the camp plunged into a stygian darkness broken only by the shouts of German guards. British watchers inside huts close to the guardroom stifled laughter behind their hands as frantic noises emerged from the building, the Germans inside thrown into complete confusion.

All along the perimeter fences, German guards called to each other, straining their eyes to see the wire and the gloomy huts within, while others stared skyward, expecting to hear an air raid siren or aero engines. Inside the cobbler's hut Searle and Moulson kept the arcing horns in place, the electrical current hissing like a cornered snake, Moulson counting off the minutes on his wristwatch. After five minutes they removed the shorting bar. There was no arcing or sparking as they had feared, but the perimeter's lights and the guardroom would remain dark for another 30 minutes until the main fuses could be replaced on the guardroom control panel. Searle and Moulson were happy to discover this delay because it confirmed that the perimeter circuits were indeed protected only by simple fuses and not by some more sophisticated type of circuit-breaker. This was important information that could be used on another occasion.

After removing the shorting bar, Searle and Moulson worked quickly to secure their electrical secret by eliminating every trace of their sabotage activities in the workshop. The arcing horns were carefully removed and the two officers meticulously replaced all the original workshop wiring, sprinkling it with dust that they had collected earlier in a small tin for just such a purpose. After a final and very careful check round, they removed the blackout curtains from the windows and quietly left the hut, locking the door behind them.

Searle's demonstration had proved a resounding success and the Escape Committee was ecstatic. The test's value to Tom Stallard's proposed wire assault was obvious, and when Stallard received details of the test informally from Searle and Moulson, he knew immediately that his idea now had a very good chance of gaining official Escape Committee approval, with their help. The Committee knew that Stallard was working on a plan involving the wire, and it was agreed that ongoing preparatory work for this wire job would, in the light of Searle and Moulson's outstanding demonstration, be accelerated.

Searle and Moulson had opened the door – now it would be up to Stallard and the others to step through it.

CHAPTER FIVE

Diversions

We knew jolly well that the guards had the power to kill,
so one was afraid of them and one kept away from them.

Captain Charles Irwin, Royal Northumberland Fusiliers

A rifle shot cracked the air, the bullet kicking up dirt at the prisoner's feet. 'Don't shoot!' yelled the young British officer, throwing up his arms in panic, '*Nicht schiessen, nicht schiessen!*' From the guard tower the sentry who had fired drew back his rifle bolt, the empty shell case clattering onto the wooden floor. He raised the rifle to his shoulder again and put his iron sights on the prisoner's chest, his finger hovering above the trigger.

The prisoner stood absolutely still, a bead of nervous sweat trickling slowly down his face, while hundreds of others converged on the perimeter fence to watch the show. Pushing through the throng, Leutnant Hager, the former schoolmaster and commander of the prisoner battalion in this sector of Oflag VI-B, yelled at the offending prisoner in heavily accented English. 'It is *verboten* to cross the line of death!' he said angrily, pointing at the single strand of wire about two yards from the main fence. 'Do you understand?'

'I was only collecting my ball, old chap', said the smiling though deathly pale officer, gingerly pointing at a football that had rolled against the main fence. 'Then you ask permission before you cross the wire, or you will be shot!' screamed a red-faced Hager. The prisoners had composed a little ditty concerning this particular security officer that they would often chant during roll call: 'I'm Hager, I'm Hager, the biggest cunt of the lager!'[1]

Pulling out his pocket notebook, Hager ordered: 'Name?' He wrote down the prisoner's name and two German sentries, their rifles slung over their shoulders, grabbed the unfortunate prisoner by both arms and began frog-marching him towards the solitary confinement cells near the guardroom, followed by the catcalls, whistles and applause of his fellow prisoners. Hager, by now extremely angry, shouted at the large throng of prisoners tapping his notebook menacingly with his pencil: 'Get back to your quarters at once or I will punish the entire battalion!'

Earlier that month, on 9 May 1942, an incident had occurred that had hardened Hager's attitude towards his charges considerably. The problem had arisen because of the British habit of deliberately messing up the *Appell* parade, where German sentries took roll call and physically counted every man in each of the five battalions.

When a bad-tempered Hager had finally dismissed the parade at 6.00pm there arose a sudden and extraordinary noise. Three young officers, two of whom would play a large part in Stallard's forthcoming mass escape, marched onto the parade square. The bespectacled 30-year-old Captain The Earl of Hopetoun of the 1st Lothians and Border Yeomanry, whose father, the Marquess of Linlithgow, was the then Viceroy of India, was blowing tunelessly on a trumpet. Hopetoun was 'the life and soul of anything he put his mind to', according to his friend Captain Hamish Forbes. As well as his interest in escaping, Hopetoun was a bookmaker along with Hector Christie, a keen rugby union player capped for the Scotland team,[2] and Brockie Mytton. These three officers would take bets on almost anything, popular wagers being the date of the invasion or the end of the war.[3]

Behind Hopetoun was Lieutenant Phil Pardoe, King's Royal Rifle Corps, who was beating an enormous drum, while behind him came Captain Martin Gilliat making a terrible racket with a large French horn. The idea was to antagonise Hager, and it worked.

Hundreds of prisoners gathered around to watch this impromptu 'musical' performance. Hager, accompanied by a guard who, according to RAF celebrity fighter ace Douglas Bader, 'was only about half the size of his rifle',[4] began chasing the three musicians through the dense crowd of jeering prisoners. Hager caught Charlie Hopetoun and snatched the offending instrument from his lips, then turned to hand the instrument to the diminutive guard while Hopetoun removed his glasses and silently stepped into the surrounding crowd of officers. When Hager turned back to take his name, Hopetoun had disappeared.

Pardoe and Gilliat, hoping to distract Hager, had continued creating a terrific din with their instruments. Hager confronted Pardoe. 'Give me that drum!' shouted the German officer. Pardoe complied, shoving the enormous drum into Hager's outstretched arms, and while the German struggled with the unwieldy instrument, Pardoe also disappeared. Gilliat and his French horn were still going strong, but when Hager marched up to him, Gilliat let the instrument slide to the ground before also merging into the crowd. The throng now numbered over 400 British officers, and they were much amused by the ludicrous sight of the little sentry, a rifle with fixed bayonet slung over one shoulder, trying to carry the trumpet, drum and French horn while Hager strode ahead with his notebook and pencil, but no names.

The crowd continued to grow until the two Germans were surrounded by almost a thousand prisoners, many wandering over from other battalions, jeering, shouting abuse and generally being a nuisance. Hager demanded to see the Senior British Officer, Colonel G.W. Kennedy.

Kennedy, red tabs at the collar of his battledress indicating his rank, pushed his way through the throng. 'I cannot understand why all these British officers are surrounding me', shouted Hager above the noise of the crowd. 'I wish to be alone, Herr Oberst.'

'Perhaps, Herr Leutnant, you might allow me to provide you with a British escort to make you feel safer?'[5] said Kennedy, a reply that brought the house down. A red-faced Hager, the sentry and the musical instruments eventually exited the camp through the nearest gate, to intense cheering from the prisoners.[6] Although the British prisoners had just been letting off steam, the potential for this kind of collective demonstration to turn ugly was not lost on the Germans. There was always the feeling that any such behaviour was probably a diversion for an escape attempt. Incidents of warning shots were fairly regular and Hager's and the other German officers' patience stretched ever thinner. *Appells* had become more serious since Hager's loss of face, and more than one prisoner who answered a guard back had received a rifle butt to the head in response.

*

One of the POWs who had witnessed the little shooting scene at the wire took careful note of the Germans' use of potentially lethal force. Major Johnnie Cousens turned to his small team of dedicated diverters. 'Our guards are not first-class soldiers, but as you've just witnessed, they shouldn't be underestimated', said Cousens, walking away from the fence as the crowd began to be dispersed by yelling German sentries.

The German garrison at Oflag VI-B, apart from Commandant Stürtzkopf and his officers, were largely the scrapings of the Wehrmacht. Although Stürtzkopf and the officers were regular army, the guards were drawn from Landesschützen Bataillon 255, a unit of reserve soldiers. The German Army contained 366 Landesschützen units, but only 86 ever served at the front. Many were soldiers who had been deemed medically unfit for the front line – men with bad eyesight, flat feet or myriad other medical problems. Some were over-age, including several veterans of the First World War. Quite a few were battle invalids, men missing fingers or eyes, or disfigured by bullet and shrapnel wounds or ugly burns. Most just wanted to go home to their families. Guarding prisoners, though not very exciting, was perfectly acceptable to many German soldiers who had been wounded in the frozen hell of Russia or in the deserts of North Africa. The POW scroungers, through an illicit trade in Red Cross chocolate, cigarettes and coffee, easily corrupted most of them. Aside from the German officers, only Feldwebel (Sergeant) Hermann Glemnitz, the senior Luftwaffe NCO in charge of guarding the 600 RAF officers in the camp, was considered completely incorruptible – but he had long experience in many POW camps and was wise to most of the tricks.

But though many of the German guards were not 'first-rate' in the British sense of the expression, they could all hold firearms and had been given permission to use them if necessary. The warning shot fired at the prisoner fetching his ball was not the first occasion when prisoners had witnessed sentries shoot at and even kill inmates. Lost balls were the usual issue that provoked gunfire. 'Have you noticed that any sort of space where we arrange football or cricket pitches is invariably bound on one side by that infernal trip wire?', said Douglas Bader, referring to the 'line of death' during a meeting to discuss diversions. 'The result is that the ball repeatedly goes into the no-man's land between the trip wire and the main fence.'

Bader, a double amputee, had proved extremely useful in diverting the attention of sentries during innumerable escape attempts. He was probably the most famous Briton in the camp, a genuine war hero and a man respected not only by his own side but also by the Germans.

One of Bader's 'party tricks' was to remove both of his false legs and, as Major Albert Arkwright witnessed, he 'amused the sentry for fully five minutes by his antics'.[7] Holding a sentry spellbound for a short time had become the party trick of more than one prisoner at Oflag VI-B, but 'Horrible' Hager was soon wise to these ruses. Hager gave orders to his men that if their suspicions were 'aroused by what appeared to be an entertainment laid on especially for their benefit they must immediately concentrate their attention in any and every direction except that one in which the entertainment was being enacted',[8] recalled Arkwright.

Bader wondered whether the arrangement of recreational facilities so close to the forbidden zone was some sort of sick joke by the Germans. 'I've yet to hear of a Hun commandant who has ever issued an order to the guards not to shoot at our chaps collecting a ball from this "dead" ground', said Bader. 'I've once witnessed with my own eyes a guard ignore a prisoner fetching a ball four or five times and the sixth time he fired at him.'[9] The Germans were also inconsistent. One prisoner who had suffered some kind of mental collapse, gone 'wire happy', 'climbed into the wire, but was not shot',[10] noted Captain Charles Irwin in his journal.

Previous shooting incidents had enraged the prisoners' British sense of fair play. Regarding the episode related by Bader, 'The astonished and incensed prisoners who had been playing the game went across to the guard who had fired and asked him what he thought he was doing that he should have ignored the incident five times and then decided to fire at the sixth', said Bader. 'The guard replied that he had been waiting until he could get a good shot!'[11]

The most recent incident had occurred on 30 April 1942, when a sentry had shot at a British prisoner who had made the mistake of throwing a few packets of Red Cross cigarettes over the wire into the Russian camp. What was going on in there was as bad as at any concentration camp, and deeply shocking to the British. 'They were relics of a much larger group of unfortunates who had walked the hundreds of miles from Moscow',[12] recalled Lieutenant G.P. Bowring of the Soviet prisoners. The young Oxford-educated Bowring, a Territorial Army officer serving in Queen Victoria's Rifles, wrote of the horrors witnessed daily. 'They were in rags, their boots gone and were replaced by bits of cloth from their greatcoats. They were starving and utterly desperate.'[13] The British tried to help the Russians, even making an official representation to Oberst Stürtzkopf demanding that their entire rations be handed over to the Russians as they could make do perfectly well on their Red Cross parcels. The Germans flatly refused. So British soldiers took to throwing packets of food over the wire to the Russians, 'but it was tragic to see them fighting for possession, like voracious animals', recalled Bowring. For Bowring, it was a far cry from the time he had taken lunch with Marlene Dietrich in Paris's finest hotel. Every day the British saw a horse-drawn wagon leave the Russian camp and slowly rumble past their own, piled high with bodies, 'many of which had been cannibalised'.[14]

The German sentry's bullet was not intended to kill the Briton who was throwing cigarettes to the dying Russians, just warn him off. Unfortunately, the bullet ricocheted through the thin wooden walls of the nearest hut and hit Australian prisoner Ken Young in the leg while he was lying on his bunk. This incident highlighted once again the dangerously trigger-happy reflexes of many of the German guards, but more than that, 'We had seen an example of the Germans' ruthless contempt of those human beings who opposed them',[15] said Bowring, who was for ever after haunted by the images of those skeletal Soviet prisoners who were forced to eat their own dead.

*

Stallard had appointed his friend Johnnie Cousens 'OC Diversions'. It was a challenging position. Cousens, his second-in-command Captain Lionel Massey,[16] who was still recovering from serious wounds received on Crete the year before and was unable to attempt an escape himself, and his small team had spent hours pacing around the camp, heads bent in concentration as they worked out the many different parts of the complex diversion scheme. Massey's father was the Canadian High Commissioner to London, and the young officer was the only Canadian in on the wire job.

Stallard had selected the north side of the camp as the site of his proposed escape because Captains Searle and Moulson had perfected knocking out the lights on this section of the perimeter from inside the cobbler's workshop. The exact location of the escape was No. 4 Battalion's area, a rectangle that constituted the north-west corner of the camp. The assault area was the section of wire running along the north side of this rectangle.

Stallard had approached Major Arkwright and his best friend, Captain Rupert Fuller, in May and asked them to work out one very important part of the plan – how to divert the German sentries from the section of wire that was to be assaulted by the escape parties. Arkwright and Fuller 'walked on air' at being taken onto the escape staff and went immediately to work. Throughout the warm days of May, the two officers could be seen around the camp, concentrating on finding a solution to the problem Stallard had set them.

Stallard had given Arkwright and Fuller the four points on the perimeter fence where the assault would take place. The plan was not yet fully worked out, but the appointed night was provisionally set for some time in September when it would be warm and there would be no moon. The escape teams would lie up inside huts close to the north perimeter wire, each carrying a climbing apparatus. Major Cousens would have watchers deployed on either flank beyond the huts and a signaller waiting in another hut on the east side of the escapers' hiding places who could be seen from the cobbler's workshop. Inside the workshop, the electrical crew ready to fuse the lights would lie concealed, one officer watching the signaller. On a signal from Cousens, the lights would be fused and the diversions, which had yet to be worked out, launched before the teams charged the perimeter fence and began escaping.

'They've a sentry tower in the north-west corner over there', said Arkwright, looking along the length of the wire to where a German soldier leaned on his machine gun, watching the camp with an expressionless face, 'then there is the 300-yard stretch of wire to the next tower to the east.' Cousens had provided some detailed information on the guarding routine gathered from his team of illicit watchers. 'The four assault points lie on this stretch of the wire.'

'The Jerries have one sentry on this stretch of wire by day', said the dark-haired and aquiline-nosed Fuller, 'and at night this is increased to three, each of whom covers a third of the distance on his beat.'

'That's close – a sentry every 100 yards', winced Arkwright, lighting a cigarette. For the next hour the two friends strolled, smoked and chatted.

Later that evening, Arkwright sketched out a section of the perimeter fence on a piece of scrap paper and marked the guards' beats onto it.

```
A←—— 100 yards ——→B←—— 100 yards ——→C   – sentries' beats
                    X                     – assault point
.....x.....x.....x.....x.....x.....x.....x.....x.....x.....x   – perimeter fence
xxxxxxxxxxxxxxxxxxxxxxxxxxxxxxxxxxxxxxxxxxxxx   – barbed wire coils
.....x.....x.....x.....x.....x.....x.....x.....x.....x.....x   – perimeter fence
```

'Points A, B, and C indicate the limits of two sentries' beats', said Arkwright. 'I've marked the assault point with an 'X'. So, we have one sentry patrolling between points A and B, and another between B and C.'

'Obviously the moment to carry out the assault is when the two sentries are at A and C respectively', said Fuller, leaning closer to see the diagram by the light of a small candle.

'Yes, but I think that it will be a mistake to attempt to draw these sentries further from the assault point than the limit of their beats', said Arkwright, rubbing his tired eyes. 'If the sentries do their jobs properly they will leave any disturbance outside their own beat to be dealt with by the neighbouring sentries on whose beats they occur.'

'Well, it seems to me that any diversions need to be carried out at points A and C', said Fuller, indicating the two points on the diagram with the stub of a pencil.

'I agree. Also, Tom has said that the assault points are going to be widely separated along the perimeter. As they have to go off simultaneously, I don't think we need to devise different diversions for each point. The same will do for all.'[17]

One of the more obvious problems that Arkwright and Fuller faced was one of timing. If the assaults were to take place at four different points, eight sentries would have to be diverted, and clearly it would be impossible to wait until every one of those sentries was in a favourable position; such an occurrence might never happen. In any case, it would be impossible on a dark night to receive information from widely separated points on the perimeter as to the whereabouts of the various sentries and at the right moment give the necessary instructions to extinguish the lights.[18]

'We will have to cater for the worst possible scenario', said Arkwright. 'That is to say, when the two sentries are standing together chatting here', he pointed with his cigarette, 'at point B.'[19] Stallard had stipulated that the duration of the escape would be just 60 seconds. This was because even though the lights would be extinguished, the guards would probably bring fire to bear in the direction of the inevitable noise made by the assault.[20] This made the successful deployment of diversions doubly important – if it came down to it, the Germans might well open fire at the diversion teams rather than the actual escapers.

Sentries were unpredictable fellows. They strolled about 'in a nonchalant way', often standing for some minutes on the same spot apparently wrapped in thought, or they chatted with neighbouring sentries at the limits of their beats. 'Their only noticeable expression was one of boredom', noted Arkwright, 'and they seldom showed any interest in life except on the arrival of their relief, when their countenances displayed a fleeting glimpse of pleasure, to be replaced almost immediately by the customary Teutonic stolidity and lack of feeling.'[21]

Fuller glanced at the hand-drawn diagram. 'The worst possible situation is that two sentries are chatting and we have to induce them to break off their conversation and move about a hundred yards to investigate something that must be interesting enough to occupy them, say, for a further two and a half minutes.'

'I've been thinking about that', said Arkwright. 'I've had an idea that we should use noise.'

'Noise?' said Fuller, raising his eyebrows.

'Yes, a suitably interesting noise should do it. The sound of someone tampering with the wire ought to engage a guard's interest.'

The next day Arkwright and Fuller were ready to present their idea to Major Cousens and Stallard.

'What about a light?' suggested Cousens, when the topic of lures came up.

'It's a possibility, though I'm inclined to think that light may turn out to be a dubious ally during the escape', said Arkwright. 'After all, the electrical team is going to a lot of trouble extinguishing the perimeter lighting.'[22] Tom Stallard nodded in agreement.

'We think that noise will be the best lure, sir', said Fuller. 'We suggest a grappling iron.'[23] It would be a relatively simple matter to manufacture grappling irons from ordinary camp objects, which, attached to the end of a long rope, could be thrown into the middle of the fence and become firmly embedded in the wire. 'Some sharp tugs on the end of the rope will sound exactly like a somewhat careless body forcing its way through the fence', said Arkwright. 'I feel sure that it could not fail to bring the sentry to the spot.'[24]

'Bravo!' exclaimed a smiling Cousens. 'However, will it keep a sentry's attention for the required time?'

Arkwright explained that he and Fuller had estimated that it would take anything up to 30 seconds for the sentry to arrive at the spot where the grappling hook was embedded in the wire. 'Obviously it will not be sufficient just to keep on tugging at the rope', said Arkwright. 'He might possibly stand rooted to the spot like a terrier at a rat-hole for a further 30 seconds, but however dark it is he will be able to see into the fence and it will be bound to dawn on him eventually that this noise is not what it seemed to be, in fact it is really nothing.'[25] By this point, the escape teams would be charging the wire, and they would also be making noise that could still bring guards to investigate – a potentially fatal situation.

'At this stage, I'm afraid I have to say that Rupert and I have yet to find the answer', said Arkwright. 'We need a little more time and then I think we will crack it.'

'That's quite all right, Arkwright', said Stallard. 'At any rate, you have solved part of the problem and I'm sure that with more thought you chaps will succeed.'

Arkwright and Fuller left the meeting and strolled back to their hut through the busy camp. Dozens of other men walked the perimeter in groups or singly, while many sat outside the huts chatting, playing chess or dozing in the weak sunshine. From the two sports grounds came the sounds of shouting, running feet and occasional bursts of applause as officers worked off some of their pent-up energy playing football or netball. The rhythm of camp life continued, this strange semi-normality, while just below the surface there lurked the conspiracies of men determined against considerable odds not to toe the German line.

On 31 May a massive Allied air raid had devastated the nearby city of Cologne, leaving the German guards in an ugly and increasingly trigger-happy mood.[26] Chief security officer Rademacher and his henchman Hager were even more determined to root out every tunnel in the camp and severely punish all officers involved. But it was good that the Germans were searching for tunnels instead of stiffening their perimeter defences. It at least gave Stallard's scheme a fighting chance.

Both Arkwright and Fuller felt frustrated but they also felt useful, and being surrounded by hundreds of their fellow officers who spent most of their days idling their time away, they felt they were standing apart from the herd, following their own course, wherever that may have led. The fence had become the focus of all their energies and their desires, the final barrier to freedom.

Two and a half minutes of diversion didn't sound like very long, but on this operation every single minute would feel like an hour. An awful lot could go terribly awry in 150 seconds – it was, to put it plainly, the margin between the success and failure of the entire enterprise. With this burden on their consciences, Arkwright and Fuller did not get very much sleep that night or for several nights afterwards until they had cracked it. But their persistence would lead to another breakthrough and take Stallard and the others that much closer to home.

CHAPTER SIX

'Big X'

*Stallard bore the responsibility of security during all
the training and it was due to his sound planning sense,
his meticulous attention to detail and his avoidance of
un-practised heroics that the scheme was a success.*

Captain David Walker, The Black Watch

The eight members of the Warburg Escape Committee sat with largely impassive expressions on their faces as Stallard and his small team began to outline their plan to cross the perimeter fences.

The Committee's chairman, Major Ken Wylie, had been elected to the position following the transfer of the previous incumbent, the 51st Highland Division's artillery commander Brigadier Eden, and most of the senior British officers to another camp in January 1942. The disappearance of the old 'war horses', as some of the younger officers had dubbed the brigadiers and colonels, had opened up the field for younger men to take a more active role in planning escapes. Wylie's arm of service, the Royal Engineers, meant that he was ideally suited to quickly grasping the more technical aspects of escaping, particularly tunnelling and Stallard's new escalade scheme. But everyone knew that Wylie, though a pleasant and well-liked officer, was a hard taskmaster and was going to be difficult to impress.[1]

Stallard needed Wylie's permission before he could progress his wire scheme any further. The Escape Committee and the wider 'X' Organisation behind it were critical components of prison camp life. Men like Wylie were generally appointed by the Senior British Officer in a prison camp, but at Oflag VI-B Major General Victor Fortune had not acted in this capacity, passing the job to a deputy, Brigadier Nigel Somerset. His successor, Colonel G.W. Kennedy, played virtually no direct part in the approval of escape attempts either. Prisoner committees appointed by the SBO were in charge of education courses, the distribution of Red Cross food and clothing, books, sports, theatrical shows and all other camp activities, even down to the arrangement of showers.

The codename 'Big X' and the 'X' Organisation were generic terms used throughout the British prison camps. As 'Big X', Wiley presided over five members who were each selected to represent one of the five battalions in the camp – four Army and one RAF. All department heads appointed and selected their personal staff.

*

The seventh person who sat with the Escape Committee was *ex officio*, 36-year-old Captain Robert Melsome, who was codenamed 'I' and acted as camp Intelligence and Security Officer. Melsome was critical to the success or failure of most schemes, and he controlled a large group of stooges and lookouts who, through complex and covert means of communication, could warn escapers of the approach of German guards. It was always to be remembered that behind every potential escaper there were sometimes dozens of men acting in supporting capacities. And for every escape attempt that was made, the Escape Committee had already considered and rejected at least a dozen other schemes.

Before the war, Melsome had been a rising star of English county cricket. Born in Christchurch in 1906, he played for Gloucestershire from 1925, the same year that he was commissioned into the Northamptonshire Regiment. His cricket career had taken him abroad, and he had played in Egypt and Shanghai. Melsome's final first-class match was for the Army against Oxford

University in June 1938. Promoted to Captain in 1940, Melsome had been captured during the Dunkirk retreat alongside most of the officers inside Oflag VI-B, but unlike his peers he was deeply involved in secret and highly dangerous communications with the War Office and MI9 in London, work so sensitive that if the Germans had discovered what he was doing he would have been arrested and probably executed by the Gestapo. MI9 was a section of Military Intelligence that aided resistance organisations in occupied Europe and helped Allied POWs to escape.

It seems almost impossible, but Melsome actually had direct communications with London at a time when mail, outgoing and incoming, was severely censored by the Germans. He achieved this through an ingenious method. Inside the German *Kommandantur* (camp headquarters) there was a small team of ten women soldiers who read every letter the prisoners sent or received and censored them to a very high standard. The women were divided into small sections, and each section dealt with the mail of one of the camp's POW battalions, so they quickly came to know particular writers from their style and to build up intelligence files on prisoners for the German field security police and the Gestapo.

Melsome was communicating with London via code-letter mail. In October 1941 the previous Intelligence Officer, Lieutenant Colonel H.R. Swinburn, had organised the code-letter mail until he was transferred out of the camp in January 1942 with most of the other senior officers. He had provided the War Office in London, through a coded letter, with a list of eight code-letter writers from among the POWs. When Melsome took over as 'I' he recruited additional writers from among the prisoners. All messages received and sent from the camp went through Melsome's hands. The number of officers involved under Swinburn and Melsome totalled 55, with 275 coded letters reaching the War Office, and 162 received in the camp from MI9.[2] In this manner, the British were able to pass on details of their escape attempts to London, as well as details of the

German administration of the camp, war crimes (one coded letter from Major W. Radford gave the names of a particular family living at Syngem near Ghent, Belgium, who hid three RAF officers for three weeks and who were betrayed and severely punished by the Gestapo),[3] treatment of POWs, the disposition of local German military units, the effects of Allied bombing, German morale and so on. This intelligence would come from a variety of different sources. Newly arrived POWs were carefully questioned by 'I' as they might have gleaned information on their way to Warburg, or had information from previous camps that to their knowledge had not been passed on. Some prisoners would chat with German sentries, hoping to glean tidbits of information from them. German civilian workers inside the camp were another excellent source of raw intelligence, particularly labourers and laundrymen. British other ranks employed in the German messes and kitchens frequently overheard interesting things as well.

British aircrew losses in raids over Germany were reported to London. Wing Commander J.R. Kayll and Pilot Officer Brockway sent coded letters on this important subject. Prior to missions over enemy territory, the RAF instructed officers in the use of code-letters, so they were able to send their names back to MI9 together with the type of code they were using and the address of the recipient of the letter. In this way the number of registered code-letter writers increased and they were listed accordingly.[4]

Captain Melsome also had a radio receiver that was smuggled into the camp in October 1941. This allowed the prisoners access to regular BBC broadcasts, so they could monitor the progress of the war against Germany. They could also pick up coded Morse messages sent from MI9. Not one code-letter writer was ever discovered by the Germans, demonstrating the efficacy of Captain Melsome's security arrangements. Most prisoners were aware that their leaders had regular contact with London, and this fact helped to keep up morale in the camp.[5]

The 'X' Organisation had, in addition to code-letter writers and stooges, a small mapping staff that dealt with maps and 'gadgets', and they took the codename 'Q' for 'Quartermaster'. Each POW battalion had a 'Q' section as well.[6] Escape materials were desperately needed and MI9 was able to smuggle certain high-value items into the camp, most notably wire cutters, maps, compasses and dyes. Unfortunately, the first maps received from MI9 were too small in scale and therefore difficult for the forgers to reproduce, high ground and woods not being marked. But later the type of map sent was excellent and was considered to be of great value. They were hidden in board games, tobacco tins, false-bottomed tins and a variety of other ingenious ways. Maps showing routes across frontiers were in great demand. Unfortunately, by the time the prisoners at Warburg actually received this information from London it was usually out of date and of doubtful value.

The officer responsible for identifying parcels that may have contained escape materials was Lieutenant C.B. Gilroy of The Black Watch. Gilroy was 'Parcels Officer' and worked with a small staff under German supervision. All books, games and so on were always taken out of the camp and examined closely by the Germans if they were suspected of containing escape equipment. Gilroy and his staff were, unbeknown to the Germans, part of Captain Melsome's 'X' Organisation, and it was Gilroy's responsibility to identify any 'phoney' packages and deliver them to the Organisation. After several months of handling parcels Gilroy and his staff were experts at distinguishing between genuine parcels containing no secret matter and those that did. Often, Gilroy was not warned by a previously delivered coded letter that a particular 'phoney' parcel would be coming, but he and his staff had developed almost a sixth sense due to long practice. Any parcels suspected by Gilroy and his men were placed to one side for further investigation when circumstances allowed by the private parcels officer, who was not always under direct German supervision. Gilroy would later smuggle out of the parcels office, in boxes with false bottoms and waste paper sacks, some escape items that he had discovered. Games, tobacco tins and the like that contained escape equipment were sent to the addressee just like an ordinary parcel and the contents later removed and hidden inside their huts.[7] In this manner, the Escape Committee soon had a veritable library of maps detailing Germany and the surrounding countries, as well as a supply of tiny compasses for navigation.

*

Forging was one of the most valuable skills in a prison camp. The most talented of the forgers at Warburg was an English artist and RAF officer, Flight Lieutenant Gilbert 'Tim' Walenn. He headed the forging department, known by the prisoners as 'Thomas Cook' or 'Dean and Dawson' after two famous British travel agencies. Documents were stolen or 'borrowed' from German guards and faithfully reproduced by Walenn and his small team of experts. Some guards were bribed with Red Cross chocolate or cigarettes to acquire cameras, film, radio parts, and even woodworking tools. The scroungers often used blackmail. Walenn was later the basis for Donald Pleasence's character in *The Great Escape*. Unfortunately, Walenn, who took part in the real Great Escape from Stalag Luft III in 1944, was among the 50 RAF prisoners shot on Hitler's direct order.

The Germans, with their love of order and administration, made sure that the forgery department was kept very busy. German prison camp papers included the *Dienstausweise* (a brown card printed on buckram, giving permission to be on Wehrmacht property), *Urlaubscheine* (a yellow form used as a leave-chit for foreign workers), *Rückkehrscheine* (a pink form for foreign workers returning home), *Kennkarte* (a light grey general identity card), *Sichtvermark* (visa), *Ausweise* (pass) and *Vorlaufweise* (temporary pass). Many of these were as complex as banknotes and required weeks of work to reproduce.

*

As Peter Stevens' two escape attempts in December 1941 had so ably demonstrated, cooperation with the Escape Committee and 'X' Organisation was vital to any real chance of success. It was important that prisoners obeyed the decisions of the Escape Committee, for several reasons. Firstly, the Committee ensured that no two similar schemes were launched at the same time. Secondly, if approved, the Escape Committee could direct its resources – such as tailors, carpenters, diggers, forgers and engineers – towards an escape, increasing its chances dramatically. By contrast, a small group of officers trying to do everything themselves would likely get caught red-handed by the Germans. Thirdly, and most important-antly from Wylie's point of view, was the prevention of what became known as 'suicide jobs' – plans that were so risky as to be virtually a death sentence. Unfortunately for Stallard, his escalade plan hovered close to this category – though all that would change when Hamilton-Baillie was unleashed upon the Committee with his little model.

*

The reaction of the Escape Committee to Hamilton-Baillie's dem-onstration was less enthusiastic than among his own little band of escapers. Wylie praised the idea and the design, though he had reservations on a number of issues.

'How many of these contraptions are you planning to build, Tom?' asked Wylie, his inquisitive blue eyes boring into Stallard's. Since the secret meetings to discuss the climbing structures Stallard had slightly reduced, on HB's advice, the number of apparatuses and the number of men that he intended to take out, but it would still represent the biggest mass escape thus far attempted from a

POW camp. Already, moves were afoot to recruit suitable men to the enterprise. An initial draft of sixteen would be trained on the first apparatus, and then each in turn would lead nine other men as team leader.

'Sixteen', replied Stallard. One of Wylie's eyebrows raised slightly but he said nothing, just jotted something down on a piece of paper on the table in front of him.

'And how many men are you planning to take out over these ... er, these apparatuses of yours, sir?' asked one of the battalion representatives, Captain Patrick Campbell-Preston, who was also one of the busiest code-letter writers in the camp.

'I'm planning on taking out 160, ten men to a ladder', said Stallard, staring at Campbell-Preston, his face set in a determined expression.

Stallard was always direct with people, and he always said exactly what he thought in a clear and concise manner.[8] His eyes seemed almost to dare the Committee to turn his scheme down. The Committee members did not appear overly fazed by the numbers of men Stallard wanted to take out, but they did make a few quiet comments among themselves.

Turning to Hamilton-Baillie, Wylie asked in a measured and friendly tone: 'Tell me, HB, how much wood is required to construct one of your climbing apparatuses?'

'Well, sir, the ladder is eleven feet long, and the stays of the ladder are made from two planks nailed together, as a single plank won't be strong enough. The bridge is fourteen feet long, and again of double thickness. The decking will be about twenty feet, so my calculations suggest a total of, say, 130 feet of timber for each apparatus.'[9]

'So, for sixteen contraptions that's ...', said Campbell-Preston, sketching on a piece of paper.

'About 2,000 feet of timber, sir', replied HB.

'You mentioned nails and rope?' said one of the battalion representatives, Australian Major Ian Bessel-Browne.

'We will need about one hundred nails and twelve feet of strong rope for each apparatus', said HB.[10]

'I don't meant to be unduly negative, Tom, but can you lay your hands on that amount of wood, nails and rope? Particularly in light of the amount of tunnelling operations we currently have on', asked Wylie, his brow furrowed.

It was a fair point, and one that Stallard had difficulty answering. However, the other facets of his plan appeared sound enough. The Committee was impressed by the fact that the German 'Deep Field', the twenty-man unit of guards that roved around outside the perimeter at night, would prevent the Germans from bringing their overwhelming firepower to bear on the escapers through fear of hitting their own men. That was a definite advantage to help sell the scheme. It was also evident that the British ability to turn off the lights on the proposed escape sector was a brilliant coup that would help the plan immeasurably.

Stallard's team was excused while Wylie and the other Committee members discussed all that they had heard and seen. After a while, Stallard and the others were invited back into the room to face the Committee's decision.

'Overall, Tom, we think that this plan of yours has great potential', said a smiling Wylie. 'There are, however, some concerns that need to be addressed before you will receive the Committee's complete blessing. Firstly, our primary concern is not to needlessly endanger our chaps' lives. The numbers that you mention taking part in the escape could be construed as a little reckless. One hundred and sixty in our opinion is just asking for trouble from the Germans. We also think that constructing sixteen climbing contraptions will be extremely difficult, and might have a detrimental effect on tunnelling operations.' Wylie paused and glanced down at his notes.

'So, Tom, we do have one important caveat before we give you the go-ahead', continued Wylie. 'You have our provisional approval, and we will be throwing the whole weight of the "X" Organisation behind you. But final permission to make the attempt is provisional on you demonstrating to us one of these contraptions in reality. We would like to see an entire team of ten men go over a full-size apparatus within the time limit that you have outlined. Do you think that's possible?'[11]

Although Stallard had absolutely no idea how such a thing could be accomplished, he swiftly realised that the details could be worked out later, and he agreed to Wylie's request.

'By the way, Tom, what name are you giving to your scheme?' asked Melsome.

'Olympia', said Stallard, 'Operation Olympia.'

'May I ask why you chose that name?' said Wylie.

'Because, like the Olympic Games, this will be an international affair involving chaps from right across the three services and the Commonwealth', said Stallard.

'Well, let's just hope you blokes win gold at the high jump', remarked Captain Bessel-Browne drily.

*

Stallard and his men left the hut and stood outside for a moment. The sun was starting to go down and the sky was taking on a slightly orange hue. The wind of the last few days had dropped, but still the air was scented with the faint odour of the open latrines and the turned earth from the fields that surrounded the camp.

'David', said Stallard, turning to Captain Walker, his second-in-command, 'I want you to find somewhere where we can set up one of HB's contraptions and start training. We also need to start thinking about obtaining the wood for the apparatuses. It's obviously going to have to come from one of the huts, but which one?'

'Okay, Tom', replied Walker. 'Some of the chaps have made some interesting suggestions and I'm going to have a look around over the next few days.'

'Johnnie', said Stallard, resting his hand on Major Cousens' shoulder, 'I need the final diversion scheme as soon as possible. If we are really going to sell this to "Big X", I need our plan to be completely watertight.' Cousens nodded and lit a cigarette, cupping his hands around the match.

Stallard's eyes settled on the perimeter fence. For a moment he seemed to drift away from his companions into a world of his own. The others watched him, expecting him to speak, but Stallard said nothing. He turned, muttered 'Gentlemen, goodnight', and strode purposefully away towards his hut, softly whistling the Durhams' regimental march, 'The Old 68th'. His companions all knew the responsibility that he felt for holding so many lives in his hands. But if Stallard had any doubts about the plan, or harboured any fears, he never revealed them to his comrades.

CHAPTER SEVEN

Operation Timber

The concentration of all British officers at VI-B
was of course the greatest bit of luck.

Lieutenant Colonel H.R. Swinburn,
1st Lothians and Border Yeomanry

Major Arkwright's eyes never left the lookout who was standing a hundred yards away in the lee of another hut. The man suddenly placed his pipe in his mouth, the signal that the coast was clear. Arkwright turned and tugged his right earlobe twice, his own signal to the next lookout, then saw a small group of prisoners walking quickly towards him from a hut near the vegetable plots. Several carried tools stuffed into their belts and two of them hauled wooden stepladders over their shoulders. Arkwright averted his gaze and settled back to staring at the pipe-smoking lookout – if he removed the pipe from his mouth that meant that Germans were on their way.

Out of sight of Arkwright – who was part of an elaborate lookout operation involving more than a dozen stooges who each had a gate or guard tower under observation – one prisoner sprinted up to the locked doors of Dining Hut No. 2. Working fast, he picked the lock in a few seconds and flung open the large double doors. Breaking cover from the nearest hut, the two men carrying stepladders dashed inside while several more gathered by the doorway, peering into the room. Suddenly, the calm of the camp was interrupted by an almighty cacophony of hammering, crashing and loud

81

thumps. It sounded as though a major construction project was in full swing, but the prisoners at Oflag VI-B were engaged in a highly organised smash-and-grab raid, led once again by the irrepressible Tom Stallard. While most of the German staff were having their dinner, Stallard and his men were stealing the precious wood needed for Hamilton-Baillie's scaling apparatuses. And, as with most things that Stallard attempted, the raid was being performed in spectacular fashion.

*

As Hamilton-Baillie had told both Stallard and the Escape Committee, constructing sixteen scaling apparatuses would require around 2,000 feet of timber, not to mention hundreds of nails and a considerable amount of rope. The Germans kept a jealous eye on any form of escape material. Hauptmann Rademacher and his staff knew that the prisoners used timber as revetments for their tunnels. Rope was an extremely valuable commodity. To counter escape activities Rademacher, Hager and the other German security officers organised frequent searches of the camp. But, as with many other aspects of Oflag VI-B, the Germans had inadvertently made life difficult for themselves. The camp was far too big for the German staff to search everywhere simultaneously, so Rademacher and his guards could only organise snap raids on a hut or two every so often.

The Germans relied to a very great extent upon guards whom the prisoners disparagingly labelled 'ferrets', whose job was to seek out tunnels. They would do this by carefully looking for signs of soil disturbance or the disposal of dirt. They also spent a large amount of time on their hands and knees, sniffing the air like bloodhounds, trying to detect foul air being vented from tunnels. When prisoners took to coupling their air vents to the hut chimneys, the ferrets spent a lot of time examining those as well.[1] It was rather hit-and-miss because the British had become masters at disguising tunnel entrances, but nevertheless the Germans still managed to discover most of the diggings.

Since the beginning of 1942, Rademacher's men had dynamited a tunnel on 4 March,[2] blasted another in Hut 29 on 31 March,[3] and uncovered a third tunnel in Hut 21 on 17 April[4] and a fourth in Hut 20 on 26 May.[5] This gives some indication of the number of tunnels begun by the prisoners, and the Germans' success rate in discovering them. During the eleven months that British prisoners occupied Oflag VI-B they began 77 tunnels. Only twelve successfully broke outside the wire, while the Germans discovered all of the remainder.[6]

Nonetheless, an opportunity had presented itself to Stallard when the Germans had suspected that a tunnel had been started in one of the two POW dining halls during the winter of 1941–42. Rademacher had led a thorough raid that had included tearing up most of the floor in the hut until his men had found the tunnel entrance. The tunnel had then been filled in with sewage and soil and the dining hall closed to the prisoners. Although the Senior British Officer, Colonel Kennedy, complained that the one remaining dining hut was inadequate for the 3,000 men held in the camp, Commandant Stürtzkopf's response was emphatic: if the prisoners wished to dig tunnels under their dining halls that was their business, but he would not replace or repair the hut.

'The abandoned dining hut is absolutely ideal for our purposes', said Stallard, when he outlined his plan to his small 'Olympia' staff. 'It's a veritable treasure trove of timber and nails. We should be able to snatch enough wood to satisfy HB's demands.'

Stallard had soon realised that if his team did not quickly strip the hut, others would. The demands for timber tunnel revetments were practically inexhaustible, so this posed Stallard and his team with a difficult choice. They could do the job by degrees – taking a little away every day until they had enough. But to do so in the long run would have increased the risk of German interference; sooner or later they would notice that the wood was being taken, and then might place a special guard on the hut to prevent any further depredations.[7] Such a *modus operandi* was not in Stallard's nature. In typically bold style, he decided to organise a raid to snatch as much wood as possible. As with everything else that Stallard attempted in the camps, this operation was also a work of inspired organisational genius.

*

'The other hut is basically identical to this one', said David Walker as he sat with Stallard, HB and some of the other Olympia escape team in the one remaining dining hall at lunchtime. The room was packed and noisy with conversation, officers sitting at long wooden trestle tables hunched over their lean rations, the constant sound of cutlery clattering on tin plates, a fug of cigarette and pipe smoke hanging above the diners. At one end stood the cooks in white aprons, doling out food from large pots to a line of officers with trays cafeteria-style. A couple of Germans stood nearby, chatting and not paying any particular attention to the noisy scene.

Stallard looked around him. The hut was identical in design and dimensions to their accommodation huts, though without the partitions that created separate rooms.

'Notice the roof?' asked Walker. Stallard looked up.

'It's a false roof', said HB from across the table. He buttered a piece of bread as he spoke. 'There's a gap between what you see above you and the actual roof. It creates a little attic space.'

'We think we should pinch the inside roof from the other hut', said Walker, sipping a mug of steaming tea. 'The timber is undamaged, unlike the flooring which was torn out by the Huns. This means we should be able to scavenge wood the correct length for the ladders.'

'Excellent. Will there be enough timber for everything we are going to build?' asked Stallard.

'More than enough – probably some left over', said HB in a low voice.

'How shall we proceed?' asked Walker, lighting a cigarette and blowing out the match.

For the next half an hour Stallard and his cohorts roughed out a daring plan. They decided that the best time to launch the raid was between 5.00 and 7.00pm. At 5.00pm most of the German staff inside the camp, with the exception of gate and guard tower sentries, went off duty and there was usually a lull of about two hours when German activity within the camp was at a minimum.

'While our Hun friends are gorging themselves on bratwurst and sauerkraut we shall strike!' said Stallard, grinning. Four groups would be involved. One group would consist of prisoners who would dig a large trench in a spot that had originally been set aside by the Germans for gardening, where the phenomenon of newly turned earth would not excite any comment. A second group would stand by to carry the timber from the hut to the hole. A third party would consist of a large number of lookouts who would watch for the approach of any curious Germans. Finally, the smallest group would consist of two highly skilled carpenters drawn from the other ranks orderlies, and they would work inside the hut dismantling the roof.

Stallard believed that the entire operation would not take more than an hour, but even so it carried some serious risks. The level of noise involved in tearing down the internal roof could not be disguised, especially as the carpenters would be working at full tilt, hacking and prising the beams loose with maximum speed. But, with the camp virtually free of Germans, and with an excellent stooge screen in position, they should be able to snatch the required timber before getting caught. In reality, Stallard realised that the operation was determined by how long it took for guards to reach the hut from the camp gates.[8] Fortunately, their target, No. 2 Dining Hall, was located in No. 4 Battalion's sector of the camp to the north-west. The nearest two gates were the west gate, approximately 40 yards away, and the main gate, a further 40 yards to the east. Any German would have to walk from a position outside of either gate, adding a few minutes to his journey time.

*

Zero hour was set for 5.00pm. A few minutes beforehand, the stooges had quietly and unobtrusively sauntered into their positions, looking like any of the other prisoners going about their usual routines. A system of prearranged signals meant that the moment a German was spotted showing any interest in their work, the raiding and burying parties could be quickly warned to cease operations, hide traces of their activities and disperse.

The burying party had already been at work for 30 minutes before zero hour, digging long trenches through the vegetable patch, carefully stacking the earth in neat piles beside the holes. Now they leaned, sweating, on their spades, waiting for the first delivery.

The carrying squad stood with the carpenters inside an accommodation hut near the dining hall. They were pent up and ready to go, casting constant glances at their wristwatches and waiting for the signal from their nearest stooge who was being carefully watched through a window.

'Right, chaps, let's go', said the watcher positioned at the window. The hut door was flung open and the carpenters and carrying squad, dressed in old clothes and woollen gloves, strode quickly towards their target.

At the vegetable patch the burying party could hear the hammering and crashing sounds from the dining hall, the noise tremendous and alarming. But their stooge did not bat an eyelid, his attention focused on another stooge some way off. Suddenly the first men appeared from around the corner carrying long planks over their shoulders like workmen, grinning wildly.

'Special delivery!' joked one of them as he carefully laid three planks into a long pit.

'Keep them coming – we've plenty of space', replied a digger, who with his mate quickly shovelled loose soil from the pile over the light-coloured wood.

'It's working like a dream', said a slightly breathless RAF Squadron Leader as he dumped his load of timber into another pit. 'Unbelievable', he added, in awe of the operation. Men arrived every few seconds, sweating and hauling huge quantities of timber, their tunics soon covered in wood chips and sawdust. The burying party filled one pit after another, covering each load of timber with a pile of rich, dark earth.

In the dining hut the carpenters, their hair almost white with sawdust, faces streaked with sweat, hammered and pulled at the roof like men possessed and 'in no spirit of uncertainty',[9] recalled Arkwright, piles of boards lying in jumbled profusion on the floor as men of the carrying party pulled out lengths and hoisted them onto their shoulders as fast as they could go.

The cacophony from the dining hut continued unabated for minute following nerve-wracking minute without any response from the Germans. It seemed too good to be true. Stallard, controlling the operation, glanced at his watch and then stared at the nearest stooge. Still no signal – it seemed inconceivable that the Germans could not notice the noise.

A stooge watching the perimeter fence suddenly noticed that a German Unteroffizier had emerged from near his barracks, straightening his uniform and side cap as he walked. But then the German stopped in his tracks and stared the several hundred yards towards the dining hut. He could, from his position, see the figures of prisoners coming and going from what he knew to be an empty and locked hut. He strained his eyes to see what they were doing, clearly aware that this was forbidden activity. The stooge watched as the German corporal jogged out of his line of vision towards one of the guard towers. Quickly, the stooge made his signal to another prisoner who was watching him, and within a matter of seconds Stallard knew that the operation had been blown. Following their prearranged procedures, the teams immediately began to cease work, covering their tracks and dispersing throughout the camp. The German corporal stood below a guard tower, ordering the guard above to report on his telephone the activity inside the camp. Within a couple of minutes a squad of armed Germans, led by the corporal, were seen striding towards the gate, some 40 yards from the dining hall.

By the time the German NCO and his men had arrived at the hut it was deserted and the door was once again firmly locked. The several hundred yards of wood that the prisoners had succeeded in filching was safely buried in the vegetable patch, where some POWs pretended to hoe and weed the freshly dug earth while keeping a weather eye on any Germans. The lookouts had dispersed and the carpenters had disappeared back into the orderlies' barracks. The only thing that remained at the hut was the faint smell of freshly cut wood and a few splinters littering the ground outside the door.

The men of the carrying party had collapsed on their bunks, exhausted, sweaty but exhilarated, their hands sore with wood splinters and their shoulders bruised from their heavy loads. Later, the wood was dug up and secretly transferred in small batches to various huts, where it was carefully hidden in the roof spaces.[10]

*

Stallard, as ecstatic as his men, knew that they had just about enough wood for HB's apparatuses. Now there remained the problem of nails and rope to hold the things together. The procurement of these articles required guile rather than brute force. Red Cross parcels arrived at the camp every week in large numbers, where they were opened under German supervision and the contents distributed to the prisoners in accordance with the

Geneva Conventions. The parcels had string wrapped around them for strength and ease of carrying, and this string was pinched. In order to make a rope the prisoners had to splice several bits of string together to make one strong cord. Three or more of these cords were then plaited together into a rope of adequate strength. It was a tedious and time-consuming job and there was no guarantee that enough rope could be manufactured, especially as each scaling apparatus required twelve feet.[11]

Nails were equally hard to source. They came from packing cases containing food that the officers' orderlies would open, again under German supervision. Orderlies would try to steal nails when the guard was not looking and smuggle them to Stallard's team in their trouser pockets.[12] To build all sixteen apparatuses, as Stallard still planned, would consume approximately 1,600 nails, a very tall order indeed. All prisoners involved in Olympia would spend months on the lookout for nails. They pulled them out of doors and walls when the guards weren't looking, found them on the ground or pinched them from the German carpenters.[13]

*

For the moment Olympia could proceed. They had enough wood to immediately construct the first scaling apparatus for training purposes and to impress 'Big X' and the Committee. They had plenty of wood removed from the gardening plot and hidden in hut lofts to construct many more, and the scroungers were working flat-out to collect nails and bits of string for rope-making. It was late May, and Stallard had provisionally set the escape for some time in September when there would be little moonlight and the temperature would be perfect for living outdoors. Three months was plenty of time to refine the plan, train the teams and gather the necessary supplies and equipment. But one major hurdle remained: to find somewhere in the camp where an escalade using the first apparatus could be practised without the Germans catching them.

'Big X' would approve Stallard's scheme only if he could success-fully demonstrate ten men raising and going over an apparatus in under one minute. The answer to Stallard's problem was, somewhat surprisingly, not military at all, but musical.

CHAPTER EIGHT

Practice Makes Perfect

My team had the record of getting over in practice.

Captain Doug Crawford, Royal Australian Artillery

Commandant Stürtzkopf stood with Rademacher, Hager and several of his other officers, including the camp doctor, beside Warburg's main sports field. It was a warm June day, with a clear blue sky. In their field-grey uniforms and polished jackboots the German officers looked smart and efficient. Oberst Stürtzkopf was rarely seen inside the camp, delegating the day-to-day running to the detested Rademacher and the other security officers and senior NCOs, but today was special. Today Stürtzkopf was answering an invitation extended to him by the prisoners.

Stürtzkopf, the prisoners' chief guard, was cordially invited to witness a competition on the main sports field. Different teams competed at athletics: the parallel bars, vaulting horse, and climbing frame. A large crowd of prisoners happily watched, cheering particular teams and having a good time. But though the 'sports day' had a friendly atmosphere, Stürtzkopf and his men were actually the victims of a clever deception orchestrated by Tom Stallard.

Operation Olympia had now progressed to a very important stage in its long gestation period – building the first of Hamilton-Baillie's climbing apparatuses. The problems were simple and revolved around where to hide it and how to train men to use it. Fortunately, Stallard and Walker's organisational genius soon solved both of these difficult questions with interesting results.

The Germans, being a highly cultured people and great lovers of music, had kindly allowed the prisoners to form several musical groups, including an orchestra, a jazz band and a choir. They permitted musical instruments to be sent into the camp. In return, the prisoners put on many performances that were well attended not only by their fellow inmates but also by camp guards, who also supported the busy theatrical society and its constant round of plays and musicals. The boredom of camp life was felt equally on both sides of the fence, but as with so many other apparently innocent diversions, music soon became interwoven with escape plans.

The Germans had set aside one small hut that they had designated the 'music room' where the various bands could meet, practise and store their sheet music and instruments. The hut itself soon became a focus for Stallard's planning, for it possessed some very useful features.

HB and his team secretly built the first climbing apparatus in late May and incorporated it into the music room in a very clever manner. The best place to hide something is often in plain sight. So on that principle, the two parts of the apparatus were attached to two walls to act as shelves, and on them the prisoners had placed sheet music and other literature. 'The ingenious part is that they can be taken down or fixed up in less than a minute',[1] said HB to Major Arkwright and Captain Fuller when they first saw inside the hut. Both men were taken aback at the simplicity of the deception, and it was soon put to the test. Rademacher himself inspected the music room shortly after the 'shelves' were put up and paced around in his usual arrogant manner, his gloved hands behind his back, his little eyes missing nothing. He had even stopped before HB's apparatus, run a finger along the wood and commented that the shelving unit was 'well made'.[2] The prisoners from the orchestra standing behind him, convinced that he must see through such an obvious ruse, quietly let out a collective sigh of relief as Rademacher moved on to complaining that the hut windows were dirty and that the prisoners must also sweep the floor more regularly.

On the day that Arkwright and Fuller visited the music room for a demonstration of the new apparatus, HB, Captain Steve Russell and Lieutenant George Cruickshank quickly stripped the sheet music and books off the shelves, took them off the wall and in a flash had assembled the whole contraption into its carrying form, with the two sections lying on top of one another.

'As you can see, sir', said Walker, 'the hut is just about ideal for our training programme. The floor is concrete', he observed, tapping his boot onto the grey surface. 'Unlike in the other huts, when our chaps start charging up and down like a herd of elephants, the noise will be much less than that generated by a wooden floor.'

Walker pointed towards the ceiling. 'You'll also notice those two beams.' Looking up, Arkwright and Fuller could see two stout wooden beams installed between the eaves. 'They're about seven feet off the floor and the approximate space apart as the two parallel perimeter fences', said Walker. 'Of course, they are not as high as the actual fence, but will do admirably for our purposes.'[3]

The room was not big enough for a full run-through of the escape, but it was large enough so that the teams could practise placing the ladder against one beam and then adjusting the bridge into position in two distinct and separate operations. 'It's the best we can hope for', said Walker.[4]

*

That night, word was sent out to the men who had been selected to join the Olympia escape teams. Stallard was still hoping to get out 160 men. But initially, because of the restricted training facilities and the need to maintain very close security over the entire scheme, Stallard selected ten officers from each of the five battalions. It was hoped that these officers would, once trained, select their own small teams from among their own battalions. At this stage Stallard decided to train only these 50 men, and they would work together in teams of ten to bring themselves to the point where they could successfully launch the apparatus and clamber over it in less than one minute.

Stallard called secret meetings in batches of ten to twelve men each, briefing each group carefully on the proposed course of action. Australian Jack Champ recalled when he first met Stallard in mid-May shortly after the 8.15am roll call. Champ, Captain Rex Baxter and ten others met in the long brick building adjacent to their own wooden hut, No. 24. The room was dimly lit and the atmosphere expectant.

'Thank you for coming, gentlemen', said Stallard, standing at the front of the group. 'My name is Stallard – Tom Stallard. Some of you I know already, but the rest of you are here because you were recommended to me. Very broadly, some people are working on a bit of a blitz out of this place, and we are selecting men from whom we can expect the fullest cooperation to be involved in the scheme.'[5]

'Now, before I go on, I must ask that each of you make a solemn oath not to repeat anything you hear today', said Stallard, his eyes drifting across each man's face. 'The plans are not to be discussed with anyone apart from those in this room, and then only in the open, well out of earshot.'[6]

Champ glanced across at his friend Baxter, who shrugged his shoulders in bewilderment. Stallard then waited as each of the twelve men gave his word.

'Please smoke if you wish, gentlemen', said Stallard after the oaths had been taken, and several men pulled out cigarette packets or pipes.

'We are going to assault the wire', stated Stallard. 'A considerable number of us are going over the double barbed wire fence at night.' For the next ten minutes Stallard outlined the scheme's bare essentials, discussing some of the problems and challenges that they faced. He asked them whether they recalled the camp lights being suddenly extinguished recently. His audience all thought it had been an air raid, but they were surprised when Stallard told them proudly: 'The method is secret but flawless, and we can put them off at will.'[7]

'I won't ask for questions at this time', said Stallard, drawing the meeting to a close, 'although I'm sure you have plenty. I do ask that you go away and think about it overnight, and I'll answer your questions tomorrow. You may even point out something we've overlooked.'[8]

'I will also need to know if you are in or out, as we'll need to look at drumming up replacements should you decide not to participate', said Stallard. 'It's going to be a risky show, and no stigma will be placed on any man who feels he'd rather pull out now. That's all, gentlemen. Thank you.'[9]

After the meeting, Champ and Baxter strolled along the perimeter wire, eyeing up the challenge that Stallard had set them. Rex smiled broadly. 'It's a bloody beauty, Champy!' he exclaimed. 'I'm sure it will work. Just what we've been waiting for. What do you think?'

'I couldn't agree more', said Champ. 'I've run it over in my mind, and I sure can't find any holes in the plan.'[10]

The next afternoon all twelve men volunteered before Stallard. At every meeting Stallard attended he found willing recruits. No one said 'no'.

*

Although the men were coming forward in large numbers, Stallard still faced several problems. He had not found a way to anchor the apparatus to enable the last man to climb over without causing the entire contraption to tip over. A solution had yet to be found to keep the guards' attention for a further two and a half minutes once they had been drawn to the fence to investigate the noise caused by Arkwright and Fuller's grapnels embedded in the wire. And a serious problem was the men's physical fitness – they would need to be in good shape to clamber over the wire and sprint off into the German countryside while carrying a heavy pack containing water and rations. Prison camp life, with its largely sedentary habits of eating, sleeping, reading, attending concerts and theatrical shows, smoking and often suffering from bouts of illness, meant that the potential escapers were mostly out of shape. They needed to toughen up their bodies in preparation for the rigours of being on the run for perhaps several weeks.

After a considerable amount of head-scratching and experimentation, the solution to keeping the scaling apparatus steady when the last man went over was finally solved. As each escaper on his hands and knees crossed over the bridge, the next one laid full length against the ladder and locked the bridge to it by muscle power. The only way this could be done when the last man was going over was for a volunteer to press himself against the ladder to steady it – in effect becoming what the RAF called a 'tail-end Charlie'. This man, christened the 'anchor man' by Stallard, would not attempt to escape, but would only hold the ladder in place.[11] This meant that the anchor men would be running the same risks of being shot or captured by the Germans without any compensating chance to escape themselves. Stallard called for volunteers, but as with so many other aspects of Olympia, prisoners willingly came forward for this hazardous job, happy to know that their efforts would mean that another comrade could escape. It was a clear case of the greater good.

*

Among the 50 men initially selected by Stallard were several who were to play prominent roles in the Olympia operation, including Arkwright and Walker. Also from Walker's regiment, The Black Watch, was Steve Russell, one of the builders of the first apparatus.

General Bernard Montgomery's godson, Captain Dick Tomes, Royal Warwickshire Regiment, was also selected, along with Captain Martin Gilliat of the King's Royal Rifle Corps. Gilliat, then 29 years old, was extremely well liked by virtually everyone, a man who thought the best of people, regardless of their background, education, nationality or skin colour, and he was also a devout Christian. Educated at Eton and Sandhurst, Gilliat joined the King's Royal Rifle Corps in 1933, serving in Northern Ireland and Palestine before going over to France with the British Expeditionary Force. Gilliat had been captured along with the rest of his battalion during the valiant but ultimately doomed defence of the Channel port of Calais in 1940.[12]

Australian gunner Captain Doug Crawford and the RAF's senior officer at Warburg, Noel Hyde, were two more high-profile members of the Olympia team. Thirty-one-year-old Wing Commander Noel Challis Hyde had been the commanding officer of 207 Squadron. On the night of 7/8 April 1941 during a raid against the U-boat pens at Kiel, Hyde's Manchester bomber had been hit by flak. With the starboard engine on fire, the crew had baled out and been taken prisoner near Hamburg. Hyde now led the 400 RAF prisoners at Warburg. Getting a senior and experienced officer like Hyde back into the war would have been a major boon to the Allied war effort, hence his inclusion on the first Olympia list.

Jock Hamilton-Baillie would not be coming along. His war injuries meant that he could not run fast enough to get away from the camp, and anyway, he was simultaneously involved with yet another tunnel.

Practice sessions were carefully guarded to prevent any German interference. A ring of watchers around the music room gave advance notice of approaching Germans, while the band covered any excessive noise made by the Olympia team by hosting very loud music sessions next to the hut, thumping away on drums and blowing trumpets and French horns.[13] Martin Gilliat took charge of the stooges when he wasn't practising. The Germans were none the wiser, for they expected noise from the vicinity of the music room. In overall charge of the training programme was Stallard's number two, David Walker.

Australians Jack Champ and Rex Baxter were mightily impressed by their first introduction to the scaling apparatus. Stallard and Walker personally demonstrated it. Champ and Baxter thought the 'shelves' on the walls of the music room really were just storage space for sheet music until Stallard went over and took them down, placed them one on top of the other and carried them over to the first beam. Stallard leaned the ladder against the beam, grasped the handles of the platform, stepped swiftly up the ladder assisted by David Walker, and deftly pushed it across. The platform cleared the ceiling by only a foot or two, dropped onto the far beam with a loud thump, and the Australians and the rest of the small audience heard the top rung click neatly into the slots on the ladder. Stallard crawled across and then, grasping the trapeze bar, dropped expertly to the floor.[14]

That day the group organised a launching team of four men. Two men would be on top of the ladder and their job was to hoist that end onto the top of the inner beam and then steady the ladder as the other two went to work. Number 1 would grasp the platform handles and step up two rungs to launch the platform. As he would be off balance and have no free hands, it was his Number 2's job, as well as that of the other two 'primaries' (Numbers 9 and 10, the last over) to hold him steady as he pushed the heavy platform up and out.[15] Six other team members would scramble over behind Numbers 1 and 2, with Numbers 9 and 10 the last to go.

Rex Baxter, tall and strong, was selected as Number 1, with Jack Champ as Number 2. Lots were drawn for the remaining positions, and Tom Stallard, who would be joining this team for the actual assault, declined any priority even though it was his show. He drew

Number 9, meaning that his chances of escaping were considerably less than Baxter and Champ.[16]

*

Stallard and the others maintained a fevered training programme throughout June and July until the men could manage to cross the apparatus within the required 60 seconds or less.[17] Major Wylie and the Escape Committee paid a visit to the music room and witnessed a demonstration. Stallard had his approval from the Committee, but a further reduction was made to the size of the operation. Even Stallard admitted that the scheme in its original conception was far too ambitious. It was foolish to have more than one apparatus completed before the day of the escape, and it would have been tempting fate to have built more 'shelves' and dotted these identical pieces of furniture all around the camp – the Germans would have been bound to become suspicious.[18] All of the other fifteen apparatuses would have to be manufactured on the day of the escape to minimise detection. And to train 160 men on only one available apparatus was logistically impossible, especially as the five teams currently under training were only able to practise on the music room apparatus at best once a week. This meant that they were not well trained enough to complete the escalade within the time limits set by Stallard and the Escape Committee.

Finally, it was agreed that only four scaling apparatuses would be used, with three built on the day of the escape, and that there would be four teams each of ten men.[19] This was felt to be the maximum number that it was possible to train to a high standard with only one scaling apparatus. Stallard then appointed the final team captains. Major Arkwright with Rupert Fuller as his second-in-command would lead Team 1. Team 2's captain was Steve Russell. Captain Rex Baxter led Team 3, while Team 4 would also eventually have an Australian in charge – the irrepressible Doug Crawford. The humble Stallard refused to make himself a team captain and was happy occupying position Number 9 in Baxter's team. David Walker, Stallard's Olympia deputy and head of training, would be with Team 2, again as an ordinary team member in position Number 5. Four men also took part in the training programme with no chance of escaping – these were the anchor men.[20]

*

The whole Olympia plan came within a hair's breadth of failure during one of Team 3's training sessions. 'Goons up!' yelled stooge Henry Coombe-Tennant at the window. Throughout the prison camp system, Germans were routinely known as 'Goons'. When a German officer demanded to know why, a British prisoner told him it was an acronym for 'German Officer Or Non-com'. In reality it was borrowed from a Disney character, a ridiculous looking fellow with a prolific growth of hair on his legs. The Goon language was unintelligible, and they were not credited with much intelligence.

When Coombe-Tennant's warning was shouted in the music room, the scaling apparatus was fully set up and Jack Champ was halfway across it, Rex Baxter having just swung down to the concrete floor. Five other members of the team were queued up behind Champ. 'Cripes Jack, move!' cried Baxter.[21]

Champ landed on the hard floor in a pile, and the Number 3, Major R.M. Young, landed almost on top of him, planting his heel on Champ's foot. Champ screamed in pain while the rest of the team cleared the obstacle in double time. Stallard whipped the platform back off the beams and with Number 10, Lieutenant Dick Page, quickly replaced them on the wall as music racks.

Coombe-Tennant sprinted to the end of the hut and dived behind the old battered piano that was pushed up against the wall, joined a few seconds later by all of Team 3, sweating and red faced. They immediately launched into a rousing and slightly breathless rendition of 'Roll Out the Barrel' as the hut door was flung open and in stepped Hauptmann Rademacher, followed by a small and pimply corporal armed with a rifle.[22]

The prisoners immediately stopped singing and stood to attention while Rademacher and his lackey prowled around. The corporal walked over to the wall 'racks', his movements closely watched by the dozen sweating prisoners, their hearts in their mouths, where he proceeded to remove several sheets of music.[23] Rademacher completed his inspection and turned to leave. But just as he reached the door and the prisoners had started to relax, he suddenly swung around theatrically and pointed directly at the 'racks'. Stallard and the others froze. Had Rademacher seen through their ruse?

'You practise for the concert, perhaps?' bellowed Rademacher. He smiled. 'Please continue; the music is good. I am sure you will give a good performance!' Then, with another flourish, the security officer strutted out, the corporal slamming the hut door behind them.

'Thank goodness!' sighed Walker. 'That was a bit too close for comfort. However, it was nice of the cretin to wish us all well with our performance. We'll perform all right, but not in the way he imagines! With a bit of luck he'll be sent to the front after our little break-out, and some lucky blighter will fire a shell up his arse!'[24]

*

Stallard decided, in consultation with 'Big X' and the Escape Committee, the provisional dates for mounting Operation Olympia. Stallard's decision was guided entirely by the state of the moon. It was also agreed that Olympia would not take place before 1 September, so that smaller escape schemes involving two or three officers would have a fair chance of success. Stallard and Ken Wylie rightly suspected that once Olympia had gone off, the Germans would institute far more rigorous security measures in the camp, to the detriment of every other scheme that was in the works. The commandant had also suddenly been changed on 20 June with the arrival of Oberst Brinkord to replace Stürtzkopf. Naturally, the new commandant wished to impress his own methods on Oflag VI-B, and Rademacher worked extra hard hunting down escape attempts and generally making life hard for the prisoners to impress his new boss.

Stallard announced that the provisional dates selected for Olympia were 7, 8 or 9 September.[25] There would be complete darkness on those nights until midnight, with the moon rising in the early hours. This meant that the escalade, once the camp lights had been extinguished from the cobbler's workshop, would be made under perfect conditions, while the later cross-country escape from the camp's immediate vicinity would be well lit by moonlight, making it faster and easier.

*

In the meantime, Arkwright and Fuller had been able to practise making the diversion, to test the practicality of their inventions. They would not be doing any diverting in person on the night that Olympia was launched, as both would be on teams assaulting the perimeter fences, but for peace of mind they made sure that the devices actually worked properly.

Fuller had manufactured two rudimentary metal grapnels each weighted with a blob of concrete. Using Red Cross string, Arkwright and Fuller had managed to make three or four stout ropes each of about 25 yards. In one corner of the camp were two huts used to store Red Cross parcels. The Germans had fenced these off from the main compound and a guard tower did not overlook the huts. The fence here was virtually identical to the inner perimeter fence. This would be their experimental ground.

Arkwright and Fuller spent a few hours one day perfecting the grapnel-launching method, and also testing the noise effect once it was embedded in the wire and given some sharp tugs on the rope.

The two officers reported their test findings to Major Cousens, who informed them of an addition to the grapnel plan. Dummy ladders would be created out of spare wood and, painted white, they would be propped against the fence at the selected diversion points with a grapnel embedded in the wire close by. A diverter would lie concealed and tug on the rope, attracting the guard's attention. Another prisoner who could speak fluent German would also be concealed close by. He would watch the reaction of the sentry when he investigated the noise and then noticed the ladder propped against the wire. At this point, from a darkened position out of sight, the German-speaking officer would start issuing orders to the sentry in the manner of one of his own NCOs. '*Hallo, Wache, was ist den hier los? Dies ist Feldwebel Jung. Wache halten die leiter! Nicht von dort zu bewegen!*' ('Hello, sentry, what's going on here? This is Sergeant Jung. Watch that ladder! Don't move from there!')[26] If successful, this little ruse would keep the German sentries immobile beside the ladders for the necessary two and a half minutes that Stallard had stipulated.

*

Fitness was a major concern for Stallard and the Olympia planners. How to improve the fitness of 40 men without drawing the attention of their jailers? Cleverly, instead of trying to hide the fitness programme from the Germans, Stallard decided to include them as well. They already formally encouraged sport among the prisoners, having provided the football pitch and netball courts, and the prisoners also played cricket, rugby, and even Australian Rules football. There were competitions between schools, regiments and nationalities. The Germans were happy – the prisoners were burning off aggressive energy in harmless pursuits that could easily have been channelled into tunnelling and other forbidden behaviour. So Stallard, using this background, decided to form a gymnastic group and sought permission from Commandant Stürtzkopf before his transfer to build a wooden vaulting horse, parallel bars and a climbing frame. Permission was duly given, and the equipment built by the camp carpenters. The Olympia teams, including the support and diversion people, took organised exercises and some competitions were created.[27] Stallard invited the commandant and his officers to watch some of the PT displays, and a large audience of onlookers joined in. In this manner, the Olympia team members were put through their paces and slowly their fitness was improved.

Other ways to improve the body involved running or walking 'The Circuit', the path that ran along the length of the camp's perimeter fence. 'I want you to run at least a thousand yards every day', Stallard had commanded. 'Walk at least three thousand, and play as much sport as you can without risking injury to yourself. You must realise that once you go over the wire you will have to run flat-out for at least a thousand yards, and you won't be in shorts and shirts – you'll be fully dressed and carrying a pack.'[28]

Major Arkwright and Captain Fuller started taking a three-quarter-mile run each morning, plus walking fifteen miles every day around the camp. The two officers religiously panted round the camp every morning when most people were still in their beds, hating every minute of it but always with the end goal fixed firmly in their minds.[29] It was impossible for anyone involved with Olympia to train with the backpacks that they would all be wearing on the night of the escape, so many of the officers fretted over the extra weight they would be carrying and its effects on their climbing and sprinting performances on the night.

By late July the Olympia teams were fast approaching optimum performance levels during training. Dick Tomes, Number 5 on Arkwright's Team 1, recalled that 'we began going over it without packs and took nearly 60 seconds for ten men – by the end we could do it with full packs in 25 seconds'.[30]

*

The next set of hurdles was now vaulted with Stallard's usual determination and thoroughness. The escapers would travel in pairs, and routes out of Germany had to be decided for each of them. Maps and compasses would need to be provided to each pair, and civilian clothing would need to be manufactured and concealed inside the camp, along with identity documents and concentrated and dried food rations. It was time for 'Q' Department to play its part in the first great escape.

CHAPTER NINE

The Road Less Travelled

Being dressed as British subjects would be an
added inducement to conceal ourselves.

Captain Rupert Fuller, Royal Sussex Regiment

'*E*s ist Aladins Höhle!' said the German sentry, reaching once more into the secret partition at the back of one of the hut lockers, pulling out one large Red Cross chocolate bar after another. The hut's British occupants stood in silence, their arms crossed, as the German continued to pull bars from the 'Aladdin's Cave', handing them to a corporal who stacked them like bricks on a table between two bunks. '*Gibt es noch mehr*?' ('Are there any more?'), asked the corporal. '*Das ist das Los.*' ('That's the lot.') '*Durchaus ein haul.*' ('Quite a haul.') The Germans had just found six pounds of chocolate carefully hidden by the prisoners as part of preparations for Operation Olympia – vital iron rations for the test of endurance that lay ahead for those who made it out of the camp.

The sentry, his arms loaded down with chocolate bars, left for the guardroom. The corporal turned to the assembled prisoners. '*Danke, meine Herren*, you are very kind', he said in heavily accented English, a huge grin plastered across his face. Pausing for effect, the corporal turned, his jackboots creaking, and marched smartly out of the door.

'I hope you ruddy choke on it', shouted a young British lieutenant at the retreating German's back.

'At least we have the satisfaction of knowing that the only

chocolate a Hun is ever likely to see comes from a British prisoner of war camp', remarked Major Arkwright drily. 'Double check all hiding places. We can't afford any more losses on this scale.'[1]

Ironically, the British had better access to luxury items like chocolate, cigarettes and coffee than their captors. The seized chocolate would be distributed among the delighted guards.

Hoarding food was one of the first elements of the Olympia plan to be enacted, and although the operation was planned for early September, it would take several months to obtain and in some cases make the necessary food to sustain the men on the march.

Each team member would be carrying around twelve pounds of provisions, designed to last for eighteen to twenty days beyond the wire. This was in addition to a washing kit, tinned cigarettes, matches, a basic medical kit, and spare socks, shirts and underpants.

All groups aimed to stay away from built-up areas as much as possible, and at the time of year they were planning to escape it was expected that they would be able to find potatoes and fruit in abundance throughout the German countryside. Unfortunately, potatoes meant cooking, and it was unknown whether circumstances would permit a fire on occasion. As servicemen, all of the escapers knew that a hot meal could restore not only the body but also the mind and soul, helping to raise morale when adverse weather, physical exhaustion and nagging uncertainty lowered it. 'A dish of newly boiled potatoes is worth all the dry biscuits in the world on these occasions',[2] remarked Major Arkwright with feeling.

Rupert Fuller invented a small oven that could be fitted to the top of his room stove. In late April, Fuller had started experimenting with creating a bulk food for the journey, based on ingredients taken from their Red Cross parcels. He created a kind of hard tack biscuit made from oatmeal, milk powder, glucose, sugar and currants that was then mixed with a little water and baked in his homemade oven slowly and thoroughly. The escapers needed something that wouldn't turn sour or mouldy quickly, and so Fuller avoided adding any fat to the mixture. The biscuits were a great success, sustaining and appetising, and Fuller baked several pounds that were carefully hidden for months.[3] For concentrated food, the prisoners mainly used chocolate and cheese.[4]

Major Arkwright's backpack would contain a typical set of rations used by the Olympia escapers, though instead of Fuller's biscuits he took Red Cross biscuits that he found more 'easily digestible'. His rations, calculated to last about twenty days, consisted of:

1½ pounds of biscuits
1½ pounds of cheese
5 pounds of chocolate
2 pounds of porridge
1 pound of sugar
Several ounces of Marmite
Large number of Horlicks malted-milk tablets
2 small tins of sardines
<u>Total</u> = approx. 12 pounds.[5]

Arkwright's rations, per day, were calculated at three biscuits, four ounces of chocolate, one ounce of cheese and, if lighting a fire was possible, a substantial bowl of porridge.[6] It was virtual starvation rations. Of course, after twenty days, the escapers' rations would be exhausted, whether or not they had managed to reach either a neutral country or one under German occupation. They would then be thrown on to their wits, and especially in occupied Holland, Belgium or France, they still could not entirely count on help from strangers.

*

Choosing a route out of Germany was the most important decision that escapers faced. Some routes were well known and had been tried many times before. Others were untried but full of possibilities. Some were considered so difficult as to be virtually impossible. It was down to each pair of escapers to decide upon their route. Tom Stallard's only guidance was that the pairs should spread out across Germany so that even if they failed to find a way out, they would nonetheless tie down considerable German military and police resources that could be used more productively elsewhere.

Three basic destinations were available to the Olympia escapers: Switzerland, Sweden or one of the occupied nations of western Europe. All three would involve mammoth overland treks of several hundred miles through enemy territory with the constant risk of discovery. Getting out of the camp was not quite the same thing as staying out of it, for many individuals and groups had successfully escaped from Oflag VI-B, including Tom Stallard himself, but no one had managed to remain free for very long.

Oflag VI-B was surrounded by farmland, flat, featureless and with virtually no cover for hundreds of yards from the wire. The nearest human habitation was the small village of Dössel, half a mile from the camp. Two and a half miles south was the pretty country town of Warburg, with its castle and timber-framed medieval houses. The first town of any real importance was Kassel, about 20 miles to the south-east. Many of the prisoners involved with Olympia carefully weighed their options and hunched over maps of Germany late into the night, after which they came to some firm conclusions.

Switzerland was an extremely attractive proposition. The distance to the Swiss frontier on foot was about twenty days' hard marching. The great advantage of Switzerland was that once across the frontier, one was as good as home, though there would be a delay of several months before any successful escaper could be returned to the UK. The disadvantage of heading for the Alps was the extensive and detailed guarding of the frontier by both the

Germans and the Swiss. As Jock Hamilton-Baillie had already discovered in mid-1941, crossing the frontier was a nightmare.

Sweden, though also a neutral country, was separated from Germany by the Baltic Sea. In order to get to it, the escaper would need to have some contact with German officials to gain passage on a ship sailing from Denmark or northern Germany. Most escapers ruled out Sweden as logistically impossible and far too risky.

The last choice was one of the occupied nations that bordered Germany to the west: Holland, Belgium, Luxembourg or France. This was the route taken by most of the escapers. Once out of Germany, locals would look upon a POW on the run as a friend rather than a foe. The prisoners did not expect any help from the population, but there was always the chance of making contact with the Underground. One had to be wary of quislings and collaborators, but the Olympia escapers believed that 90 per cent of the population would look the other way when they saw them.[7]

*

The challenges of remaining on the run inside Germany itself were huge, and the recent case of two RAF escapers from Warburg had highlighted the problems that the Olympia teams would be facing once they were beyond the wire. Intelligence Officer Captain Melsome and Major Stallard both recommended that the RAF report on the escape be studied carefully by every man involved with Olympia and its lessons absorbed.

The RAF prisoners, believing that they had made sufficient plans to make it out of Germany, had first noticed in late April 1942 that at 7.00 each evening the sentries at Warburg were withdrawn from the main gate, presumably to have their supper. Interestingly, they were not replaced until 9.00pm, and during that two-hour hiatus the main gates, firmly locked, were guarded by only one sentry in the overlooking wooden guard tower and by another inside a second tower on the camp's south-east corner. These sentries were also charged with looking into the camp and along the perimeter wire in both directions.

A South African Air Force pilot bravely crawled up to the main gate one evening, just as Stallard was starting serious planning for Olympia and absorbing the lessons from his own few days on the run after cutting through the wire with Dick Page and James McDonnell. The South African managed to bend back the bottom wire from the gate and excavate a shallow scraping, creating a hole just big enough for a man to crawl through. Carefully replacing the dirt and bending the wire back into place, he quietly crept away to report his findings. 'Big X' and the Escape Committee gave the go-ahead for an attempt using this fascinating new method.

At 8.40pm on 27 April, the South African officer repeated his wire bending and scraping exercise at the camp's inner main gate. The camp was quiet, with just the sound of sentries walking along the perimeter fence, their jackboots crunching on the gravel path. Searchlight beams from the tower played across the camp, periodically sweeping assigned sectors. A complex lookout system was put into place for the escape, the RAF leaving nothing to chance.

This time the South African had three British companions, each officer dressed in dark clothing, his face and hands blackened with soot from their hut stove, and carrying a homemade backpack containing 15½ pounds of concentrated and dried food, Horlicks and Ovaltine tablets – the men believing that this food could last for 24 days on the run.

They pushed under the two gates like dogs burrowing under a garden fence, the last officer through carefully covering their tracks so that the Germans would be none the wiser. The Escape Committee hoped that this method could be used more than once before the Germans caught on. Once under the outer gate, the four men quickly crawled to a ditch six feet from the perimeter wire, clearly visible to the guards on patrol. The moon had risen, but fortunately the German sentries were looking into the camp, rather than out, and they failed to spot them.

For the next hour the men slowly crawled between sheds and piles of timber outside the camp until they arrived at a partially completed hut. Inside, the group quickly changed out of their escape clothes into a mixture of military and civilian garments, the idea being to portray themselves as foreign labourers, then a common sight throughout Germany.

After shaking hands and whispering 'good luck', the group divided into two pairs and struck off in different directions. The South African and his partner managed to walk for seventeen days, covering 275 miles before being caught just short of the Swiss frontier. The other pair, one of whom spoke a little French, decided to pass themselves off as Belgian labourers. Their harrowing story eventually provided Stallard and the Olympia escapers with a series of 'dos' and 'don'ts' when attempting to walk out of Germany.

They had decided to travel only by night, and to hide and sleep during the day. Unfortunately, at that time of the year darkness was limited to seven hours a night, so they had to push themselves hard to make the distance. Before dawn the two men, completely exhausted after covering up to twenty miles, would face a nerve-wracking time trying to find somewhere quiet and safe to lie up in. Favourite places were woods and general undergrowth, though they often had to make do with ditches, hiding under rotting leaves, rubbish or even brown paper carried as a kind of *ersatz* camouflage. As soon as they stopped moving they froze, as the air temperature was still wintry, and because their packs had had to fit through the shallow scrapings beneath the camp gates they had not been able to bring greatcoats, blankets or groundsheets. Lighting fires for cooking was also largely impossible, so they tried to make do on ten ounces of concentrated or dried food each day, plus some tablets. If they were lucky they managed to scrounge a few swedes from farmers' fields, but these were eaten raw.

Unable to wash or shave, they soon looked and smelled more like vagrants than foreign labourers, and naturally they tried to stay well away from other people.[8] Unfortunately, even in the German countryside they were bound to run into locals, providing for some very sticky moments.

On their second night of freedom the two officers were travelling south on a minor road when a German civilian on a bicycle had ridden up beside them and started questioning them. The escapees quickly recounted their 'Belgian workers' cover story in bad French, explaining that they were walking to the next village. The German continued with his questions in an increasingly persistent manner, so the two Britons quickly branched off onto a smaller track to the south-east and lost him.[9]

The escapees were averaging only three or four hours' sleep a day. Because of the month and the air temperature, they didn't stop violently shivering until around midday, shortening further the amount of sleep that they could snatch. When they woke each night their feet and legs were terribly stiff, and walking was extremely painful for the first several miles.

Day 8 was spent hiding in a wood about a mile from the autobahn near Butsbach, a small town 22 miles north of Frankfurt am Main. The two men had just started eating their 7.00pm 'meal' when a German NCO and his girlfriend literally stumbled upon them. The German was looking for somewhere quiet for a little fun with the girl, but all passionate thoughts were quickly expunged from his mind when the two British officers emerged from the undergrowth beneath his jackboots. Their hair and clothes were matted with leaf litter and dirt, their beards straggly and their eyes red-rimmed from exhaustion.

'*Was zum Teufel*!' ('What the hell!') exclaimed the German. '*Sie sind Russen*?' ('Are you Russians?') '*On ne parle pas allemand*', said one of the escapees. '*Alors, qui êtes-vous*?' said the German. '*Nous sommes des travailleurs belges*', stammered out the French-speaking prisoner, trying to stick to their Belgian workers story. '*D'où venez-vous?*' asked the German, wanting to know where they had come from. At this point the RAF officer's schoolboy French was exhausted, his mind freezing under stress. The German repeated the question in perfect French. He took a step closer to the escapees. '*Montrez-moi vos papiers d'identité*', he said, demanding to see their papers. '*Ausweispapiere*', he repeated. The evaders stood staring at him with blank expressions on their faces. '*Sie sind mit mir*', declared the German, indicating that the two RAF officers should come with him. Fortunately for the Britons, the German was dressed in his best walking-out uniform and was unarmed, so they simply took to their heels and ran like the wind. '*Halt!*' screamed the German, '*sofort stoppen!*'[10]

Day 15 found the two evaders 150 miles from Warburg. They were just outside Karlsrühe, on the road to Stuttgart. They were so exhausted and half-starved that they could no longer think straight, leading them to make a stupid decision. They agreed that they would push on for an extra few miles *after* daybreak, violating one of their cardinal rules. However, they escaped detection on this occasion.

The day after Captain Few's failed escape attempt from Oflag VI-B in the back of a tractor trailer, the two RAF officers finally ran out of luck. This was their sixteenth day outside the camp and they were soaked to the skin by a violent thunderstorm and heavy rain. The next day, 14 May, their clothing was still sodden and the ground was too waterlogged for them to lie down and sleep. They decided to try for the French frontier just beyond Nagold, bordering the Black Forest in south-western Germany, that night.

In the evening, the pair approached the town of Wildberg very cautiously. There were many civilians about, walking or sitting in the streets smoking pipes and chatting. The two evaders soon found themselves moving through the centre of Wildberg and attracting a fair amount of attention from curious locals. They looked bedraggled. Though both men had managed to shave that morning, their clothes were soiled and very worn after seventeen days of living rough. They were also wearing what were evidently homemade backpacks. Just as they reached the end of the town a German policeman rode up to them on a bicycle and ordered them to halt. The 'Belgian worker' story did not survive even a few seconds' questioning by the policeman, and any thoughts of making a run for it were scuppered by the appearance of another policeman behind them. Both were armed with automatic pistols. '*Britische Kriegsgefangene*', said one of the RAF officers as he raised his hands above his head, declaring that they were prisoners of war. The pair had averaged sixteen miles a night and on 19 May they were returned to Warburg.[11]

Although recaptured, the experiences of the RAF escapers helped enormously with Stallard's planning. Carefully debriefed by Captain Melsome, the two men outlined some of the problems that they had encountered. A report prepared by Melsome was circulated to Stallard and his team leaders and made the following suggestions for future similar escapes:

1. Two people are the ideal number for this type of trip, especially for keeping up each other's morale.
2. Loss of morale was caused by physical weakness, the feeling of being hunted, and hunger and/or thirst.
3. Although the backpacks were getting lighter, the escapees never felt that this was the case.
4. Both escapees suffered from constipation and even small scratches quickly turned into festering sores. They recommended future parties carry more fruit.
5. Both men suffered dramatic weight loss, one losing 18 pounds, the other 10.
6. Army boots were completely unsuitable for long-distance travel and they hurt both men's feet.
7. Capture was caused by slight mental imbalance attributed to

being cold and wet and having no dry clothes. Both men said that if they had had groundsheets and rubber-soled boots they would have made it to the frontier.[12]

Stallard and his Olympia teammates drew one conclusion from the RAF officers' experiences: to remain free on German soil it was absolutely essential to keep out of contact with the German people. It was also plainly obvious that a shortage of food, adverse weather conditions and other unforeseen circumstances tempted POWs on the run to make decisions that they knew were foolhardy, and nine times out of ten this led to their recapture.[13] Even if a prisoner was a first-class German speaker dressed to look the part, if he entered a town or loitered at a railway station he had very little chance of not falling under suspicion sooner or later. For an amateur, mingling with Germans was nothing short of disastrous.[14]

*

The Olympia pairs started choosing routes. Major Arkwright and Captain Fuller decided, as did several other officers, to head for occupied Holland. If you draw a line from Warburg north-west to Münster and south-east to Kassel, all of the country south-west of this line up to the Dutch frontier is heavily populated and built-up, forming part of the Ruhr industrial heartland of Germany. However, Arkwright and Fuller discovered that on the frontier west of Osnabrück a loop in the border bulges out to the east. A line was drawn on their map from this bulge east through a gap between Osnabrück and Münster, thence east by south-east till you arrived at Kassel. Along this strip of Germany there were few large towns and much of the country was hilly and wooded. The Dutch–German frontier at the end of their map line was partly marshy and thinly populated.[15]

Team 3's Rex Baxter and his partner Jack Champ also decided upon Holland as their initial destination, in the hope of contacting the Underground and making it to Spain and thence to Gibraltar.

The captain of Team 4, Doug Crawford, decided that he would head south-west for France via the Black Forest with his partner Jack Hand. From there they also hoped to get over the Pyrenees and into neutral Spain. He had been told that if his team went towards Holland, Belgium or France, and the Gestapo didn't pick them up and the Underground did, they would be all right. 'I personally didn't think it was worth prejudicing the Underground',[16] he said. It was a fair point, for the punishments handed out to the citizens of occupied nations who helped escaping Allied prisoners were severe and often fatal, and having that on one's conscience was hard to bear.

Team 1's Dick Tomes and his partner, Lieutenant Fred Corfield, Royal Artillery, intended to go to Denmark and thence Sweden, and they would strike north-east from Warburg via Höxter on the banks of the River Weser, then Holzminden and Hannover. Tom Stallard's target was Holland, a popular choice as it was slightly over 100 miles from the camp.

In total, the plan was for twenty pairs of escapers to fan out from Warburg and head out across Germany – north, south and west. Stallard was certain that some would get through. The whole operation absorbed the lessons learnt by the RAF officers, and precautions were being taken to make changes to equipment and supplies.

None of this would have been possible without good maps, and because of MI9's provision of escape equipment through parcels sent into the camp, the Escape Committee was not short of them. Maps were printed on very fine tissue paper and were exact in every detail. 'Q' Department's Mapping Section had cleverly constructed a printing press to make multiple copies. Heavily strained jelly provided the base, and once the jelly had set hard, they were able to etch the map details onto it in very fine relief. The forgers used ink made from indelible pencils and could run off as many copies as needed on their press.[17]

Maps were all well and good, but without a reliable compass they would be useless. An ingenious solution was soon found to this problem. Compasses were manufactured consisting of a magnetised needle set on a cork swivel. A small speck of luminous paint from a broken watch face was glued to the tip of the needle to indicate north at night.[18]

*

Clothing was an essential component of the plan, and it was imperative that the Olympia escapers not make the mistake of the RAF group who carried completely inadequate clothing and suffered badly from exposure to the elements because of it.

The first items made by the Olympia escapers were backpacks to carry their provisions and spare clothes. The Germans, because of their obvious use, strictly forbade any kind of haversack. A few officers had managed to smuggle one in, but there were not nearly enough to equip the members of a scheme as large as Operation Olympia.

Stallard instructed the team members to make their own. Major Arkwright's design was typical of those made by the prisoners. It consisted of two thicknesses of thin twill cloth stitched together. A single thickness was not waterproof but two layers actually managed fairly well, even in a severe thunderstorm. Arkwright's backpack was wide at the top and tapered to the bottom. Shoulder straps were made from the same material as the bag, with the addition of a strip of soft blanket to prevent rubbing. To prevent sideslip, a string belt was attached to the bottom of the bag and could be adjusted around the waist for comfort.[19]

The main requirement was that the clothing should be comfortable to walk in and as far as possible waterproof without being hot or heavy.[20] A mackintosh was the obvious choice, but there were few available at Warburg as the Germans had realised their value to escapers and confiscated most of them. Friends of Arkwright and

Fuller promised them a scarce mackintosh each if they managed to reach the final selection for the Olympia team. With Arkwright's appointment as captain of Team 1, the two escapers would at least have a waterproof coat each.

For headdress the prisoners turned to 'Q' Department, which had a section of tailors who were able to create civilian clothing from odds of material that had been smuggled into the camp. Fortunately for Stallard and the others, one of the tailors was a pre-war employee of Herbert Johnson Ltd of New Bond Street, London, a famous hatter that made both uniform hats for the armed services and civilian headwear. He instructed the Olympia team members in making a flat cap each out of some very handsome tweed blankets. Each evening for several nights, the tailor monitored successive teams as they cut, stitched and sewed the hats. They were waterproofed by the addition of a lining made out of a piece of mackintosh taken from a kit bag.[21] Captain Crawford in particular excelled at the tailoring challenge, and he quickly became one of the main manufacturers of caps.[22]

As for the rest of their escape outfits, that was left to the individual prisoner to create from his own stock of clothing. As all of the teams intended to stay well clear of settlements and German civilians they were not too worried whether they mixed military and civilian garments together. The escapers would largely wear old battledress or flannel trousers, the more battered and stained the better, but gave up on making coats as too difficult. Rupert Fuller had a pair of grey flannels that the Germans had dyed a dirty mustard-colour to prevent their use in escapes. He discovered that by boiling them two or three times they reverted to a fairly reasonable hue. Arkwright used a pair of very old battledress trousers that were so greasy as to be virtually waterproof.[23] They would carry their donated mackintoshes rolled up on their packs except during inclement weather.

Fuller, after much indecision, and after exploring the idea of manufacturing a coat out of some blue blanket, decided instead to just wear his khaki service dress tunic, and to hell with it. He removed all unit badges and his pips. Fuller believed that 'being dressed as British subjects would be an added inducement to conceal ourselves'.[24] Arkwright agreed, as did many of the other escapers who eschewed fully dressing as civilians. The escapers would take along spare underwear, woollen jerseys and spare socks, and each had a good pair of new boots from their Red Cross parcels. The boots had rubber soles and each man wore them around camp during their daily exercises to ensure that they were adequately broken in.

Jack Champ swapped one of his precious blankets for a grey Greek Army greatcoat. This he then shortened to just above knee height. He would also wear a pair of dyed battledress trousers and one of Crawford's homemade caps. Champ was unusual in that he had managed to retain his army haversack. This he also dyed and converted into a smaller backpack.[25]

*

The apparatus training programme was well advanced, provisions gathered and concealed, bags and clothing made, maps printed and compasses manufactured. Provisional assault dates had been set. It appeared to everyone involved that Olympia was on track and that nothing could stop it now. But at the eleventh hour a wild card was suddenly thrown down before Stallard and everyone involved. The entire finely tuned operation was suddenly faced with a profound crisis beyond the control of the prisoners, a crisis that had the potential to render Olympia stillborn.

CHAPTER TEN

Pack Up Your Troubles

*I had this horrible vision of myself hopelessly ensnared
on the coiled barbed wire between the fences.*

Lieutenant Jack Champ, 2/6th Australian Infantry

'Gentlemen, from now on you are on twelve hours' notice to commence the escape',[1] announced Tom Stallard on 28 August 1942, his eyes beaming before the assembled members of Team 3. He had already visited the other teams with the same order. A ripple of excitement ran through them all at his words. Stomachs filled with butterflies and mouths went dry, furtive glances were made at partners and teammates – the moment they had been waiting and planning for had finally arrived.

Stallard's announcement would presage many nights with little sleep for the Olympia escapers, nights dominated by visions of the double perimeter fences, the scaling apparatuses that they had all come to know so intimately, and the Germans watching them from their lofty wooden towers. Fears, both well founded and irrational, would dominate all of their minds. 'Will I be up to it when the time comes?' 'Will I freeze with nerves or panic?' 'Will the platform remain steady?' 'Will the guards shoot?' 'Will I let the others down somehow?'[2] During those dark summer nights, lying in their bunks, eyes staring into the blackness, those kinds of thoughts, the self-doubt, the fear of failure or cowardice, preyed upon their minds relentlessly. Very few were immune. In Team 3 their illustrious captain, Rex Baxter, exuded confidence and buoyed up the others, dispelling many of the worries with his sense of humour and stolid countenance.

Stallard's shock announcement was due to their captors. The Germans had left him with no choice but to launch Olympia at a time not of his own choosing and under less than ideal circumstances. The Germans didn't know it, but they had just taken a wrecking ball to Stallard's intricate operation, and it remained to be seen if the British could salvage it.

In early August the new camp commandant, Oberst Brinkord – thanks to his rotund build disparagingly nicknamed 'Bulk Issue' by the prisoners – had suddenly called the Senior British Officer, Colonel Kennedy, to his office in the *Kommandantur* and announced that Oflag VI-B was being dissolved. The German experiment with creating a single enormous camp housing virtually all of the British and Commonwealth officers that they had captured in France and Greece was at an end. The 450 RAF prisoners would be sent to a new camp, a 'Stalag Luft', run by the Luftwaffe, the German Air Force. Five hundred of the older army officers were to be sent to a new camp 30 miles from Warburg on the other side of Kassel at Rotenburg an der Fulda. The remainder of the prisoners would go to Oflag VII-B at Eichstätt in southern Germany.

Brinkord's announcement was a major blow to Operation Olympia, because the four escape teams contained officers destined for all three of the new camps, and the same applied to the electrical, stooge and diversion teams. Infuriatingly, the Germans refused to give any specific dates for the moves, except to say that the first group to go would be the older officers before the end of the month. Brinkord had the lists placed on the camp noticeboard, showing all the officers' names and the parties they would go with. There was widespread consternation among the prisoners; for not only was Olympia under threat but several major tunnelling operations might not be completed in time.

The prisoners' mood was often combative with the Germans, resulting in some punishments. On 29 July Brinkord had announced that because German prisoners were not receiving regular mail in British and Dominion POW camps, mail to prisoners at Warburg would be severely restricted. This was a major psychological blow to the prisoners. On 8 August Brinkord ordered many prisoners to be interviewed for writing 'insulting letters' criticising the new mail restrictions. Several were threatened with court martial. The same day Hauptmann Rademacher sentenced 40 RAF officers to five days' solitary confinement in the cooler for being late on parade.[3]

*

Tom Stallard faced a terrible quandary. It was clearly no longer possible to launch the escape attempt in early September, as originally agreed by the Escape Committee, because one or more of the three parties of prisoners would have already left the camp by then. Any earlier escape date would mean that the condition of the moon would not be favourable. Stallard, Walker and the team leaders fretted over the decision. Experience and available information suggested that the first party to go, containing the older officers, would move at very short notice. When the lists were consulted on the camp noticeboard, Stallard and Rupert Fuller's names were in that first party.

Stallard had to decide between putting his plan into operation perhaps prematurely or being caught napping if the Germans moved him and several other vital Olympia members at short notice.

The solution to Stallard and Fuller's problem was substitutes. Two officers volunteered to impersonate Stallard and Fuller. It was agreed that three weeks after arrival at their new camp these two substitutes would reveal their true identities to the German authorities, and then leave them to work out what had happened.[4]

But no one knew what kind of precautions the Germans might be taking to prevent this kind of ruse, and whether the substitutes could pull it off in front of Rademacher and his team. Stallard was already well known to Rademacher because of his previous escape attempts.

Stallard had to consider whether the Olympia teams were ready to go on short notice. They were highly trained after spending most of the summer scrambling over Hamilton-Baillie's apparatus in the music room. Rations and clothing were ready. The three other apparatuses were not yet built and this would require at least two hours' covert labour. The electrical team was ready and would need to be in position almost an hour before the assault began.

Captains Searle and Moulson had not been idle since they had proved their theory by shorting the perimeter lights in May. They had made a technical decision to change the shape of the arcing horns. Their earlier demonstration meant that they had a good idea of the probable magnitude of the electric current involved, and also of the likely main fuse rupture capacity. They modified their original horn configuration, making it more like a pair of shallow hooks with a built-in hinged shorting link incorporated. This would eliminate the somewhat cumbersome T-bar and, more importantly, would later enable them to disengage the shorting link from outside the cobbler's workshop by means of a long remote-control string.[5]

Searle and Moulson explained to Stallard that they would still be able to control the flow, though they now intended to leave the area of the workshop immediately the perimeter lights were out, and thus well before they came under random fire from panicking trigger-happy guards along the wire. 'We reckon we can leave the hinged link in position for as long as it helps to continue to cause Hun chaos, thereby aiding our chaps already safely over the wire', said Searle. 'After that, the sooner the shorting link can be removed, the better because of our chances of preserving the cobbler's hut secret for further use.'[6]

The two RAOC men had discussed the idea of having more lookouts on the electrical team, as Stallard's plan required such precise timing to work. Johnnie Cousens had explained that once in position inside the workshop, they were to await a lamp signal from him and were then to cut the power immediately. Searle and Moulson decided that in the interests of preserving the cobbler's workshop secret they would make do alone on the night of the assault, but they would allow themselves extra preparation time to reinstall blackout curtains, electrical equipment and so on well before Zero Hour. A larger team might be spotted moving into position as they crept towards the cobbler's hut after dark.[7]

Reacting to Commandant Brinkord's declaration to disband the camp, Major Stallard judged that, moon and weather conditions aside, the Olympia teams were ready to go at short notice. Several team members were in the party that was going to be sent to Eichstätt. These men told Stallard that they would give up their Olympia places because their best chance to escape would be from the new camp located close to the Swiss frontier. They asked that their places be given to older officers who were to be moved first. This decision, though magnanimous, created a problem. There was no time left to train new men as replacements. They could receive only basic instruction on the apparatus in the little time remaining.[8] Stallard decided to put most of the replacements, mainly from the RAF, on to Team 4 under Captain Crawford.[9] Henry Coombe-Tennant lost his partner, who was going south to Eichstätt with the third party, so he asked permission to join Major Arkwright and Captain Fuller to make a trio. This meant that Team 1 would number eleven members.

The final teams would consist of the following officers:[10]

Team 1

Position	Surname	Nationality/Arm of Service
1	Arkwright (team captain)	UK/Army
2	Fuller	UK/Army
3	Coombe-Tennant	UK/Army
4	Corfield	UK/Army
5	Tomes	UK/Army
6	Oldman	UK/Army
7	Hunt	UK/Army
8	Quill	UK/Royal Navy
9	Hanrahan	UK/Royal Navy
10	Heisch	UK/Army
11	Symonds	UK/Army
Anchor	Jamieson	UK/Army

Team 2

Position	Surname	Nationality/Arm of Service
1	Russell (team captain)	UK/Army
2	Johnston	UK/Army
3	Leah	UK/Army
4	Campbell-Preston	UK/Army
5	Walker	UK/Army
6	Ross	UK/Army
7	Macleod	UK/Army
8	Gilliat	UK/Army
9	Pardoe	UK/Army
Anchor	Rawlings	UK/Army

Team 3

Position	Surname	Nationality/Arm of Service
1	Baxter (team captain)	Australia/Army
2	Champ	Australia/Army
3	Young	UK/Army
4	Bartlett	UK/Army
5	Mytton	UK/Army
6	Hyde	UK/Royal Air Force
7	Kayll	UK/Royal Air Force
8	Morris	UK/Royal Air Force
9	Stallard	UK/Army
10	Page	UK/Army
Anchor	Barr	UK/Army

Team 4

Position	Surname	Nationality/Army of Service
1	Crawford (team captain)	Australia/Army
2	Hand	Australia/Army
3	Bain	New Zealand/Army
4	Cooper	New Zealand/Army
5	Bisset	UK/Army
6	Smith	UK/Royal Air Force
7	Driver	UK/Royal Air Force
8	Evilt-Jones	UK/Royal Air Force
9	Kritland	South Africa/Royal Air Force
10	Williams	UK/Royal Air Force
Anchor	Hamilton	UK/Army

With the reshuffle complete, discussions now centred on bringing 'Zero Day' – the day of the escape – forward. The Germans announced that the first party containing the older officers would hand in their kit for inspection on 27 August and would depart on the 30th. Stallard decided that 30 August would be the first *possible* day to launch Olympia. The Germans had frequently told the prisoners in the past that a party would leave on such-and-such a date and that kit would be handed in and searched two days before. The prisoners would duly hand in their kit, but then the evening before the agreed moving day the Germans would announce that the transfer was postponed indefinitely.[11] This uncertainty meant that if Stallard were to launch Olympia on 30 August, when the moon was unfavourable, he might be premature. The Germans might delay the move, allowing Stallard to stick to his original schedule and launch Olympia on 7 September, the first day when the condition of the moon would be perfect. The choice of dates might be the margin between the success and failure of the entire enterprise, an enterprise that had been five months in the planning. Some prisoners suspected that the Germans deliberately changed their plans in order to upset escapers' calculations.

Although Stallard had decided that the escape would take place on 30 August, he added a caveat. If by 29 August there was still no news of the first party's impending move, then Zero Day would be postponed from day to day until 7 September, the originally agreed upon first escape day.

On 27 August the first party's kit was duly handed in for inspection. The Germans also announced that the second party, consisting of RAF prisoners, would leave on 1 September and the third party, going to Oflag VII-B in southern Germany, on 3 September.

Stallard visited each of the Olympia teams on 28 August to personally brief them on what was happening. He met with his own team in David Walker's room.

'We have decided the actual assault area will be between Huts 20 and 21.' These were two accommodation huts that stood side by side in the north-west corner of the camp next to the hockey field and perpendicular to the perimeter fence. 'Some rather noisy diversions have been organised for when the lights are put out, and I can assure you that the place will be in complete uproar while our escape is in progress',[12] said Stallard. Up to this time, for reasons of security, the team members had not been privy to Johnnie Cousens' diversion programme.

'Our departure will be timed so that the guards on patrol will be as far from the assault area as possible', continued Stallard, 'and we're quite convinced that all the Germans will panic, having no idea what the hell is going on.' Several officers laughed at this satisfying vision.

'As you know, Hut 20 is empty, and this is where our team will assemble. Those on Number 2 ladder will also assemble there, while the remaining two teams will be in Hut 21.' Stallard paused. 'When we go over we will fan out, and David will show each of you the direction you should take.'[13] Walker nodded and fumbled with a clutch of notes in his hand that detailed precise compass bearings for each pair of escapers.

'Now one important thing', said Stallard, his eyes scanning the faces of his team. 'We know there is a German standing patrol in the hayfield beyond the camp, but they change their position every night. Should you be unlucky enough to run into this patrol you are to surrender immediately and try and occupy them for at least three minutes to give the others a chance to get away. Understood?'[14] The men all muttered their agreement. Stallard's reference to 'Deep Field' was of concern, because it was the one aspect of the plan that the prisoners could not control. Having twenty or so heavily armed Germans wandering around the fields through which 40 men planned to run to freedom was worrying and frustrating in equal measure, but there was no way this patrol could be diverted. Stallard's order to surrender immediately if any of them stumbled into 'Deep Field' was wise. Under the circumstances, the Germans would be well within their rights to shoot first and ask questions later.

'In conclusion', said Stallard, 'Major Cousens will be in charge of the entire operation from the compound, and his word is law. He will give you the signal to start, and if he feels it is necessary he will call a halt.' Cousens' job of 'Controller' was paramount, for on the night Stallard would be simply team member Number 9 and would not be in any position to influence the overall operation. Cousens would weigh the risks, time the escape and try to prevent the guards interfering. It went without saying that Cousens and his team of stooges and diverters would be running the same risk of being shot as the scaling teams, without the bonus of actually making an escape. Stallard would later characterise Cousens' team as 'tireless, faithful and courageous'[15] without any understatement.

'That's about it, gentlemen', said Stallard, a broad smile crossing his face. 'No more practice sessions, and word will be passed to you when it is on.'[16] Stallard left the hut and Walker immediately went to work issuing instructions to the escaping pairs on which direction they should follow once across the wire. Nothing was left to chance – the plan was complete. Nothing more could be done to prepare the men for Zero Night. Now it was simply a waiting game.

CHAPTER ELEVEN

Fifteen Yards to Freedom

*Olympia was a tremendously exciting business, not
only in computing risks, but in adjusting plans to
chances that were deteriorating all the time.*

Captain David Walker, The Black Watch

'Dear God, help him!' yelled Michael Borwick, his face streaked
with dirt and sweat. 'There's been an accident!' Borwick
had crawled out of the darkened tunnel beneath Hut 13 and into
the chamber at the bottom of the vertical entrance shaft. He was
virtually hysterical, his body smeared with mud, his eyes wild.
Lieutenant George Cruickshank, who was operating the tunnel air
pump, was aghast. A few seconds before, Borwick had started yelling down the tunnel, ordering Cruickshank to turn off the electrical
current that supplied the lighting. It was 30 August 1942 – Zero Day
for Operation Olympia – and a terrible tragedy had just occurred.
Death had come to Oflag VI-B, throwing the final preparations for
Tom Stallard's brilliant scheme into serious doubt.

30 August had begun very early for many of the prisoners at
Warburg. At 2.00am the Germans had begun processing the officers
who were due to leave with the first party. The Germans made them
pass through a wicket gate into the German area of the camp. They
had set up a bright arc lamp so that each prisoner could be seen
clearly by three German officers sitting at a table. As each prisoner
stood in front of the lamp before the table, he gave his name and
prisoner of war identity number. A German officer then compared

the prisoner's face with a portrait photograph taken when he had first arrived at Warburg.

For the two substitutes who would attempt to pass themselves off as Tom Stallard and Rupert Fuller, the scrutiny by the German officers was a major test. The officer pretending to be Stallard went through first. After giving his name and number a German found the relevant photograph and carefully scrutinised it, his eyes passing backwards and forwards from the photo to the officer's face under the harsh light. Unfortunately, Stallard was probably the best-known British prisoner in the camp because of his numerous escape attempts and periods of solitary confinement. The German officer rifled through Stallard's file and seized on a particular detail.

'Raise your shirt', ordered the German. The file noted that Stallard had a large appendectomy scar. His substitute did not. The fake Stallard was quickly dragged out of the line by German soldiers and marched off to the guardroom for further questioning.[1]

Fuller's substitute watched the fate of his companion with barely disguised horror. He lost his nerve, left the line and went to see Arkwright and Fuller in their hut. He told them that it was impossible and that he saw no point in making a fool of himself trying. Arkwright and Fuller tried to restore the man's confidence with hot tea and common sense.[2] Fuller explained that unlike Stallard he was unknown to the Germans, as he had never attempted an escape or broken any of the camp's rules. It also helped that Fuller's substitute bore an uncanny resemblance to him. Eventually Arkwright and Fuller won the man over and he agreed to give it another go. He passed through the gate and passed the inspection without a single problem.

*

While his substitute was getting himself caught at the wicket gate, the real Tom Stallard was lying under a bunk in an area of the camp that he did not usually frequent, being carefully watched over by a team of stooges. When he received word from Arkwright that his identity switch had failed, he moved on to another well-protected hide. Walker visited him briefly and Stallard ordered him to take command of Olympia if the Germans managed to discover him before the operation began.[3]

By 7.00am the Germans had processed the last of the prisoners who were leaving that day. Immediately afterwards German sentries began banging on every accommodation hut, ordering the prisoners outside for a roll call. During this parade the German security officers repeatedly demanded to know where Stallard was. They were met by sarcastic replies from the prisoners. 'Tom died and was buried last night', shouted one wag. 'He was last seen going through the wicket gate an hour ago', said another. 'I saw Tom leaving the camp with a bag under his arm two weeks ago, old chap', shouted another. After an hour of futile questioning the Germans dismissed the parade. Fortunately for Stallard, they had their hands full providing a heavy escort for the prisoners who were leaving and could not spare the staff to conduct a search of the camp for the phantom major.[4]

*

It was at lunchtime that the camp erupted into frantic activity and word began to circulate that a terrible tragedy had occurred. For several months Jock Hamilton-Baillie and a team of diggers had been slowly excavating a tunnel beneath a coal cellar just off Hut 13's kitchen. HB had kept the tunnel's dimensions to a minimum because of the difficulty of getting rid of the spoil.[5] It was extremely narrow and very dark, lit by just a single bulb hanging from some poorly insulated piecemeal wiring that ran along the roof of the tunnel.[6] Since the announcement of the impending moves from Warburg, HB and his co-workers had been frantically trying to complete the tunnel in time, hoping to escape at the same time as Stallard and the Olympia teams. Some of HB's original tunnellers had already gone through the wicket gate with the first group to be evacuated and he had been forced to accept new, untrained volunteers for the dangerous work.

On the morning of 30 August the excavation team consisted of a new recruit, Lieutenant John Dupree, Seaforth Highlanders, who was working at the face, passing back mud and stones to his partner Michael Borwick. Lieutenant Cruickshank was manning the air pump. Dupree was lying in about an inch of water as he worked.

As soon as Borwick emerged into the entrance chamber shouting for assistance, Cruickshank crawled straight down the black hole, quickly locating Dupree's inert body. Dupree had been hauling up a muck disposal trolley on the little railway that HB had laid inside the tunnel. The trolley had contained a new length of air pipe that Dupree was going to install. One end of this air pipe caught in some live wire that had been coiled to enable the light to be moved progressively as the tunnel became longer. This wire had fallen on to the track and become entangled with the trolley wheels. Dupree, sweating, cursing and worming his way like a snake, crawled back to the tangle to try to clear it when a joint in the makeshift wiring broke and a live cable fell onto his naked back, electrocuting him.

Cruickshank pulled desperately at Dupree's ankles, trying to pull his body out of the tunnel, but it was too heavy.[7]

'We'll have to sacrifice the tunnel', gasped Cruickshank to Borwick. Cruickshank scrambled out of the tunnel into the coal cellar where the rest of the day team waited and started pounding on the locked cellar door like a maniac. A startled British orderly opened it. Cruickshank quickly explained what had happened, sending some of his diggers to alert the Germans and others to inform the Escape Committee. When the Germans arrived they agreed that the quickest way to get Dupree out was to dig down into the shallow tunnel from the compound.

HB and his team attacked the ground like madmen, digging frantically in the hope that Dupree might still be alive. In the meantime Captain Frank Weldon ran into the coal cellar with a rope, squirmed up the shaft and tied the rope around Dupree's ankles. Back in the air pump chamber Weldon and another officer, Johnnie Johnstone, hauled on the ropes for all their worth, eventually managing to drag Dupree's body out.[8] Other prisoners and German guards helped to lift Dupree onto the coal cellar floor where British and German camp doctors tried desperately to revive him. Weldon, streaked in mud and sweat, collapsed from his exertions. Sadly, Dupree was dead.

'Big X' and the Escape Committee held an emergency meeting within an hour of the tragedy. They faced a difficult and delicate decision. Colonel G.W. Kennedy, Senior British Officer, also attended and would have the final say in the matter. Each Escape Committee member was asked to state his thoughts about the launching of Operation Olympia that night, in light of the Dupree tragedy. Some thought it unseemly to allow Stallard's plan to go ahead after the death. Others made the point that the camp was being split up, the operation was ready, and it should proceed as planned. Kennedy made the final decision after listening to 'Big X' and the others speak. Stallard was also present.

Kennedy mulled things over for a few minutes and then turned to Stallard. 'You go, Tom', he said. 'You go because that's what young Dupree would have wanted you to do.'[9] It was a sentiment that was wholeheartedly echoed by Major Arkwright and the other team captains when they heard about Dupree's death and the discussion about whether to allow Olympia to proceed. Arkwright felt no sympathy for talk of cancelling the show, and he was backed up to a man by his teammates. 'It will be difficult to find a more timely and fitting tribute to Dupree's unsuccessful attempt to escape than to bring our own effort to a triumphant conclusion',[10] he stated to his team.

Hamilton-Baillie was upset by Dupree's death but also dismayed by the loss of his project. The German decision to move out part of the camp meant that he had been forced into accepting the inexperienced volunteers, 'so we lost a tunnel perhaps rather unnecessarily',[11] as he later said.

Tom Stallard quickly left the hut and returned to his hiding place, issuing orders to his team leaders to begin construction of the final three scaling apparatuses. Dupree's death had shocked them all. 'Zero Hour', the moment when Operation Olympia would swing into action and the 40 prisoners would storm the wire, had been set for 9.30pm.[12] In less than nine hours Stallard and his men would also be facing death in their attempt to escape, not from bad wiring but from rifles and machine guns. Dupree's demise caused every man to pause and reflect on what he was about to submit himself to. Most had already suffered several sleepless nights filled with imaginary fears and doubts since Stallard had placed them on notice. The sudden death of a brother officer who was engaged in an escape attempt was depressing and deeply unsettling. But at least they now had something to do. The waiting was over, and building the scaling apparatuses would take their minds off Dupree, death and failure for a few hours.

*

Rex Baxter joined Stallard and Jack Champ from Team 3 in Hut 27. Arkwright and Fuller from Team 1 arrived shortly afterwards. The team captains and their Number 2s would be responsible for building their scaling apparatuses. Since the tragic death of Lieutenant Dupree and the loss of the Hut 13 tunnel, Hamilton-Baillie had secreted himself in the loft of Hut 27, where timber, nails, rope and purloined tools had been assembled. The parts for the apparatuses had already been cut out – it was just a case of assembling them.[13] A well-concealed trapdoor in the ceiling allowed access to the loft, and the five escapers carefully climbed up. An elaborate screen of stooges was in place around both Huts 27 and 28; inside the latter loft, Captain Crawford and Jack Hand from Team 4 awaited instruction from HB in constructing their own apparatus. Team 2, led by Captain Steve Russell, would use the apparatus concealed in the music room, so instead they supplemented the stooges who were guarding the huts.

Soon, the sounds of sawing and hammering could be heard coming from the lofts as the teams worked quickly, trying to build the apparatuses within their cramped confines. It was hard work, but thrilling to see the brilliant design take shape. There was the chance that the Germans might launch a sudden inspection of the camp, but it was a chance that the Olympia teams were prepared to risk. Twice the stooges gave the warning shout 'Goons up!', meaning that a German had strayed to within earshot of the construction projects.[14] On this command all work ceased and the escapers kept completely still until the German had wandered off and the stooges gave the all clear.

*

Afternoon roll call was called for 3.00pm, but none of the teams had quite finished making their apparatuses. Once they had gone through the motions of being counted by the Germans, the teams slipped back to the huts and completed their work. By 4.00pm three more apparatuses had been built, dyed purple with indelible lead dye for camouflage and stashed in the roof spaces until they could be moved into final assault positions once the light began to fade from the sky. The Olympia escapers were exhausted by their labours in the confined roof spaces and returned to their huts for tea. Some, like Arkwright, retired to their bunks for a few minutes' sleep before evening roll call at 6.00pm.

Assembling on the sports ground for roll call, the prisoners were surprised and slightly alarmed when Hauptmann Rademacher appeared to personally take the parade. Some were worried that his presence signalled that the Germans were aware something was brewing, but as it turned out Rademacher's appearance was nothing special – he strutted, shouted and generally behaved in a hateful manner, but clearly had no idea of the covert preparations for Olympia.

Once dismissed from parade, the escapers were permitted by Stallard to make their goodbyes to their friends, who up until that time had not known that the escape was on. The Olympia members told their friends two at a time out in the open. Then they returned to their rooms to pack their homemade backpacks and make last-minute preparations for their departure. Nervous tension pervaded their huts like some infectious miasma, and very few of them were unaffected by it. 'What's up, Arkwright? You haven't touched a thing', asked Rupert Fuller as Arkwright picked at his supper of porridge and tinned meat.

'Dentist's pain',[15] replied Arkwright, using the prisoners' euphemism for being in a blue funk.

Fuller was unmoved. He tucked into his supper with the enthusiasm of a man who had just finished a hard day's labour. Arkwright, out of shame, forced himself to eat, even though he had to force down every mouthful with an effort. Nerves aside, he knew that in a few hours' time the food would stand him in good stead.

Baxter and Champ's close friend, Second Lieutenant Mark Howard, a former Australian jackaroo who had worked the sheep stations before the war, prepared for them a special celebratory meal. They dined on tinned steak and onions followed by pudding made from ground-up biscuits, margarine, powdered milk and raisins.[16]

*

At 8.00pm the Olympia teams dressed in their escape outfits and a little before 9.00 they made their way to Huts 27 and 28, where they had stashed the scaling apparatuses. A wide ring of stooges was laid on by Johnnie Cousens to make sure that no Germans came close.

In Hut 27 Arkwright and Baxter's teams carefully took down

their new apparatuses from the loft. It was dark outside, and the Germans permitted prisoners to wander around the camp until 11.00pm. Cousens' stooges pretended to be taking a last stroll or enjoying a final smoke before turning in. Cousens would take command of the operation from Stallard as soon as all four teams were safely ensconced in the huts. He used 'Camp Police', a system of sentry observers, a patrol system for helping the watchers, and a signal system between his control point and the cobbler's hut.[17] If a German so much as scratched his head, Cousens would know about it.

Teams 1 and 3 were to move into Hut 20, just fifteen yards from the perimeter fence. This hut was under observation of one of the ground sentries who was patrolling on that portion of the perimeter. Cousens arranged to carry out the move when the sentry was not in a position to see. Inside the darkened Hut 27 the two teams were ready. Four men carried each ladder assembly while the others waited in a line behind, one man looking out of the window waiting for the nearest stooge to give the 'all clear' signal.

At the fence the German sentry paced along, occasionally glancing into the camp, his boots crunching along the path just outside the perimeter. He stopped, adjusted the rifle strap over his shoulder, ran a finger around the inside of his tunic collar and proceeded on his beat. As he neared the end of his patrol sector, he was temporarily without line of sight of Hut 20. At this moment a signal was passed like lightning between the stooges. In Hut 27 the man at the window turned and muttered one word: 'Clear.' As silently as possible, the 23 men, including the two anchors, left the hut and scampered across the patch of open ground to Hut 20, crossing the main road that bisected the camp east to west, almost bent double as they ran. Within a few seconds everyone was inside, smiling, panting hard and wiping sweat from their faces. No alarms had sounded. Teams 2 and 4 also transferred their apparatuses to Hut 21, standing to the left of 20, without incident. Zero Hour was set for 9.30pm, in less than an hour's time. Another agonising wait ensued.

*

While the four teams moved quietly into position in Huts 20 and 21, some distance away to the east Captains Searle and Moulson made ready to play their vital role in Operation Olympia. Donning dark clothing, balaclavas and backpacks containing their equipment, the two electrical specialists knew that they would need plenty of time to prepare inside the cobbler's workshop. They set off well before 9.00pm, flitting from hut to hut and shadow to shadow, towards their objective. At one point they found themselves pressed into the deep shadow beside a hut as a German walked past on his way to the camp's lower gate. Not daring to move or breathe, Searle and Moulson waited until the German, who briefly glanced in their direction without seeing them, meandered his way to the gate and thence into the guards' compound on the other side of the wire from the cobbler's hut.[18]

Once it was clear, Searle and Moulson charged up to the cobbler's workshop door. While Moulson kept watch, Searle quickly used the fake key to unlock the door before both men slipped inside. Working methodically, Moulson once more hung the thick blackout cloth over the windows, then using a weak torch beam the two men carefully attached their newly designed shorting hooks to the exposed wiring, played out a long string through the window, and concealed themselves once more in deep shadow outside the workshop, with Searle holding the string in both hands. Both men peered towards the huts far away to the west, waiting for the lamp signal at which point the string would be pulled tight and the lights shorted.

Searle and Moulson sat in complete silence and waited and waited and waited. Time dragged by as if in slow motion, and their limbs grew stiff. But their eyes never left the far-away huts, whose northern ends were slightly illuminated by the perimeter fence lighting. The lazy beams of the guard tower searchlights occasionally played across the open ground and the huts, a harsh and unforgiving light.[19]

*

Inside Huts 20 and 21 the tension was as palpable as that being experienced by Captains Searle and Moulson outside the cobbler's workshop. All teams carefully greased the apparatuses' runners using dripping.[20] Other than this job there was nothing more to do except wait. Waiting was torture, and all the men involved suffered in those silent huts.

The men soon became fidgety, making minute adjustments to their clothing and backpacks. There was a little desultory conversation but for the most part the men were quiet and reflective. Rex Baxter in Hut 20 sat as still as a statue on the end of a wooden bench plucking microscopic bits of lint off his trousers. Jack Champ, his Number 2, felt cold in the pit of his stomach, a peculiar empty feeling. When he glanced across at Major Arkwright, captain of Team 1, he could see Arkwright's blue eyes darting around the room, always returning to the silent sentinel who stood by the window gazing steadfastly out into the compound, waiting for the signal to begin the assault. Champ watched as Arkwright bent down and slowly retied his bootlaces.[21]

Arkwright was desperately trying to control his racing pulse and the sudden hair-raising spasms of panic that assailed him, and to fight down the waves of dread that everything was going to end in a ghastly and bloody fiasco.[22]

Champ tried to think of home, of Australia. He closed his eyes and a dark image of Corio Bay, Geelong danced into view. As Champ concentrated, the scene lightened until the water turned azure blue. He could feel the slight swaying of his small yacht as he turned into a pleasant breeze. Reflected light danced across the water's glassy surface, sparkling and glinting under the sun. Champ

143

imagined the gentle waves slapping against the yacht's bow, while overhead a single seagull cawed as it circled the mast.[23] But when one of his teammates stifled a cough he opened his eyes and was brought sharply back to reality. He felt calmer now, more resolved and stronger.

In Hut 21 the same scene played out. Team captains Steve Russell and Doug Crawford and their men waited, daydreamed or simply stared into space. Every man knew that they could be facing the last few minutes of their lives. Many suffered from Arkwright's feeling of dread – that somehow Tom Stallard's wonderful plan would be dashed on the cold steel mesh of the perimeter fences, and that many of them would be shot down attempting to cross or fall in between the fences to be left wriggling in a mass of barbed wire that would tear their clothes and flesh to ribbons. Every man believed in Stallard and they believed in Olympia, but if anything went even slightly awry, men could die. They had all weighed the risks when Stallard had first proposed the plan to them, and they had decided to gamble with their lives. More than one man said a silent prayer.

David Walker, Number 5 on Team 2, sat and watched. Occasionally someone eased the weight of his pack against the wall with a creaking sound. Walker looked out at the wire. 'The lamps on the perimeter stood barely against the night, each making its own small pool of brightness.'[24] Walker watched as every now and then a searchlight beam played on the flat ground beyond 'and reduced the lamps to their proper status'.[25]

Tom Stallard remained a pillar of strength, refusing to reveal any indecision or fear as the minutes ticked down to the assault. In Hut 20 he went from man to man on both teams, shaking their hands and wishing each of them good luck and Godspeed. Stallard had brought them to this place, and he would deliver them over the wire to freedom – in that simple fact all wanted to believe.

*

Walker sat on a wooden bench with two Scotsmen, Ross and Macleod from the Queen's Own Cameron Highlanders. The Scots chatted away about nothing in particular.[26] Walker could say nothing – he was too tense.

As the last few minutes bled slowly from their watches, some of the men went to the coal box beside each hut's stove and covered their hands and faces in soot. Most already wore balaclava helmets and they now pulled on dark woollen gloves. At 9.20pm the team captains turned to their men, telling them to take their positions. The scaling apparatuses were made ready, four men holding each. Behind them, the remaining team members stood in a quiet queue, each in his assigned numbered position, all eyes fixed on the window, waiting for the lights to go out. Pulse rates increased, nerves fluttered through stomachs or made men shudder with cold even though it was a warm night. They were like racehorses champing at the bit, on a knife-edge of readiness, adrenalin pumping through their systems. 'Come on ... come on', they muttered under their breath, constantly scanning watches and staring at the window, 44 men whose faces had taken on hard, determined expressions, totally focused on the task ahead. The scaling apparatuses grew heavy the longer the men stood holding them; everyone's breathing had increased, blood pumping in their ears, stomachs hollow, mouths dry.

Arkwright licked his lips and whispered urgently: 'What time is it?'

'9.25 sir', came a reply. Then the lights went out ...

CHAPTER TWELVE

Zero Night

So far as we could see, the Operation worked like clockwork.

Captain Rupert Fuller, Royal Sussex Regiment

'Go! Go! Go!' hissed Captain Ron Moulson. Kenneth Searle quickly pulled the string and engaged the shorting hooks on the exposed cobbler's workshop wiring. The perimeter was plunged into darkness, the floodlights and searchlights going out in an instant.[1]

In Huts 20 and 21 the four Olympia teams tensed, straining their ears for the signal from Major Cousens' controllers to begin the assault. Nothing happened – the seconds ticked by and no order came. The men, sweating heavily, ready in their assault positions, couldn't bear the suspense much longer. In Hut 21 Captain Doug Crawford, leading Team 4, heard the controller say something through the open door. 'You heard "Go!"' whispered his Number 2, Jack Hand. 'Was that "Go!" or did he say "No"?' asked Crawford.[2] He waited a few more seconds, wracked by indecision, then made up his mind. 'To hell with it, we go', he said. Team 4 thundered through the hut door followed closely behind by Steve Russell's Team 2. David Walker followed his escape partner Pat Campbell-Preston through the door and down the steps. 'It was even quieter than before. Only fifteen seconds ago we had begun to move. Now we had action and the time of waiting had gone. This was reality and clear.'[3]

Four men in each team ran forward holding the scaling appa-ratuses like firemen while the rest followed behind in their allotted places. Moving in line, the men looked straight ahead. 'I saw the others in front of me', said Walker, 'the fence above, and through it the flat plain and the little hut which would guide us when we were over.'[4]

In Hut 20 also, confusion over the signal reigned. Major Arkwright's Team 1 and Captain Baxter's Team 3 stood holding their apparatuses, blackened faces swept by doubt. Arkwright never heard any order to go; instead, through the gloom outside he saw Crawford's Team 4 come pounding out of Hut 21 next door and decided to simply follow them. 'Go, go, go!' he whispered, and the two teams came through the hut doorway and charged the wire, fanning out to launch their apparatuses at their agreed places.[5]

The Number 5 man on Team 1, Captain Dick Tomes, was struck by how light it still was, even though the perimeter lights were extinguished. The moon was not fully up but it was not pitch black either. As Tomes ran along behind the apparatus he could clearly see the nearest German sentry, some 50 yards away in the gloom.[6] He was examining the fence. Johnnie Cousens' diversions were working like a dream – the sentries were being held some distance from the assault point by the noise of grapnels embedded in the wire being vigorously pulled by unseen hands. The fence was actually rippling as the wires thrummed and vibrated through the holes in the supporting posts. Two white-painted ladders leaned against the fence, one on each wing of the assault point, adding to the effect.[7] The sentries were confused and had not left their positions to investigate the new noises being made by the four assaulting teams, obeying the stream of fake orders being issued to them by two unseen German-speaking British officers. Added to the noise from the wire and the shouted orders were musical instruments that some of Cousens' diverters were banging or blowing tunelessly, creating a cacophony designed to further disguise the sounds of the scaling apparatuses being raised into place on the wire, and 40 men clambering over.

At the wire the assaulting teams quickly leaned their ladders against the inner fence and began preparing to haul the heavy bridges across the barbed wire-filled gap between the two fences, sweating and panting as they worked. The men were in a state of complete concentration; their long hours of training inside the music room had paid off, and most were hardly aware of what the other teams were doing. The extent of their world was the back of the man in front and the tall ladder standing solidly against the fence in the gloom.

Team 1, on the extreme left of the assault sector, quickly emplaced their ladder, Rupert Fuller slamming the butt ends into the ground with all his strength. The claws at the top of the ladder successfully engaged with the top strand of the fence, just as Hamilton-Baillie had designed. Arkwright, leading, took the handles of the decking, stumbled over the 'line of death', the trip wire that prevented prisoners from getting too close to the perimeter, and put his foot on the first rung of the ladder. But then he froze. For one shattering moment he felt completely powerless to move, but then strong hands gripped him on all sides and he began to climb, pushing the decking up and outwards in front of him as he had been taught.[8]

Team 2 stepped over the trip wire, which had been surreptitiously whitewashed by the diversion team to prevent the heavily loaded teams from tripping, and leaned their ladder against the fence. In position Number 5, David Walker could see the ladder silhouetted against the sky, his eyes quickly adjusting to the gloom.[9]

Doug Crawford, leading Team 4, quickly hooked his ladder onto the wire and also began heaving the heavy bridge decking up, straining under the weight. Rex Baxter, leading Team 3, did likewise, his body held in position by Jack Champ, Major Young and Lieutenant Dennis Bartlett, who had already proved his courage by winning a Military Cross for bravery in Greece.[10] Baxter's great strength enabled him to heave the brutally heavy platform over the wire until it clicked satisfyingly into place. Team 2's Steve Russell managed to launch his decking without incident, the bridge engaging with the top of the ladder and the guide ropes coming taut to form a strong joint. 'I heard the click of the sockets and then the tingle of the wire as the bridge lay across it.'[11] Russell went up at once, with his Number 2, Johnston, close after him. The rest of the team crowded in number order at the bottom. Walker looked to his left and right and saw the other three teams starting to go over. The wire rattled and twanged.[12]

Walker shuffled forward, ready to begin climbing. 'This was the thing we had practised so often. This was the thing we could do with our eyes shut. Easy it was ...'[13]

The Olympia escapers could clearly hear the diversions continuing from both sides, as well as the confused shouts of the German sentries in the nearest guard towers. Teams 1 and 4 suddenly ran into problems. Crawford heaved the decking up and out but jammed the end into the electrical wires that were mounted three feet above the top of the fence. 'Strewth!' exclaimed a puffing Crawford, his booming Australian voice clearly heard by all the other teams. 'Come on, you bastard!' shouted Crawford, pulling the bridge decking backwards and simultaneously climbing down the ladder, in the process almost losing his balance. He would have fallen if the appropriately named Jack Hand, who was right behind him on the ladder, hadn't placed both of his hands under Crawford's seat and held him up while the team captain repositioned the bridge.[14] Finally, after a few seconds of hectic struggling and swearing, they heard the bridge click into place with the top of the ladder.

Major Arkwright made the same mistake as Crawford, and cursed himself for it. For months he had been saying he would not snag the bridge in the electrical wiring above the fence, but in the heat of the moment and in the poor lighting conditions that is exactly what he managed to do. Fortunately, the bridge disengaged from the wires almost immediately and with a final thrust Arkwright launched it across the void to its fullest extent, seeing it drop onto the far side of the obstacle.[15]

The moment the bridges were over the fences and locked into place, the team members began crossing. Arkwright, exhausted from hauling the bridge into position, took a deep gasp of breath and then scuttled over the decking on his hands and knees. Grasping the trapeze bar he dropped down to the ground, kicking up a cloud of dust as he landed. Just as his boots hit the earth, the first gunshot went off close by. The Germans were beginning to recover from their confusion and opened fire randomly at the shadows of men scaling the fences and running off into the darkened sugar beet and corn fields beyond. Arkwright glanced to his right and saw Rex Baxter on the next team hit the ground and take immediately to his heels.[16]

Doug Crawford was going so fast when he came over the bridge that he somersaulted on landing. He quickly picked himself up and started running as fast as he could.[17] Jack Champ was three feet behind Rex Baxter. He was halfway across the bridge when he heard the first rifle shot. German sentries were screaming almost hysterically, both into their field telephones inside the towers and also at the flitting forms of prisoners. Champ's training paid off, for he did not hesitate but immediately followed his team captain, gripped the trapeze bar and swung down. He sprinted after Baxter, who was fast disappearing into the night.[18] Dick Tomes was fifth over on the Team 1 ladder behind Arkwright, Fuller, Henry Coombe-Tennant and Fred Corfield. They had all gone over like cats and Tomes hit the ground on the far side of the fences almost without realising it.[19]

Walker and Campbell-Preston were halfway down their team of ten men. The escalade seemed to go faster than it ever had during training. Walker remembered little of the actual wire crossing – 'only a climb, a scramble, a grip on the dropping bar and down on the other side'.[20] Campbell-Preston was already down, and the two of them immediately streaked off past the little hut as bullets whipped by.

Within 40 seconds 32 men had cleared the wire and were running for their lives across the fields surrounding the camp. Tom Stallard had been one of the last to go, Number 9 on Baxter's Team 3, but he made it and joined the others in sprinting the first 50 yards to put as much distance as possible between himself and the Germans.

Tragedy struck Crawford's Team 4. Perhaps it was the inexperience of many of the RAF officers that Stallard had hastily recruited to fill the gaps caused by the German evacuation of prisoners from Warburg. Perhaps someone had fouled up when constructing the apparatus, or perhaps the wood was in some way defective or weakened. David Walker asserted that the ropes that locked the bridge to the ladder failed.[21] Whatever the cause, with a sickening crunch the ladder suddenly collapsed. Only Crawford and Hand had managed to clear the perimeter fences before the apparatus fell apart.[22] The rest were left on the wrong side of the wire with a splintered and broken ladder. At this point Major Cousens signalled the end of the operation, his team of controllers calling out orders into the dark. Cousens had allowed only 60 seconds for the assault, knowing that the Germans could fall on them at any time. Those officers from Team 4 still inside the perimeter were ordered back by Cousens and attempted to make themselves scarce before the guards arrived. They were bitterly disappointed but obeyed to a man.

The anchor men had all done their jobs splendidly, allowing for three of the apparatuses to work perfectly. They had remained at their posts even under German fire before Cousens released them and they too ran for cover among the nearest huts.

By now, extensive German fire had broken out all along the camp's northern perimeter. Sentries screamed '*Halt*!' or '*Hände hoch*!' at the fast-retreating shadows that flitted and darted across the fields like wraiths. As expected, the sentries in the towers did not turn their fast-firing MG34 machine guns onto the fields for fear of hitting the 'Deep Field' patrol, but they and other Germans did use their rifles, the bullets whining over the heads of the Olympia escapers who were charging along like men possessed.[23] Other shots kicked up the earth around them, throwing up plumes of dust.

Stallard was almost hit several times as he, along with the other escapers, ducked, swore and zigzagged, all the time feeling that they would be hit in the back as they ran. The near misses passing by their heads sounded like buzzing hornets. Fortunately, the Germans were firing almost blind into the darkened fields, but the intensity of fire was nonetheless lethal and it was the prisoners' most frightening experience since capture. If not for Deep Field, the machine guns in the towers would have mown the Olympia escapers down like ripe corn.

Captains Searle and Moulson, some distance away, were waiting to clear the shorting hooks from the cobbler's hut wiring, and they could hear and see what appeared to be a small battle going on, the muzzle flashes of the German weapons lighting up the perimeter fences. Throughout the camp, hundreds of prisoners had come to their hut windows and doors to watch and listen to the uproar, unsure of what was going on.[24]

Searle and Moulson, from their position outside the cobbler's hut, had a perfect view of the tremendous activity occurring in the German barracks area.[25] Dozens of Germans were running from their quarters, pulling on steel helmets and loading weapons as officers and NCOs screamed orders above the din, sending squads of guards off in all directions carrying hand-held torches as well as rifles and machine pistols.

*

Walker and Campbell-Preston sprinted 50 yards, then hit a patch of beans – tall beans, thick and tenacious. From there they emerged onto a stretch of grass and turned left over ploughed fields, running along almost parallel to the camp.[26] 'Pat forged ahead going well, much too well', remembered Walker. 'I was dead tired already and I saw him fading into the dark. Then he stopped and came back.'[27] Panting wildly, Campbell-Preston forgot, as Walker recalled, 'his English accent' and said in a hoarse Scottish whisper: 'Arre ye wounded, Davie?'[28] Walker straightened up and clapped his friend on the back. 'No, let's go!' The two men ducked as a rifle bullet whizzed past. On they ran, idiotic grins plastered to their sweating faces.

Nearly every one of the escapers ran straight into a single strand of barbed wire that the Germans had secretly installed 50 yards from the perimeter fence. Slamming into this practically invisible obstacle, positioned at hip height, at full tilt in the dark was a painful experience. Arkwright went down hard, the wind knocked out of him, falling flat onto his face, too pumped up with adrenalin to feel any pain. His partners Rupert Fuller and Henry Coombe-Tennant quickly caught up with him, Coombe-Tennant stooping and helping to disentangle Arkwright's trousers from the wire. They then quickly spread out again, running along in single file about five yards apart, as German bullets continued to pass over their heads or smack into the earth around them, occasionally ricocheting off stones with a metallic whine. The group covered another two or three hundred yards under fire, seeing no one else but hearing above the din from the camp other escapers moving along parallel to them in the near darkness.[29]

Jack Champ managed to catch up with Rex Baxter and slowed down to his team captain's pace. They also ducked as bullets whistled past. But heedless of the danger, Champ felt elated – he was free at last, free for the first time in eighteen months, free of Warburg. He felt exultant.[30] They all did. Tom Stallard belted along at breakneck pace, grinning wildly, his partner Dick Page, an officer in the Royal Horse Artillery, just behind him. Stallard could hardly dare believe what they had just done. He had seen all eight men in front of him successfully clear his team's apparatus, and he knew that some of the other teams must have managed the same number. He knew that these men were now fanning out across the darkened landscape,[31] the Germans for the time being almost powerless to stop them. Stallard, ducking involuntarily as each German bullet cracked past, felt reborn.

Dick Tomes collided with the strand of barbed wire and went down hard. His trousers and coat were both torn and he was considerably shaken up. He looked for his partner, Fred Corfield, who was only a few yards ahead, struggled to his feet and ran on, the night air carrying not only the flat reports of rifles, but also the constant cries of German sentries, still screaming into the open fields in a vain attempt to stop the escapers.[32]

The German rate of fire was heavy and sustained, but by a miracle none of the Olympia escapers was killed. Unfortunately, Lieutenant Hunt, Royal Tank Regiment, the Number 7 on Team 1, took a bullet ricochet to his heel. In agony and bleeding profusely, Hunt didn't stop but carried on running as best he could with his partner, Lieutenant Brooke Oldman, who had been captured in Norway in 1940, helping him along.[33]

*

The Warburg escapers entered large fields of corn a few hundred yards from the camp perimeter, the crop already cut and standing in stooks. Arkwright, Fuller and Coombe-Tennant slowed to a rapid walk and crouched low so that their heads were no higher than the stooks. Occasional German bullets continued to pass over but they appeared to be out of immediate danger.[34]

Baxter and Champ also slowed to a jog when about 1,000 yards from the camp. Suddenly, a large group of Germans stepped out from behind some stooks and levelled rifles and pistols at the pair of Australians, shouting '*Hände hoch*!' Baxter and Champ, out of breath and bent over with exhaustion, quickly raised their hands above their heads. They had had the bad luck to run straight into Deep Field.

Within a few seconds two more escapers were thrust into the circle of German guards that now surrounded Baxter and Champ. These were Wing Commander Kayll and Flight Lieutenant Morris of the RAF, Numbers 7 and 8 on Baxter's team. All four prisoners were panting from running so hard, choked with fear and with deep frustration at having been caught so quickly. But Baxter and his men realised that they must follow Stallard's order that if captured they were to try to divert the guards' attention for at least three minutes, to allow other escapers time to get clear of the camp.

The German sergeant in charge of Deep Field strode up to Baxter, shoving his Luger into the Australian's heaving chest. 'How many have escaped?' he demanded in English. 'How many away?'

Baxter, still winded, stalled for time. The German sergeant was furious.

'Answer me, or you will be shot!' he bellowed into Baxter's sweat-streaked face.

'Four men', gasped Baxter. 'Four men is all. You have us all!'

The sergeant put his face even closer to Baxter's. 'How did you get out? How did you get past the wire?'

'We jumped over it', gasped Baxter. 'It was easy!'

'You lie!' screamed the sergeant. 'That is impossible!'[35]

For several minutes the sergeant raved at the prisoners about how unbelievable their story was. The other guards stood around leaning on their rifles, listening and waiting for orders. Baxter's ruse worked. He had bought some time for his comrades. The Germans marched Baxter and his companions back to the camp with their hands raised above their heads. On arrival they were taken straight to the guardroom for further interrogation. There, two more escapers who had been recaptured in the fields joined them.

One of the men who joined Baxter's group in the guard-room was Lieutenant Jack Hand, Number 2 on Team 4 and Doug

1. The officers of 2nd Battalion Durham Light Infantry in September 1939 before setting out for France. Tom Stallard is third from the right in the front row.

2. Picture taken from Albert Arkwright's book *Return Journey* (1948), in which the caption reads: 'Captains Norman, White, Fuller, Todd, Few, Arkwright and Symonds, and Major Clark taken after we have been at Laufen nearly a year. It will be seen from our appearance that Red Cross parcels must have been arriving some time.'

3. A group of officer prisoners. On the far right is Jock Hamilton-Baillie, the 'Camp Brain', standing next to his friend Lieutenant Kenneth Jacob (at rear).

Prüf-Nr. 150

OFLAG XVII A 15378

4. Jock Hamilton-Baillie's identity card from Colditz Castle, where he was sent following the Warburg Wire Job and Eichstätt Tunnel.

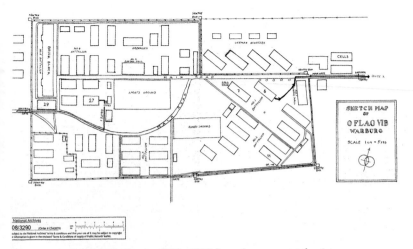

5. MI9 sketch map of Oflag VI-B from the top-secret dossier prepared by British Military Intelligence.

From 'Oflag VI-B', WO224/73, courtesy of The National Archives (Public Record Office)

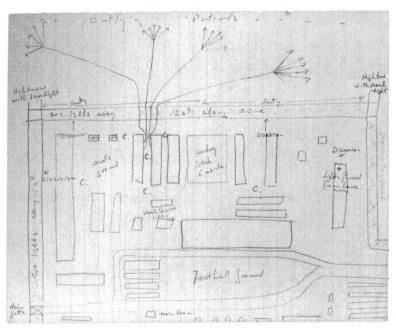

6. Maurice Few's hand-drawn map of the section of the camp where the Wire Job took place, showing the planned routes of the four escape teams.

From 'Operation Olympia: Escape from a Prison Camp', a paper by Major Maurice Few, May 1991, within Few's IWM papers

7. One of Hamilton-Baillie's ingenious scaling contraptions photographed across the fences the day after the escape, 31 August 1942.

8. A further view of the escape contraptions left *in situ* by the German camp authorities the day after the escape.

9. Andrée De Jongh, 1941.

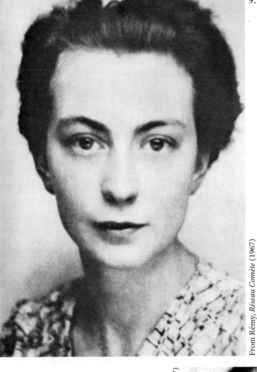

From Rémy, *Réseau Comète* (1967)

From Rémy, *Réseau Comète* (1967)

10. Andrée De Jongh and her father
Frédéric in Paris, late 1942.

11. Baron Jean Greindl (aka 'Nemo'), one of the key leaders of Comet Line.

From Rémy, *Réseau Comète* (1967)

From Rémy, *Réseau Comète* (1967)

12. Jean-François Nothomb (aka 'Franco'), who took over the running of Comet Line after Andrée De Jongh's arrest in 1943.

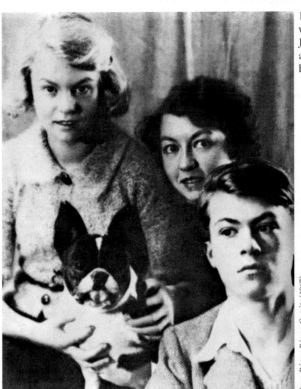

13. Elvire De Greef with her children Janine and Freddy, and her dog 'Gogo', before the war.

From Rémy, *Réseau Comète* (1967)

From Rémy, *Réseau Comète* (1967)

14. Photo from Albert Johnson's identity card, Anglet, 1940, in the name of Albert Jonion.

15. Picture taken from Albert Arkwright's book *Return Journey* (1948), in which the caption reads: 'Rupert, Henry and myself taken during our stay in Liège.'

16. (L. to R.) Andrée De Jongh (Dedée), Micheline Ugeux (Michou) and Elvire De Greef (Tante Go) visit the Ministry of Defence in London as guests of the Royal Air Forces Escaping Society, January 1967. They are talking to Group Captain Bill Randle and Air Commodore Denis Crowley-Milling, whom they once helped to escape.

Crawford's escape partner. When Crawford and Hand had hit the free side of the perimeter fence they had been among the last men over in the whole operation, Crawford having expended several vital seconds struggling to free the bridge decking from the overhead electrical cables. Once in the field they had been subjected to intense rifle fire. Crawford and Hand had split up, running hard, weaving and ducking as bullets stitched the ground all around them. Hand had swerved into the cornfield and run into a section of Deep Field and been captured. Crawford made it through unscathed and decided to go on alone.

Stallard and Page had avoided capture, along with Martin Gilliat and Phil Pardoe. David Walker, Stallard's second-in-command, and his partner, Escape Committee member Pat Campbell-Preston, also made it safely away from the camp. Altogether eight men had failed to get over the perimeter fences; 32 had vaulted the wire but six of them had been recaptured within minutes. The remaining 26 were 'gone aways', as the prisoners described successful escapers. These men were now fanning out across the German countryside along pre-arranged compass bearings towards their target countries. But although 26 were free, they still had a long way to go before they would be safe.

*

Dick Tomes and Fred Corfield made a sharp left turn after getting across the sugar beet field intact. Once over the single strand of barbed wire, the two men ran a further 300 yards through more beet and cabbage fields but then slowed down to a fast walking pace. Their packs seemed to weigh several tons on their backs, their throats were as dry as sandpaper, and Tomes' legs seemed to have lost all their power. Tomes had almost missed inclusion in Olympia due to a bout of diphtheria that had kept him in the camp hospital for six weeks. His recent illness had impaired his physical strength and stamina. He worried that he would not be able to go on until he heard Corfield's heavy huffing and puffing. He was as exhausted as Tomes, and he had not been ill. Suddenly the going became easier and the pair recovered a little from their exertions.[36]

As Arkwright, Fuller and Coombe-Tennant jogged further and further from the camp, the gunfire stopped and the noises behind them gradually died away until they moved through the stillness of the night.[37] They had no idea how many of their comrades had escaped but they felt sure that Olympia had been a resounding success. Before leaving the camp, every escaping group had carefully studied their printed maps and committed the topography and landmarks to memory so that they would not have to constantly stop and divine their bearings during the first night, when it was imperative that they travel as fast and as far as possible before first light. All of the groups were exceptionally well supplied with detailed maps. For example, Arkwright's group possessed a rice paper map of the whole of Germany, another covering western Germany, Holland and France, and a map printed in camp in five sections using the ingenious jelly printer, to the scale of six miles to the inch, showing the entire route that they planned to cover.[38]

Arkwright, Fuller and Coombe-Tennant's plan was to travel almost due north and make for a heavily wooded area about ten miles from the camp. The first obstacle that all of the Olympia escapers would face was a main road three quarters of a mile from the camp and just below the village of Hohenwepel. Stallard and Page were following a similar route, also aiming for the Dutch frontier, along with several other pairs. But Stallard had made sure during the planning stages for Olympia that no pair would take exactly the same route, increasing the chance that some of them would successfully get out of Germany.

Arkwright's group approached the road with extreme caution – it was quite on the cards that the Germans had sent out patrols on bicycles from the camp to guard all the roads, bridges and railway lines in the vicinity in the hope of netting a few more evaders before daybreak.

When they were about 50 yards from the road Arkwright's group stopped and listened. 'Can you hear anything?' whispered Coombe-Tennant, as the three men crouched in the darkness. After a while Arkwright replied: 'I think it's all clear. Let's go.' There was no sign of any movement, so they quickly crossed the road and continued north. From their maps they knew that the next obstacle in their path was a railway line one mile ahead and running parallel with the road. Adjusting their heavy packs, Arkwright's group marched quickly towards the railway across the silent, darkened German countryside; the only sounds were their boots on the ground and the occasional movements of nocturnal creatures in the hedgerows and undergrowth.

*

Tomes and Corfield also crossed the road without incident. Two hundred yards into yet another cornfield they ran into Hunt and Oldman. Hunt was sitting on the ground, blood oozing from the bullet wound to his ankle, while Oldman bandaged it as best he could. 'Looks as though my dance card is going to remain empty for a while', quipped Hunt stoically, his voice hitching as he spoke, his face wet with perspiration and strained with pain.

'Dashed bad luck, old boy', said Corfield, trying to catch his breath.

'Are you going on with it?' asked Tomes, a concerned look on his face as he watched Oldman working on the wound. 'I'll bally well crawl out of Germany if I have to', said Hunt grimly. 'Anyway, I've got Brookie to lean on.' The wounded officer tapped Brooke Oldman on the arm. 'Quite so', replied Oldman.

Brooke Deare Oldman was already a seasoned escaper. Before being captured in Norway he had tried to help a British NCO to avoid capture. Because the NCO was ill, Oldman, who himself was wounded, requested help from a Norwegian local who promptly betrayed them both to the Germans. Shipped to Germany, Oldman next tried to escape in August 1941 from Oflag IX-A/H at Spangenburg, in company with another officer. They planned to descend to the ground by means of a hosepipe hung from a loft; the pipe broke and Oldman was caught immediately.[39]

In September 1941, when Spangenburg was being evacuated and all the prisoners sent to Warburg, Oldman, with eight others, hid beneath the dining hall. Although some sentries remained, he and his companions managed to get through the main gate. Oldman, with three other officers, headed for Holland but after eight days their unusual civilian clothing led to their arrest near Münster. This time Oldman, with the wounded Hunt, was heading not for Holland but for Denmark, a journey of 250 miles north.[40]

'Right, old chap, that should do you for the time being', said Oldman, helping Hunt to lace his boot. The four men spoke for a few more minutes before shaking hands and wishing one another good luck. Then Tomes and Corfield continued on their way.[41] Hunt struggled to his feet, helped by his partner, and the two men also started trekking north-west, Hunt moving as fast as he could, his sock and boot already soaked through with blood. Oldman carried Hunt's pack for him, and somehow they kept moving all night, both men driven by fierce determination.

*

Doug Crawford soldiered on alone, having no idea what had become of his friend and companion Jack Hand. He headed west and soon came to an obstacle – a footbridge over a small river. Walker and Campbell-Preston were also headed in roughly the same direction, intending later to hook south and head for Switzerland.

Like Arkwright's group, Crawford suspected that Germans on bicycles might have already thrown a cordon around the area by placing sentries on nearby roads and bridges. It was too dark to see clearly along the length of the bridge and Crawford had no intention of trusting to blind luck and just walking across. Instead, he removed his boots, socks and most of his clothing and climbed down the riverbank to the water. Tying his clothes and boots to his backpack, he gingerly clambered into the freezing cold river and quickly swam across to the far bank, attempting all the time to keep his pack out of the water.[42] Once on the other side he quickly dried himself off as best he could, shivering violently in the chilly air. He dressed and then shouldered his pack, setting off once more towards the west.

*

Arkwright's group arrived at the railway line after skirting a small circular wood. The tracks ran through a deep cutting. Just as they were clambering down the side of the cutting, a train came hurtling around the corner at full speed, the noise of its approach deadened by the high banks and the curved track. The great black engine seemed to be coming straight for them, belching clouds of smoke into the cold night air. All three British escapers threw themselves against the wet grass as the train thundered past inches from them, the wheels and bogies crashing and clanking past their heads. All three prayed that neither the driver nor the engineer had spotted them, but with the train's speed and the darkness, Arkwright thought it was extremely unlikely.

Once the train was out of sight, Arkwright and his companions picked themselves up and scrambled over the railway line. Once again Arkwright ended up flat on his face when he tripped over some signal wires on the far side. They turned north-west and began to ascend a gentle slope. As they climbed, the moon rose as if by magic behind them. It was a beautiful sight. Exhausted and tense, the men stopped and lay down for a few minutes on the grass, which was wet with dew, and looked at the moon and the countryside bathed in silvery light.[43] A slight breeze was getting up, cooling them down. Looking at his watch, Arkwright noted that it was approaching midnight. Soon they would shoulder their packs once again and trek slightly west of north until they struck a branch railway line that ran due north to the town of Paderborn. Sunrise was in just under six hours. But for a few minutes the three British officers lay on the sweet, damp grass on a nondescript hill somewhere in Germany looking up at that huge moon. It was their first night of freedom in over two years.

CHAPTER THIRTEEN

'Another British Evacuation'

One thing we can be certain: our captors never did
discover how we had been able to engineer such a
precisely timed and all-embracing blackout.

Captain Kenneth Searle, Royal Army Ordnance Corps

'Take off your clothes!' bellowed a German corporal to the six British and Australian escapers who had just entered the darkened guardroom at Oflag VI-B. The camp lighting was still out, and as the recaptured prisoners slowly stripped off their escape clothes a German hung two hurricane lamps from hooks on the corridor walls that flickered and danced, casting eerie shadows. '*Schnell!*' shouted the impatient corporal, five other agitated guards standing before the prisoners, fingering their rifles. Fully naked, the prisoners stood in silence, one arm length apart from each other and well away from the wall. Suddenly the door at the end of the corridor was flung open and in strutted Oberst Brinkord, the commandant, a malevolent and infuriated look on his plump face. '*Achtung!*' screamed the corporal, and the prisoners sprang to attention.

Brinkord, in a large greatcoat with green velvet collars, looked even more rotund and pompous than usual, amply living up to the prisoners' nickname of 'Bulk Issue'. But there was nothing humorous about his demeanour on this night, as he slowly walked along the line of prisoners, his face almost demonic under the hurricane lamps' baleful glare, his eyes boring through each prisoner in turn. He said nothing, just contemplated each man with a cold gaze.

Brinkord was in almost as much trouble as Stallard's erstwhile escapers. The German high command took a dim view of mass escapes, and there was no denying the fact that 32 POWs climbing over the wire was extraordinarily bad, as he would soon discover. No one, neither the commandant, his chief security officer Rademacher nor higher command, had imagined a situation where the prisoners would make such a bold escape attempt in the face of overwhelming German firepower – it had simply not been attempted before on such a scale. It was particularly embarrassing for Brinkord, who had been appointed to the command only on 20 June, replacing Oberst Stürtzkopf. Even the prisoners had known that the Germans were afraid of large escapes.[1] Any more than twenty meant the involvement of higher command and probable action against the commandant.

*

In the guardroom at Warburg, during that warm night of 30 August 1942, Commandant Brinkord suddenly turned from the naked prisoners and strode off towards the door, his jackboots echoing on the flagstone floor, a stream of German expletives erupting from his fat lips, the door slamming behind him with grim finality.

For now, the prisoners would wait in the cold corridor. They would await whatever fate Brinkord decided for them. The Germans generally abided by the terms of the Geneva Conventions when administering Allied POWs, but Stallard's escape had also caused enormous loss of face. The prisoners expected some form of retribution.

The first indication that retribution would be forthcoming was the appearance of the camp's chief security officer, Hauptmann Rademacher. Accompanied by a large retinue of torch-bearing guards, Rademacher had spent the last few hours walking along the camp perimeter, carefully inspecting the electrical wiring and trying to determine without success how the prisoners had managed to short out the lights.[2]

When Major Cousens had stopped Olympia and recalled the men still on the wrong side of the wire, Captains Searle and Moulson had left the shorting device in place for a few more minutes and then gently tugged on the string that ran from the electrical circuitry to their hiding place in the shadows. The shorting link was lifted and the short circuit cleared. Searle and Moulson then relocked the door of the workshop, slipped quietly back to their hut and climbed into their bunks while pandemonium reigned outside. Both men lay in their beds feeling very pleased with their efforts.[3] But their part in Olympia was not over yet. Once the sun rose they would have one more hazardous mission to complete in order to preserve the secret of the cobbler's hut. Both men snatched only a few hours' sleep, often awakened by the sounds of vehicles starting up in the German area of the camp as Brinkord dispatched patrols to try to apprehend more of Stallard's escapers.

*

Back in the cold guardroom the naked escapers waited, shivering not only from the chill air but also from their exertions during the escape. They had all been running on adrenalin and little else for almost 24 hours, since the German selection of prisoners who would leave the camp had begun at 2.00am the previous night. They were exhausted, thirsty and hungry.

Just as Major Arkwright's little escape group was lying on the grass looking at the moon, Rex Baxter and Jack Champ were the first recaptures to be interrogated. They were ordered into a small, dimly lit room. Before them was a table where the Germans had carefully laid out the contents of the two Australians' backpacks, their precious food, maps and compasses. Seated behind the table was Rademacher, his face red with fury.

Rademacher evidently took some pleasure in the discomfort that the two cold and naked Australians were suffering. He relaxed slightly and leaned back in his chair, which creaked, crossing his arms as he did so. 'You have been brought here for interrogation', said Rademacher in a level tone. 'I am sure you will cooperate, just as I am sure you know the consequences of your stupid attempt.' The German paused, his cold eyes surveying Baxter and Champ. 'You have read the notices warning you what might happen', he continued, 'so you have nothing to lose by answering a few questions. It might even save your lives!'[4]

Baxter and Champ said nothing, just stared straight ahead at a position on the wall about a foot above Rademacher's head. The security officer picked up one of the maps from the table in front of him, glancing at it briefly before his eyes fell once again on Baxter and Champ.

'We have already examined your escape equipment, and we know how you got out', said Rademacher in a nonchalant tone. 'Where did you get the ladders, and how many of you were there? Where did you get these maps, and how did you plan to get to Holland?' Rademacher stared at the Australians, waiting for an answer.

Baxter took a deep breath and spoke. 'My name is Captain R.R. Baxter. My army number is VX136.'[5] Champ followed suit, stating his name, rank and number.

Rademacher sighed. 'You are being very foolish', he said, his tone slightly more threatening. 'Why not answer my questions? We will soon know it all anyway, so let us save some time.' Rademacher paused and then tried again: 'Come along, gentlemen, if you give me some details now it will be a lot easier for you when we have to decide the punishment, and I am sure you know what the punishment may be. You are facing some very serious charges, so you must cooperate.'[6]

'Baxter, Captain, VX136', replied Rex, his eyes never leaving the wall above Rademacher's head. 'Champ, J.W.K., Lieutenant, army number VX707.'[7] Champ had scarcely finished speaking when Rademacher jumped up from his chair, his face contorted with rage, screaming in unintelligible German, and began pounding with clenched fists on the table before him, knocking most of the escape equipment to the floor. His eyes blazed with fury and not for the first time he appeared to have lost his mind in front of prisoners. Baxter and Champ thought the man was a raving lunatic. Rademacher's right hand grasped the black leather pistol holster on his belt, and for a horrifying moment the two Australians believed that he was crazy enough to shoot them dead on the spot. Instead Rademacher snatched up Baxter's fine Dunhill pipe from the table, threw it on the floor and stamped on it.[8] '*Raus*! *Raus*!' screamed Rademacher, and the two stunned prisoners were quickly herded into the corridor by an equally alarmed sentry.

After a few moments Rademacher appeared at the door to the interrogation room. He was once again calm. He spoke briefly to a guard, who then hustled Wing Commander Kayll and Flight Lieutenant Morris into the room, slamming the door behind him. After a few minutes the prisoners in the corridor could hear Rademacher's muffled voice shouting from behind the door. All six escapers received the same treatment that night, but all six refused Rademacher's entreaties and threats, giving only their names, ranks and numbers.

*

At 6.00am the camp lights suddenly flickered back on. An hour later the Germans gave the prisoners back their clothes. While this was going on, Searle and Moulson had unfinished business in the cobbler's workshop.

As the two electrical specialists walked across the camp in the early morning chill they passed the spot where Stallard's men had launched their escape. The four scaling apparatuses still lay across the wire, with Team 4's ladder broken against the fence. A single disgruntled sentry, armed with rifle and fixed bayonet, guarded them. Massed in front of the fence were several hundred British prisoners, jeering the sentry and a Wehrmacht cameraman who had been ordered by Brinkord to photograph the escape apparatuses before they were taken down and destroyed. The final insult to the Germans was a large hand-painted sign that someone had attached to the inner perimeter fence, announcing in tall black letters, in a pointed reference to Dunkirk: 'Another British Evacuation'.[9]

Such was the general hubbub at the wire that no one noticed Searle and Moulson sidle up to the cobbler's workshop, unlock the door and slip inside. Working quickly, Searle replaced the German wiring and carefully disguised all traces of tampering with his little tin of dust, while Moulson took down the blackout curtains from the windows and stashed them for later retrieval. Stuffing the small electrical shorting device into a battledress pocket, the two officers left the hut, carefully locked the door behind them with their duplicate key and strolled back to their accommodation without a single German noticing anything amiss.[10]

At 7.30am the six prisoners in the guardroom, now suitably dressed, were escorted to the camp's main gate. Passing into the camp, the corporal commanding the escort told them, much to their amazement, to return to their huts. They had all been expecting a lengthy sentence in the cooler, but it seemed that punishment was suspended, as the whole camp was shortly to be moved. Hardly believing their luck, the prisoners walked along chattering excitedly about the night's events. They too witnessed the large crowd at the fence, and saw for themselves the four apparatuses *in situ* and the sarcastic sign. Although their joy was tinged with regret that they were not still free, they felt deep pride and satisfaction that they had played a role in a successful escape – and an escape on a massive scale, made in such a unique and bold manner.

Rademacher, in order to take some measure of retribution for his humiliation at Stallard's hands, immediately instituted a series of severe 'bastard searches' throughout the day, the idea being to cause maximum disruption and destruction of property among the remaining British prisoners in the camp. Groups of guards entered accommodation huts at random, most of their inmates having had nothing to do with Operation Olympia, and ransacked lockers. In Captain G.P. Bowring's room a German guard picked up a tin of Red Cross sardines, opened it and proceeded to pour the contents over a suitcase full of clothes. This was then shaken up and heaved out of the open window onto the dirt outside.[11] All through the day, when the prisoners were not being subjected to roll calls, German guards smashed up their rooms while clothing, possessions and even furniture piled up outside windows and doorways. Rademacher's men went through each hut with a fine-toothed comb, confiscating anything remotely useable for escape purposes, to the fury of the prisoners who could only watch the infliction of wanton destruction and damage. Fortunately, the one item the Germans failed to find was the camp radio, carefully concealed by Captain Robert Melsome, the Intelligence Officer, through which the prisoners received news of the progress of the war.[12]

*

Out beyond the wire, 26 men scarcely had time to enjoy their first night of freedom. They moved through the silent German countryside with grim determination. Only a few hours remained until daybreak, a few precious hours in which to put as much distance as possible between themselves and the hated camp, to elude the inevitable cordon of searchers and to find somewhere to hide during the hours of daylight. It was the beginning of an ordeal the like of which few of them had faced before. Many factors would determine whether any of them would make a 'home run', and the greatest factor of all was one over which they had absolutely no control – luck.

CHAPTER FOURTEEN

A Walk in the Woods

Running into the night, we made our way, against heavy odds, towards our common goal – to fight again.

Major Tom Stallard, Durham Light Infantry

Since leaving the wounded Lieutenant Hunt in the care of Brooke Oldman, Dick Tomes and Fred Corfield had found the going easier through freshly cut cornfields. When the moon rose shortly before midnight, they too were refreshed and rejuvenated by the cool breeze that followed, the same as Arkwright, Fuller and Coombe-Tennant who were at that moment flat on their backs resting on a small hill a few miles away. Glancing back in the direction of Warburg camp, Tomes and Corfield could see occasional pinpricks of light moving on the horizon – these they took to be torches shone by the guards. The northern perimeter lighting was still out, as well as the watchtower searchlights, which was a happy sight.

Tomes and Corfield slipped unseen across the railway line where Arkwright's group had almost been run down by a speeding German goods train and trekked for a further three miles before deciding to take a rest. They crept into a thick copse of firs and nestled down among its tangled, dark undergrowth. Each of them ate a teaspoonful of glucose from their travelling ration packs and drank some water from their bottles. The glucose was wonderfully reviving and Tomes and Corfield would ration themselves to three or four doses a night to help keep them going.[1] Their nerves were still as taut as piano wires – every noise or shadow near them seemed like German pursuers. But, like all the other little groups of escapers speeding through the enemy countryside that night, Tomes and Corfield felt a tremendous sense of exhilaration. They felt like the escape had been worthwhile, if only for the excitement of the actual breakout, the mad scramble over the fences followed by the crazed dash through the fields pursued by German bullets.[2] It was a lovely summer's night and the sweet smells of the countryside filled their nostrils, replacing the stench of the prison camp, the perpetual odours of latrines and mud. They could have wept with joy.

Tomes leaned down to fill his water bottle in a little stream. Once he had filled it, he dropped his head down to the clear, cold water, cupped his hands and drank the refreshing liquid in great gulps that ran down his chin and through his fingers. The strong smell of wild thyme growing along the stream banks was intoxicating. Tomes and Corfield were so enraptured by the beauties of nature that they completely failed to hear the noise of approaching bodies across the dark field that surrounded them until it was almost too late. The two escapers froze mid-drink, the water trickling from their cupped hands as their eyes bored into the darkness, straining to see who was coming. It sounded like the whole German Army, the thud and crunch of dozens of heavy jackboots on the grass. With a terrible sense of dread, both men realised that they had stupidly let down their guard for a wild few moments, revelling in nature like day-trippers instead of the hunted men that they were. The noise came closer until out of the gloom stepped not a German soldier but a large black dairy cow, followed closely behind by the rest of the herd. Tomes and Corfield, who were about to raise their arms above their heads, instead collapsed into nervous laughter, the tension suddenly broken. Picking up their equipment, the two officers continued quickly on their way.

*

Doug Crawford, after his little swim in the river, had continued on his lone journey south-west towards Frankfurt am Main and the Black Forest area. Exhausted by the escape and the cold swim, Crawford found a little wood to hide up in and burrowed down under some branches and leaves well before daybreak.[3] Like all of the Olympia escapers, Crawford had great difficulty sleeping through the hours of daylight. His body clock was still attuned to sleeping at night, and like the others he was tense and nervous, constantly worried whether he was concealed adequately and whether someone might chance upon his hide. He had the added stress of being alone, as Hauptmann Rademacher in the Warburg camp guardroom was then grilling his travelling companion, Lieutenant Jack Hand. Crawford knew that he faced weeks of loneliness and solitary fears if he was to reach Spain and freedom. But his mental toughness and determination to get home would sustain him through the trials ahead. His thoughts often drifted to his wife Rae back in Australia and the one-year-old daughter he had never seen.

*

Captain Martin Gilliat and Lieutenant Phil Pardoe struck directly north from Warburg, their plan being to head for the northern German city of Hamburg, and from there into Denmark and then neutral Sweden. Theirs was one of the more ambitious routes chosen by the Olympia escapers – virtually every other team was headed for occupied Holland or France, all in the hope of reaching Spain. But against all odds, Gilliat and Pardoe managed to make good time by following the North Star, lying up in woods during the day. Captain Ronald Leah, Number 3 on Steve Russell's Team 2, was heading north-west. By the end of the first night, 30/31 August, 26 men remained on the run inside the Reich, an incredible achievement for Stallard and a major security headache for the Germans.

*

Major Arkwright's group arrived at some woods near the small historic town of Willebadessen at around 4.30am on 31 August.[4] The town, with its large Benedictine convent founded in 1149, is located on the edge of the Eggegebirge, a southern extension of the vast Teutoburg Forest in North Rhine-Westphalia, just over fifteen miles from Paderborn and two hours by train from Warburg.

Arkwright's group had followed a branch railway line that ran towards Paderborn, knowing that this would eventually lead them to the thickly wooded region near Willebadessen that they were looking for. As they trudged on through the night, walking parallel to the railway tracks, though not always in sight of them, their thoughts turned to other issues. Water was the most pressing. It was summer and though there was still a chill in the air at night, all of the evaders sweated with nerves and from the sheer effort of walking so far after years of enforced idleness inside prison camps.

Carrying water was difficult because of a lack of suitable containers to be found inside the camp. The Germans had long ago stripped nearly all prisoners of their military water bottles because of their use to escapers, but by great fortune Arkwright's batman, Private Leyden, had managed to retain his. After being severely wounded in the face by a German grenade while shielding Arkwright from the blast during the fighting in France, Leyden had transferred from hospital to Oflag VI-B, bringing his water bottle with him, and he gave this precious item to Arkwright a few days before the escape.

Arkwright's two companions and indeed most of the other Olympia escapers had to make do with *ersatz* water containers. Rupert Fuller had a half-pint tin with a screw top, while Henry Coombe-Tennant carried a larger receptacle that had been manufactured in the camp by 'Q' Department, consisting of two tins soldered together using tiny blobs of solder from the inside of tobacco tins, also with a screw top. This soon started leaking and

Coombe-Tennant would throw it away on the second night, demonstrating the limitations of homemade escape equipment.

When they broke out of the camp, only Fuller carried any water. The other two officers left their water bottles empty, because of weight considerations. Between the assault on the wire at 9.30pm and 3.00 the next morning, Arkwright's group had virtually nothing to drink until they stumbled upon a watering place for cattle in the corner of a field fed by a reasonably clean-looking stream. Arkwright and Coombe-Tennant filled their bottles and they all drank deeply, then rinsed their hands and faces clean of sweat and dirt, before resting for ten minutes.[5] Then they wearily continued on their way, determined to reach the woods near Willebadessen before dawn. They always moved cross-country, refusing to take even the most deserted-looking country road. The moonlight meant that they could see hundreds of yards ahead and spot any farmhouse or dwelling long before they reached it.

'What's that?' asked Coombe-Tennant, pointing to the other end of the grass field that they were walking through. All three men stopped and stared into the gloom, the target of Coombe-Tennant's attention standing in the shadows a few hundred yards off, just out of clear sight.

'A cow, maybe?' replied Arkwright uninterestedly.

'I thought cows lived in herds', said Fuller. The three men stared and stared.

'Crikey!' said Coombe-Tennant, breaking the spell, 'it must be a bull!' As they strained their eyes attempting to make out the animal's species, it began moving towards them in a very purposeful manner. Whatever it was, it was big, and it could clearly see them.

'Right, chaps, run!' hissed Fuller, and the three officers took to their heels across the field while behind them the sounds of the huge animal grew louder, its feet pounding on the grass, snorting as it thundered along. Arkwright's group reached the fence on the opposite side of the field almost as one and vaulted it in unseemly haste, collapsing into a panting pile on the other side. Looking up, they saw the animal's head peering over the fence, its huge black eyes staring at them. It was a very large carthorse![6] He was friendly too, and the three officers, giggling at the absurdity of it all, stood for a few moments waiting for their heart rates to return to normal, stroking the horse's great black head and snuffling nose.

They found the woods as dawn approached and flopped down into what they thought was good cover, all of them dog-tired.

*

Tom Stallard and Dick Page, moving in roughly the same direction as Arkwright's group towards Holland, though on a slightly more northerly track, also found some woods to hide in just before dawn. They had trekked twenty or so miles from the camp without incident. But finding a suitable hiding place in the dark was extremely difficult, and was a constant worry for all the escapers attempting to 'boy scout' across country inside Germany. Stallard had already experienced this problem when he briefly escaped with Page and James McDonnell on 9 April 1942.

The hiding place had to provide a screen from any prying eyes. One couldn't just walk into a wood during the night and hope for the best come the sunrise. All woods appear deserted at 4.00am, the time when most of the escapers would begin searching for a hiding place. But German woods were probably the best maintained in the world, with very little undergrowth between the neatly ordered trees. Woodsmen were often seen in very out-of-the-way places and the Nazis also operated a system of firewatchers mounted on platforms 30 feet above the canopy. Stallard and the others often felt under observation from these platforms, though the strain on manpower in wartime Germany probably meant that they were not always in use.

Among the biggest dangers for the British escapers were groups of German children. Stallard and his fellow Olympians soon developed a healthy dislike for children, who were usually encountered suddenly, and very often miles from their homes, playing, exploring or involved in some other activity. Indoctrinated through membership in the Hitler Youth or League of German Girls, the children of Nazi Germany were trained to be suspicious of outsiders and to report people to the police. They were a useful adjunct to law enforcement at a time when many Germans were afraid of the large numbers of foreign workers living among them, most press-ganged from the occupied territories.

If the escaper chose a poor location for a hide during the predawn, he might end up spending the hours of daylight covered in bracken or lying still in a ditch with no chance of a fire and a hot meal. The escapers soon discovered that the ideal hiding place was a young fir plantation where the trees were only ten or fifteen years old. The foliage was dense, difficult to penetrate and low-lying, making it ideal for concealment.

*

Tomes and Corfield were exhausted after having walked over fifteen miles. Tomes particularly was nearing collapse, still weak from his bout of diphtheria six weeks earlier. Just before dawn they spotted what looked, in the dim light, to be a thick wood about one mile to their right. Both men were longing to reach a hiding place, desperate to lie down and sleep. But as they got closer to the 'wood' it gradually became a grassy slope on top of a low ridge. Feeling a little desperate as light began to creep into the sky, Tomes and Corfield struggled on through several hundred yards of tall crops, ending up soaked to the knees by heavy dew. They skirted what looked like a wireless station, later revealed to be harmless electricity pylons, and eventually found a patch of thick woodland. In the half-light the two exhausted British officers crawled into the undergrowth, which was spread over a steep slope. As the light increased they discovered that the wood was not very thick after all, and they had also inadvertently made camp only a few hundred yards from a farmhouse.[7]

Tomes and Corfield watched as dawn turned into a bright, hot and sunny Monday, 31 August 1942. They made porridge and ate biscuits, raisins and nuts and spent the day sleeping in shifts, one man always on watch, due to the proximity of the farmhouse.

*

Although young fir plantations were ideal hiding places from the perspective of concealment, they were less so regarding comfort. Because the foliage was so dense, no sunlight penetrated to the ground, which was covered in damp moss and fir needles. This in turn was often infested with mosquitoes, spiders and other creepy-crawlies. The timber was also unsuitable for fire-lighting. The evaders needed dry wood that would burn at a high temperature and create little or no smoke. Any dampness in the wood would produce thick, heavy smoke, drawing civilians to investigate as it was expressly forbidden to light fires in German national forests.[8] Sternly worded signposts were mounted along roads and paths announcing this rule.

The very best type of hiding place was a young fir plantation in the middle of a larger wooded area. The escapers could lie on the edge of the plantation basking in the sun, cook potatoes and other food, and sleep comfortably. If anyone came too close they could slink into the denser cover of the fir trees and hide.

In Arkwright's group the practice was to settle in their hiding place around 5.00am, take off their backpacks, put on all of their spare clothing against the early morning chill, and sleep for two hours. Whoever woke first would check to see if their hiding place offered sufficient concealment. If it did, breakfast would begin.

Working as a team, Arkwright's group soon had a routine for fire-lighting. One man would excavate a hole out of the dirt, into which the fuel for the fire was placed. Another would quickly make a tripod out of sticks, 'Red Indian-style' as Arkwright termed it, from which to suspend their only cooking pot, an aluminium saucepan minus the handle that could hold just over a pint of water. The fire was lit for only fifteen to twenty minutes, but they would be able to cook porridge and tea.[9] Sometimes it was possible to have a fire in the morning and during the evening. If that were the case, the group would bake potatoes that they had gathered during their cross-country treks. Before the morning fire was lit they placed a layer of potatoes in the scooped-out fire hole and covered them lightly with earth. The fire was then lit and their breakfast porridge and tea was made. The potatoes were left among the ashes all day and before the evening fire was lit they were turned over; thus by the time the tea was prepared after supper the potatoes were well cooked on both sides. They were then pulled out and eaten piping hot.[10]

It would not always be possible to light fires, and over the coming days there were several occasions when the miserable little bands of evaders lay all day in ditches while Germans worked in fields close by, able only to eat some homemade hard tack biscuits carried with them from the camp.

Stallard and Page picked a bad location on their second night of freedom, camping on the edge of a forest full of large trees. When the sun rose they discovered to their horror that there was almost no undergrowth, and in broad daylight their hiding place was actually as flat as a billiard table and they could easily be seen from a hundred yards away. Arkwright's group faced the same problem – their first hide was discovered in the morning to be only 50 yards from a well-worn path leading into the forest. They remained extremely tense until darkness once more fell and they could move on.

*

All of the evaders had an excellent idea of where they were in

Germany at any given time, day or night. Their maps were fantastic, and for the first three nights the fugitives navigated by the stars to avoid constant stops to consult compasses. Celestial navigation proved remarkably simple. As long as they could see the North Star they could find their way without too much trouble. They rarely became lost. During the day when they were not sleeping, cooking or repairing their clothes and equipment, they studied their maps carefully, planning each night's march in detail.

*

Arkwright's group left their hide early on the evening of 31 August, starting out before 9.00pm. They kept going north through the woods, crossed and then recrossed the railway line that they had been following north-west and finally stopped about 5.30am on 1 September in more woods near the village of Schwaney, a district of Altenbeken just over nine miles east of Paderborn. Normally they would have found cover earlier, but they had great trouble finding water. Eventually they found a drainage spout in a railway embankment and filled their water bottles from that.[11]

*

The night of 1/2 September was the evaders' third night on the run. They were all still quite close to Warburg and needed to start putting a lot of miles between themselves and the camp, and the inevitable German searches.

Tomes and Corfield started off across fields to continue following the railway line for several miles. It was a beautiful, starlit night. At one point the two men looked south and could see antiaircraft searchlight beams stabbing into the night sky, the lights moving steadily across the blackened heavens searching for British bombers.

The two officers walked along the railway line until they came to a small village situated between steepish hills – it looked to be virtually impossible to skirt. They had to clamber over dozens of small fences, struggling to negotiate a maze of back gardens that ran up a steep slope. Both men were struggling also against tiredness, for like all of the escapers, their bodies had yet to adjust to sleeping during daylight and working at night. Sweating in the humid air, eventually they passed out of the slumbering village and into an inky black wood that ran for several miles.[12]

They emerged into a little misty valley with a good stream and a path in the bottom. Tomes was struck by the valley's beauty. He imagined what a pleasant place it would be to picnic, under different circumstances.

After a mile or two they emerged onto a main road that ran in the direction they wanted, so Tomes and Corfield followed it until dawn. Out of the gloom suddenly emerged a German civilian pushing a bicycle up the hill. It was a tense moment, for the two evaders had been chatting away in English until they stumbled into the German, and they had no idea whether this man had heard them and raised the alarm on arriving home.

Tomes and Corfield turned off into a large forested area and climbed a steep track away from the road, sitting down for a few minutes to rest before starting to look for somewhere to hide. Unfortunately, they were both so tired that they dozed off in the open. Luckily they slept for only a few minutes before waking and managing to drag their weary bodies into some nearby cover. Tomes got into a nettle bed and wedged his body under a rotten log, falling into a deep sleep almost immediately. He was comfortable, but wet.[13]

When it became light Tomes and Corfield moved a few hundred yards into thicker cover and spent 2 September lying among young firs on a carpet of needles. They slept on and off, passing the rest of the day observing German harvesters working in fields next to the woods.

*

'*Halt!*' shouted a German policeman at David Walker and his travelling companion Patrick Campbell-Preston just outside a small-town railway station. It was ironic that Walker, the man who had organised all the intensive training for Olympia and acted as Stallard's second-in-command, should have been the first of the escapers to be caught beyond the immediate vicinity of the camp. Walker and Campbell-Preston had strayed too close to a railway station on the night of 1 September and been spotted by locals who thought their appearances and manner suspicious. A policeman had quickly appeared on a bicycle to question the pair.

'*Zeigen Sie mir Ihre Papiere*', commanded the country policeman, demanding to see their papers.

Understanding only basic German, Walker attempted to bluff it out, claiming that they were Belgian labourers going to the next village. A few minutes of intensive questioning and unsatisfactory answers later and the Britons came clean, admitting that they were escaped POWs. Placed under guard in the station waiting room, the two evaders handed over their prison camp identity tags and awaited a military escort back to Warburg. Walker and Campbell-Preston's quick recapture illustrated the danger of getting too close to population centres. In order to remain at large, the lesson of previous escapes had clearly demonstrated that one must avoid any contact with Germans.

*

Arkwright's group left their hide in woods near Schwaney at 6.00pm on 1 September and moved into a deserted hut at a disused quarry. Later they cooked up some potatoes for supper behind one of the many sheds that littered the abandoned workings. As they were eating the steaming hot potatoes they heard noises. A German in uniform walked right by their hiding place with its still smoking fire, passing only ten yards from the three Britons, who were squatting on their haunches in a little huddle. Coombe-Tennant said later that the German looked straight at him. But far from being the vanguard of some larger group of soldiers come to capture the escapees, the German looked considerably displeased at seeing them in their cloth caps and tatty clothing. Arkwright's group soon realised why. Trailing behind the German was a young woman, and they surmised that the German was as annoyed to see the evaders as they were shocked to see him. Clearly, he took the three Britons to be quarry workmen and was hoping to find the vicinity abandoned for a private liaison with the girl.

Packing up their kit as quickly and as quietly as possible, the three waited until the two Germans had passed out of sight and earshot. Moving fast, Arkwright's group dived into a fir thicket higher up the hill and crouched there until it was dark.[14] They were badly shaken by the encounter, but it taught them one thing: it was pure folly to move around in daylight.[15]

Following the railway once more, Arkwright and his companions walked on the sleepers. Because the sleepers were not set at regular intervals the three evaders made a lot of noise, often dislodging the stones that filled the gaps in between. They discovered that road and railway bridges were generally not guarded, but that railway level crossings normally had an old man stationed there.

'*Wer ist da?*' boomed out a guttural German voice as Arkwright's group approached a darkened signal box beside the track. '*Wer ist da?*' came the man's voice again, demanding to know who was there. '*Es ist verboten, auf der Bahnstrecke gehen!*' ('It is forbidden to walk on the railway line!') A hand-held torch was suddenly switched on, but before its beam could be shone at Arkwright's group they quickly dived off the tracks, tripping over the signal wires as they ran, disappearing into some woods. They spent the day in hiding east of the town of Altenbeken.[16]

Arkwright's team had suffered two close calls, and both occasions, at the quarry and on the railway line, had demonstrated that it was incredibly difficult to remain concealed from the local population and still manage to cover sufficient ground each night. The solution in the case of Arkwright's group was to stop walking on the railway line and instead try to follow its course more discreetly from the woodland that often ran parallel to it. But because of the density of woodland and a lack of paths, this tactic drastically reduced the number of miles that they could walk each night.

*

Oflag VI-B fell within the jurisdiction of Wehrkreis VI (Military District 6), headquartered in Münster. All POW camps within the district came under the command of Generalmajor (Brigadier) Georg von Döhren. Once Commandant Brinkord had informed Döhren of the mass escape, he would have issued instructions to all towns and villages within a 30-mile radius of the camp. All police officers, mayors, Nazi Party officials, Hitler Youth and railway station personnel were informed and told to be on the lookout for young civilian men of military age travelling in small groups through the countryside or along railway lines. This vigilance had already netted Walker and Campbell-Preston. All German military units within the 30-mile zone were placed on high alert and patrols were dispatched to search woodland and other obvious hiding places.

The problem for the Germans was that several of the groups of evaders, including Arkwright's team, Stallard/Page and Tomes/Corfield, were heading into one of Germany's largest areas of forest, the Reichswald. There simply wasn't the manpower to search everywhere; so vigilant civilians were essential to the hunt. In two nights' marching the escapees should have left the 30-mile cordon, but they were never out of danger while still inside Germany.

*

Doug Crawford had spent the second night steadily heading southwest. As the first tendrils of light began to appear in the sky around

184

dawn he started looking for a suitable hiding place. He saw a hay-stack in a nearby field and he thought it looked inviting. He climbed inside the hay and fell into a deep, dreamless sleep. Two hours later he awoke suddenly, his skin itching and crawling. He was covered in lice.[17] For the rest of the day Crawford was forced to remain immobile inside his lousy hide, dozing fitfully and unhappily. He made a mental note to avoid all haystacks in future.[18]

At dusk Crawford set out south. Two hours later he paused for a drink of water only to discover that he had lost his bottle. Cursing, he soon realised that to go on without it would be both difficult and foolish, so with a heavy heart he turned around and started to retrace his steps. Over two hours later he came to a small stream where he had last filled the bottle and soon found it lying beside a bush. This incident had cost him virtually the entire night, and so he had no choice but to find a hide before sunrise. He spent the day concealed near the stream, fretting over the time that he had lost.

Once night fell, Crawford's target was the village of Wilhelms, near the town of Kassel on the Fulda River in northern Hesse, historical home town of the Brothers Grimm. Crawford's jour-ney since leaving Warburg had been less of a fairytale and more of a nightmare. Like Hansel and Gretel, Crawford and the other Olympia evaders wandered through the thick, dark German for-est, sometimes afraid, often cold and hungry, always oppressed by the feeling of danger behind every tree and around every bend in the road.

CHAPTER FIFTEEN

'*Hände hoch*!'

The trouble with these damned Germans is that
they neither hunt nor shoot pheasants!

Captain Fred Corfield, Royal Artillery

Doug Crawford grunted in pain as the German corporal smashed his rifle butt hard into the Australian's stomach. He almost collapsed onto the recently reaped cornfield. Gasping for breath, Crawford, half bent over, gingerly raised his hands above his head as the German swiftly cocked his rifle bolt, its metallic sound harsh and uncompromising, and levelled the weapon squarely at Crawford's chest. He managed to gasp '*Nicht schiessen*! *Nicht schiessen*!' His voice was a breathless rasp and his cheeks burned with frustration and embarrassment. As he recalled later, he felt like a 'complete bloody idiot'.[1]

Crawford was the third of the 'boy scouts' to be recaptured but he would not be the last. Every day that the Olympia evaders remained at liberty was another day when the odds narrowed a little more against them.

*

Major Arkwright's group, after being seen by a German soldier in the abandoned quarry and shouted at by the railway signalman, had decided to start looking for a hide earlier than usual on the night of 1/2 September. They would sacrifice an hour or two of marching for the safety of a really good hide. By 3.00am on 2 September they had reached a railway junction somewhere to the east of the town of Paderborn, 31 miles south of Bielefeld. The branch line that they had been following for three nights running north–south continued into the main east–west line at the junction. Arkwright's group struck north-west and headed for their next landmark.[2]

After hiding all day, the group started out during the evening of 2 September. They expected to cross the east–west railway within a short time but walked two or three miles without finding it, climbing all the time. They were sure of their map reading, and after another mile they began to descend. Suddenly, they realised that the railway was still there; it was just running underground through a long tunnel beneath their boots. Relieved that they were not lost, Arkwright's group followed a bridle path into the foothills of a small and unimpressive range running west-north-west. Fuller's plan was to cling to the southern edge of these hills until they struck another railway line that would steer them in their desired direction. They followed the bridle path for five or six miles through the deserted hills, emerging onto an empty country lane where they started looking for a suitable hide.

The place they chose was rather too close to a nearby farmhouse, but the cover was first-rate, with a good water supply. They were unable to cook any food or tea, but several foresters and workmen who wandered past during the day did not see them.[3]

*

Dick Tomes and Fred Corfield faced their biggest test so far when they came to cross the wide River Weser. They had awoken from their deep slumber in the undergrowth above the town of Beverungen. 'What's that noise?' Tomes had asked Corfield, his pulse racing. Loud thumps and taps close by their hide sounded like forestry workers chopping down a tree. Corfield cocked his head like a gundog and listened. Then he reached forward and gingerly parted the foliage. The 'tock, tock, tock' sound continued. Corfield let go of the branches and turned to Tomes. 'It's a damned wood-pecker in the tree next to us', he said, smiling. Tomes also smiled and visibly relaxed. 'Let's get moving. It will be dark soon.'[4]

Setting off just before dusk, the two evaders kept to the edge of the wood above Beverungen, which stands on the River Weser in the eastern corner of North Rhine-Westphalia, bordering the prov-inces of Hesse and Lower Saxony. The night was cloudy with no moon, making it virtually pitch-black. Tomes and Corfield skirted Beverungen, but the going was slow in the dark across rough ground with steep banks and sunken paths. They climbed several six-foot-tall rabbit wire fences and as they passed through orchards they collected apples and plums, gleefully filling their pockets with this unexpected bounty.

Picking up the railway line, Tomes and Corfield followed it to the town of Höxter on the Weser. Höxter stands on the left bank of the river, 32 miles north of Kassel. It is famous as the scene of a great battle in antiquity between the Emperor Charlemagne and the Saxons.

The two Anglo-Saxons, Tomes and Corfield, faced a great challenge at Höxter. They had to cross the river using the main road bridge that ran through the town. This was extremely risky. To make matters worse, the clouds parted and the moon came out, bathing the sleeping town in a pretty grey light. Before they entered the town the two evaders washed in a small river. Then they followed a riverside promenade for half a mile that had a row of houses on one side. They neither saw nor passed a single person. Reaching Höxter's road bridge, they strode quickly to the other side, passing the end of the main street. Fortunately, the Germans had left the bridge unguarded. Looking back, the whole picturesque medieval town was laid out before them, its timber-framed houses and church spires bathed in moonlight. Tomes was reminded that the town of Hamelin was only a few miles away along the Weser. 'It seemed as if the Pied Piper had visited

189

Höxter too, spirited all its inhabitants away and left it silent as the grave.'[5]

On the far side of the Weser they walked through a deserted factory area and then struck out across an open meadow beside the railway line. They took a short rest by the railway bridge that also crossed the Weser just below the town, watching trains rolling across, trying to make out the different types of wagons and thinking about hitching a ride 'hobo style'. They followed the line above the gorge and tunnel that it passed through, struck a main road and covered several miles into Lower Saxony, once or twice hiding when they heard Germans approaching on foot or bicycle.

Towards the morning Tomes and Corfield couldn't find any good wooded areas for a hide. Retracing their steps for over a mile, they decided to sleep in a small depression on the edge of a field, as the woodland was too well ordered and lacking in undergrowth. This infuriated Corfield, who remarked caustically: 'The trouble with these damned Germans is that they neither hunt nor shoot pheasants!'[6] The depression would have to do. It was filled with bracken and nettles and the two evaders settled beneath a canopy of foliage as best they could. They had a homemade stove that burned smokeless firelighters, so they could at least make a hot meal before turning in. Tomes remarked on the date – Wednesday, 3 September 1942, the third anniversary of the start of the war.[7]

*

Other groups of escapees continued along similar routes. Stallard and Page were only a few miles from Arkwright's group and planned to arrive in about ten days at the town of Gronau in Westfalen, North Rhine-Westphalia, right on the frontier and six miles from the Dutch town of Enschede. Gilliat and Pardoe, the two King's Royal Rifle Corps officers, were still pressing almost directly north and were somewhere in the wooded country between Willebadessen and Bad Driburg. Royal Tank Regiment officer Lieutenant Hunt, though still bleeding from the bullet wound to his heel, was also managing to keep moving along with Brooke Oldman, though they were not making as much distance as the other groups. Hunt's determination was impressive, but even Oldman could see that he wasn't going to make it. They faced a difficult decision over the coming days.

*

Arkwright's group spent 3 and 4 September wandering through country that ended up as something of a challenge. They had continued on the route they had been following since 2 September, along the range of foothills, and entered what appeared to be an area entirely given over to forestry. No watercourses were marked on the group's maps, but they reckoned that they would find plenty of water running off the hills to the north. Then they discovered that they were in fact inside a large German Army training area that consisted mostly of sandy soil, heather and a poor type of conifer.[8]

By the night of 4 September, the trio was running out of water. Driven on by their increasingly frantic attempts to locate a watercourse, they stumbled across a field firing range off to their right. At 8.00pm rifle fire broke out, so they knew that the area was full of German troops on exercise. Their desperate water situation was alleviated by some rather unappealing stagnant water that they discovered in a deep cart rut in a path through a wood. They boiled the water and made porridge and tea, then filled their bottles.

*

Tomes and Corfield had an even worse time than Arkwright's forlorn group. The idea of hitching a ride on a goods train was still in their minds when they set out on the evening of 3 September. Arriving at the railway line they found a slight incline where passing trains would have to slow down. Waiting beside the track, a suitable train soon appeared, puffing up the hill, a long string of wooden boxcars with black tarred roofs rattling along behind. Tomes and Corfield broke cover and sprinted as fast as they could along the track beside the train, stumbling over the sleepers and the flints that filled the gaps in between. Carrying their heavy packs and water bottles it was an impossible task – the train was still too fast and the two evaders were soon out of breath and struggling just to keep up, let alone jump aboard. All notions of riding the train Old West-style were swiftly abandoned, the two officers collapsing in a panting heap beside the darkened track as the train pulled out of sight, its whistle giving a single eerie blast as it disappeared around the corner into a tunnel, a red tail light glowing like a malevolent single eye.

Lying on their backs staring at the starry sky for a few moments, breathing like exhausted carthorses, Tomes and Corfield considered their options. It appeared that finding a shortcut to days and days of footsore hiking would have to be forgotten. Gritting their teeth, they set their minds to walking and, heads down, strode off, their hands hooked into their haversack shoulder straps.

They spent a very long night wandering through an area of young fir plantations, criss-crossed by numerous bridle paths. They had lost their way trying to find the original railway line they had been following, and in the dark had become turned around. It was easily done over hilly and unfamiliar terrain.

The morning of 4 September found Tomes and Corfield out of the maze of firs but very far from their correct route and close to a small town that was just starting to awaken. The two evaders took shelter in some thick bushes on a large open heath and waited out the day. They studied their maps and discovered that they had walked about twenty miles during the night, but actually advanced in the direction they wanted by only five. Germans constantly walked by close to the hide, including a pair of armed soldiers.

Tomes and Corfield decided to move north-east that night until they struck a road and then work out their exact location from a signpost. They inadvertently wandered up a long driveway in their search for a sign and almost stumbled upon a garden party behind a country house. The two British officers, unshaven, hollow-eyed, their clothes and hair soiled with mud and leaf litter, stared through the bushes at the party. German officers in immaculate uniforms mingled with young women in pretty summer dresses, chatting, laughing and drinking cocktails, music from a gramophone wafting on the night air like some exotic scent. Burning torches set among the flowerbeds provided light. It was a surreal moment for the fugitives, a glimpse of the kind of life they had enjoyed before the war. They couldn't help but stare after their years as prisoners and remember what it felt like to be free and relaxed, in pleasant company, one's head a little light from alcohol. They were spectres at the feast, peering at this vignette of normality like ragged forest trolls from the safety of the wilderness.

Tearing themselves away from the garden party, Tomes and Corfield contented themselves with a wash and a shave in a little nearby stream, in the process somewhat restoring their spirits. They found the signpost they had been looking for, and it read 'Holzminden'. Consulting their maps, they realised how much time they had wasted the night before. Holzminden was a small town in Lower Saxony, just a few miles north of Höxter, and ironically considering its nocturnal visitors, the site of a prison camp for British officers in 1917–18.

The evaders pressed on up the road, going directly through mostly sleeping villages. But at one, someone suddenly shone a torch at them. Tomes and Corfield, fearing a police control post, dived off the road into a back alley and skirted around the rest of the village.

By 3.30am they were approaching Eschershausen, a village twelve miles north-east of Holzminden and 31 miles south of the city of Hannover. Tomes and Corfield gave the place a wide berth, hooking right off the road into fields, and crept through a built-up area of fairly widely spaced houses. A large kitchen garden provided them with lettuces, young peas, apples, pears and plums.[9] But locals were starting to wake up, and the occasional cyclist was seen on the road. It was time to hide. After a difficult trek through a field of wet potatoes they reached a hilly, wooded area and burrowed down in the undergrowth halfway up a steep slope and enjoyed their free food.

*

Once darkness had fallen on 4 September Arkwright's group, deep inside a German Army training area, started off. They had gone barely half a mile when they began to hear voices in the distance. Listening intently, they could make out 'Lili Marlene' being sung by marching troops. The German soldiers were either returning late from the ranges or setting out for a night exercise.[10] This encounter was just the start of the most stressful night Arkwright's group had experienced since Zero Night at the camp.

The group hid for a couple of hours until the sounds of German soldiers had disappeared, and then, around midnight, they continued. Almost immediately they came to the edge of a small village. They could see two or three people still walking around on the main street, even though it was late. Arkwright's group had probably already been seen, so they faced a choice – either dive into cover, which would look extremely suspicious, or, in Arkwright's words, 'brass it out'[11] and walk through the centre of the village. They decided on the latter course of action, and started boldly strolling through the little settlement, soon realising that the village was a billet for German soldiers on exercise. Suddenly, someone shone a torch directly at them. Arkwright and his friends kept walking while the torch beam followed them for a few inquisitorial seconds, the evaders all the while expecting the order to '*Halt*'. But nothing was said and the Britons walked out of the village into open countryside, their hearts in their mouths. Their homemade cloth caps and ragtag assortment of 'civilian' clothing had evidently fooled the military policeman wielding the torch.[12]

Once out of sight of the village, Arkwright's group quickly dropped off the road and, navigating using the North Star, continued along small tracks and paths over a wide marsh and heath interspersed with patches of woodland. Their fear was that the German military policeman might have changed his mind and sent a patrol on bicycles to waylay the trio.

Making excellent progress, the group came upon a motor track used by tanks and other heavy vehicles, bringing them unexpectedly to a large, open entrance gate flanked by stone pillars and a noticeboard. Coombe-Tennant read the sign in mounting horror – it was a German barracks and vehicles were ordered to slow down to 10kph. Suddenly, from the road behind them came the sound of marching jackboots. Arkwright's group leapt into a ditch beside the road and froze. After a few seconds a German soldier emerged out of the darkness and tramped between the pillars into the barracks. Detouring noisily around the camp, Coombe-Tennant becoming mired in a pile of abandoned tin cans, the evaders thought they were clear of trouble when out of the gloom loomed another entrance gate. At that exact moment the air was rent by the banshee wail of a siren loud enough to freeze the blood.[13] Completely terrified, they headed off at a trot into some agricultural land as the air raid siren continued to wail, the noise shockingly loud and penetrating.

Crossing a stream, Arkwright's group paused to drink deeply and refill their water bottles. Then they came upon an orchard and ran riot through the trees, plucking down apples, taking a bite and casting them aside as they searched for sweeter fruit. They filled their haversacks and pockets with this bounty before hitting a railway line that Fuller, their chief navigator, decided to follow for the next two or three nights. They strode through rich and fertile moonlit land dotted with farmsteads. It was time to find a hide before the milkmaids rose early to tend to their herds.

*

After hiding all day, Doug Crawford had emerged and spent the evening of 4 September hiking towards Frankfurt am Main. Nearing a small town, he turned under a railway bridge and found himself walking into a built-up area. A young woman strolled past on the street, looked at him and smiled. 'It may have been better if I'd accepted the smile', joked Crawford years later, 'but I was getting home, that was my aim in life then.'[14] He decided that it was safer to avoid people and buildings altogether and retraced his steps, carefully skirting the town by walking up a steep, bare hill through recently cut cornfields.

By the early morning of 5 September Crawford found himself in an area with virtually no cover. The stars had begun to pale and he needed to find shelter quickly. Coming upon a small brick building by the side of a road, he tried to break in but the padlock was too stout and he gave up. Looking around desperately, Crawford saw a few scattered mounds of kale in the fields. His heart sank – after his previous experience of sleeping in a lice-infested haystack the last thing he wanted was a repeat performance, but it would be dawn soon and there was nowhere else to hide. 'Well, I've just got to do it!' he said to himself. Rounding the nearest stack, he got the surprise of his life.

After picking himself off the floor, raising his hands above his head and imploring the German corporal not to shoot him, Crawford had a few seconds in which to gather his thoughts. In his haste to find a hide, Crawford had stumbled, literally, upon a German soldier who had been happily whiling away his hours on guard duty sitting inside a foxhole behind the kale stack. The soldier was as surprised by the encounter as Crawford. The German's presence was a bit of a mystery to Crawford, but he would later discover that the whole area was studded with sensitive equipment and secret factories.

The German decided to march him down the hill to the little town.[15] '*Sie sind verhaftet!*' bellowed the corporal – he was under arrest. Crawford didn't understand much German, but the Mauser rifle pointed at his chest needed no translation. '*Fuss vor mir*', said the corporal, indicating with his weapon that Crawford should walk in front of him. '*In Bewegung setzen!*' said the German, impatiently shoving the rifle's muzzle into the small of his back to get him moving.

As Crawford was marched along the dusty road back into the town he reflected on his adventure. He had managed to remain free for seven nights, which was an amazing achievement. But it was hard to realise that he would not be seeing his wife and child any time soon – that particular dream was well and truly over. Any thought of overpowering the guard was soon dispelled – the German was savvy enough to remain several paces behind, with his safety catch thumbed off.

When Crawford arrived outside the town's little police station there was considerable excitement. His bag was taken from him and he was forced to turn out his pockets before the desk sergeant. Everyone seemed to be talking at once in a language Crawford did not understand. Then he was escorted to an empty cell and shoved roughly inside. A guard was placed on watch outside the cell door and soon Crawford could hear telephones ringing and muffled conversations as the wheels of Nazi bureaucracy began to spin.

Later in the morning a stony-faced policeman brought Crawford a thick slice of black bread and a little dripping as well as a cup of cold, weak and bitter coffee. Crawford was glad of it. For the rest of the day he languished inside the uncomfortable cell, listening, trying to rest and waiting for something to happen.

Towards the evening of 7 September, Crawford heard the squeal of brakes as a vehicle pulled up outside. Car doors slammed and hard boots strode through the station doors and down the hall outside the cells. '*Geheime Staatspolizei*',* someone announced in a loud and authoritative voice.

Crawford's cell door was hurriedly unlocked and in strode two immaculately dressed German officers. Both wore the field-grey open-necked tunics of the SS, with brown shirts and black ties. The black right collar patch was ominously empty while the left carried their rank insignia. 'Poison green' shoulder boards completed their outfits. With rising horror Crawford saw that each man had a diamond-shaped black badge on his left cuff containing the letters 'S.D.'** picked out in silver thread.

The Gestapo had arrived.

---

* 'Secret State Police'. Shortened to 'Gestapo'.

** *Sicherheitsdienst*, or 'Security Service'.

CHAPTER SIXTEEN

The Bitter Road

I was glad our enemies were having
a taste of their own medicine.

Major Albert Arkwright, Royal Scots Fusiliers

Doug Crawford sat between two German soldiers on the back seat of a black Opel. Beside the driver was a uniformed Gestapo officer. No one spoke during the journey to Kassel; Crawford, his hands shackled in his lap with iron cuffs, looked out of the window at the green countryside flashing by. It had been a long time since he had moved anywhere other than on foot, and a car journey was almost a novelty. He felt tired but this was tinged with deep apprehension about what was to come. Everyone knew the reputation of the Gestapo for torture and brutality.

*

Arkwright's group had set off on the evening of 5 September and walked up the railway line north-west of Paderborn until they reached a road that passed under the autobahn. They spent 6 September hiding from small groups of children who were out in the woods playing and picnicking. Children were to prove the undoing of more than one of the Olympia evasion groups.

That night, Arkwright's team made it to the outskirts of Bielefeld by 11.00pm, north of the huge and dark Teutoburg Forest, the green shoulder of western Germany. There were many people still about but because it was so dark, few paid the group any attention. They blundered into a city suburb that was not marked on any of their maps and had a start when an old woman suddenly opened her front door as they were passing, gasping loudly at them in surprise.[1] They lay up on 7 September just beyond the village of Halle on the River Ems, nine miles north-west of Bielefeld.

*

Tomes and Corfield spent 5 September in perfect safety. Their hide was dry and they feasted on the fruit that they had gathered, and also made a vegetable soup. Looking at their map, their position was on a spur of the Harz mountains that they would have to traverse in order to reach and then cross the Hildesheim–Hannover road and railway. They started off before dark, keeping to woods and making for a quarry with an overhead railway that clanged and clattered away with a constant stream of little trucks passing up and down, to and from Eschershausen.[2] A line of pylons ran up over the hill. They intended to follow them. Filling their water bottles in a lovely bubbling brook, the two evaders started to climb.

It was a hot, muggy night and the going was rough and steep. Twice the men startled roe deer that were sleeping on the slopes, the animals crashing through the undergrowth in fright. After two exhausting hours Tomes and Corfield reached the top and began to descend through thick bracken on a steep and slippery slope. They hoped to strike the autobahn but couldn't find it, though they managed to find and plunder another excellent orchard.

Saturday 6 September was spent lying up in a beech wood on the edge of a field. They watched a large family party harvesting corn all day. It was a jolly affair, and pangs of homesickness for summer days in England crept up on them. That night, they reached the west bank of the River Leine and followed it downstream until they found a bridge. Then they boldly strode straight through the town of Elze, nine miles west of Hildesheim and 39 miles from

Hannover, fortunately without being seen, and found a good hide in the middle of open woodland.[3]

*

Though Tomes, Corfield, Arkwright's group and many of the other evaders continued on successfully towards their target destinations, the number of Olympia escapers who remained free had begun to thin. Captain Ronald Leah, Number 3 on Team 2, was caught north of Münster on 6 September.[4] Major R.M. Young, who had been third over on Team 3 behind the unfortunate Rex Baxter and Jack Champ, was caught the next night, 7 September.

Lieutenant Hunt's evasion also came to a grinding halt on the evening of 7 September. He was in agony from the bullet wound to his heel. Though his escape partner, Lieutenant Brooke Oldman, had fashioned a crutch for him out of a tree branch, the younger officer was clearly unable to go on. Every time his injured foot touched the ground violent pain shot up his leg, causing him to cry out. If he kept moving he would either bleed to death or gangrene would set in and he could lose his foot.

'Just leave me behind', Hunt gasped, his skin sickly pale in the evening light, his young face a sheen of cold sweat. 'I can't make it and I see no reason why both of us should end up back in the bag.'

'Nonsense, old boy', said Oldman. 'We can still make it. We'll just slow down a bit. Perhaps we could even stop for a few nights to let you rest properly?' Oldman knew that what he was saying was senseless, but it was extremely difficult to accept the inevitable truth. He would have to go on alone and leave his friend to the tender mercies of the Germans. It went against his entire training, experience and personality to abandon a wounded comrade, but if he didn't, both of them would be recaptured and all of their sacrifices thus far would have been for nothing.

'Look, Brookie, you've still got an excellent chance', said Hunt.

'Just leave me somewhere for the Huns and get moving. You know it makes sense.' Gingerly he unlaced his bloodstained boot.

'We've made it this far', said Oldman fiercely. 'I'm sure if you could rest for a day or two we could carry on.'

'I'm sorry, Brookie', said Hunt sadly. 'It's dashed bad luck, and I hate to let you down. I'd keep going if I could, but I simply can't. I'm pretty banged up and I need a quack.'

Oldman knew his friend was talking sense. Slowly he nodded his head in agreement.

'All right, Hunt, how do you want to play this?'

'Take my rations and water – you'll need them. When we passed by that last village, do you remember the little station?' Oldman nodded. 'Leave me in the waiting room – I'll be picked up at first light and it will give you a few hours to get clear.'

A plan was soon thrashed out, and two hours later Hunt was sitting on a hard wooden bench in the darkened waiting room. Oldman had done what he could for his friend. Hunt was wearing his khaki service dress tunic and Oldman had replaced his rank pips on the shoulder straps. Hanging around his neck was Hunt's POW identity disc. It was clear that he was a British officer.[5]

Oldman made his friend as comfortable as possible and then stood before him.

'You'll do', he said.

'If you make it, don't forget to send a postcard', said Hunt, his eyes misting over.

'It's been a hell of a ride, old chap', said Oldman, stretching out his hand.

'I'm not one for long goodbyes, so I'll say the very best of luck to you', said Hunt intently, grasping his friend's hand.

Oldman smiled and nodded slowly. 'And to you, old chap, and to you. When all this is over, we'll have that drink we've been talking about.'

'Quite so', said Hunt, his voice faint from exhaustion. 'Though

I'd trade all the whisky in Scotland for a shot of morphine right now.'

'Chin up. You'll be between clean white sheets in a few hours with a beautiful blonde fraulein dabbing at your fevered brow', quipped Oldman. Hunt laughed weakly.

'Well, I'd better shove off now', said Oldman slowly. He stood and the two men shook hands one last time in silence, their eyes locked in fierce comradeship. And then Oldman was gone, out into the dark night. Hunt leaned back against the cold wood and closed his eyes. All he could hear was the steady ticking of the station clock on the wall above him. 'A hell of a ride', he muttered to himself, smiling broadly, 'a hell of a ride.'

*

By the evening of 7 September at least thirteen of the original 32 that successfully crossed the wire on 30 August were still on the run inside Germany. Arkwright, Fuller and Coombe-Tennant were near Bielefeld. Tomes and Corfield were on the road to Hannover, with the Baltic coast as their target. Tom Stallard and Dick Page were still on their way towards the northern Dutch border and Brockie Mytton and Noel Hyde were edging towards Aachen on the Belgian frontier. Lieutenant Dennis Bartlett remained on the run, while Lieutenant Oldman would continue his solo march north. On a slightly different route but headed in the same direction were Martin Gilliat and Phil Pardoe, trudging towards Hamburg in northern Germany.

*

Sunday 7 September passed without incident for Tomes and Corfield. During the night they trekked across deadly dull flat country. They planned to cross the Hannover–Brunswick railway line and hoped to reach another railway line running north out of Hannover before morning. But the scale of their map was too small and they became lost amid many smaller branch lines. A tiring march was made across fields of greens and potatoes. All the paths and roads seemed to run east to west instead of north to south as they needed, forcing them to walk 'against the grain'. Barking dogs and people in villages threw them off further. They blundered into the centre of a small town trying to find a bridge over a small but deep river and were forced to cut across back gardens in daylight to get out again.

*

Arriving at Kassel jail on the evening of 8 September, Doug Crawford was thrown into a crowded cell. His cellmates were four very young shaven-headed Russians who had been drafted into the Wehrmacht, two Belgians and a few German civilians.[6] No one spoke very much and Crawford soon fell into an uneasy sleep on a lice-infested bunk. The uncertainty of his situation was deeply worrying. He was no longer under the authority of the German Army and POW administration and it seemed clear that the Gestapo had plans for him. His fellow prisoners didn't speak English and so Crawford was unable to communicate with them. He could only stare at the grey concrete ceiling and wait.

*

Tomes and Corfield spent the early hours of 8 September lying unhappily on soggy ground covered in reeds and willows. Heavy dew, wet crops and streams soaked their clothing. Insects relentlessly pestered them. Unsurprisingly, they failed to sleep but could at least take heart from the fact that since leaving Warburg they had averaged twenty miles a night, an impressive feat of 'boy scouting'.

That night this run of luck almost came to an abrupt end. Walking across a field, they suddenly heard planes overhead and then anti-aircraft batteries opened up some way off, the thud and boom of the guns extremely loud. Then, all of a sudden, six searchlights were switched on, the nearest less than half a mile away. If not for the British air raid they could easily have blundered into one of the German positions and been captured. Quietly thanking the RAF for their deliverance, the pair moved on.

Tomes and Corfield struck the Mittelland canal that night, the principal east–west inland waterway in Germany. They passed a sign giving directions to a Marlag, a prisoner of war camp for naval personnel. The sounds of trains shunting and a mass of bright arc lamps led them to a huge goods station at Lehrte, six miles east of Hannover. They decided to try to jump another train that was headed north. They needed to get to Stralsund in Western Pomerania, a city on the coast of the Strelasund, a sound of the Baltic Sea.[7] From Stralsund they could take a ferry to Rügen, the largest island in Germany. There were connecting ferries from Rügen to Bornholm in Denmark and Trelleborg in neutral Sweden.

But once again, jumping a free ride north proved impossible. The rail yard was crawling with workers in flat caps and blue overalls. At one point Tomes and Corfield almost lost each other as a long goods train separated them. They couldn't locate a train that looked like it was going north, so they eventually gave up an hour before dawn and found shelter. The plan was to try again the following night at the goods yard at the next station.

*

Arkwright's group reached Doren on 8 September where they rested for 48 hours. They made some futile efforts to snare a rabbit, and tried to sleep as much as possible.[8] They also witnessed anti-aircraft fire and searchlights in the direction of Münster and Osnabrück and took heart. 'I was glad our enemies were having a taste of their own medicine',[9] remarked Arkwright.

*

Doug Crawford was having a taste of quite different medicine. On the night of 9 September he was hauled into an interview room that contained only a scratched and battered wooden table and three chairs, a bare bulb hanging from an electric cable providing little light. Two Gestapo officers laid some papers on the table in front of them. The older one stared at Crawford, his small brown eyes piercing and snake-like. The Gestapo bombarded him with questions in German, but Crawford could pick out only a few familiar words. They shouted, banged the table with their fists, all the time repeating the questions. Crawford eventually worked out that they thought he was a spy. Each time the Gestapo men yelled a question Crawford responded in English with his name, rank and number. This was carefully written down. Crawford pulled out the two sets of dog tags that he wore around his neck – one set from the Australian Army and the other his prisoner of war tag issued to him at Oflag VI-B. The Gestapo officers carefully examined both tags and made more notes. Then they abruptly stood and left the room. Crawford was put back into his cell until the next morning.

*

While Crawford was being sweated down by state security, Tomes and Corfield rose and stole some milk from churns left near their hiding place. At 10.00pm they arrived at the level crossing at Burgdorf, a village thirteen miles north-east of Hannover. They crouched by the side of the tracks, waiting for a suitable train to come along. For two hours the evaders waited, watching several trains pass by, but only one was a goods train and it was hauling sealed oil wagons. Stymied again, they decided to move on and spend the next night in Celle goods station.

*

Crawford's interrogation resumed early on 10 September, with one Gestapo officer accompanied by a young Army lieutenant acting as interpreter. It was clear that the Gestapo still thought Crawford was an enemy agent.

'You are a British spy, Herr Crawford. Do you know what we do with spies in Germany?' said the Gestapo officer, leaning forward under the light, his face long and vulpine.

'I'm not a spy, I'm an Australian prisoner of war', replied Crawford, staring defiantly at the two Germans.

'If you are a prisoner of war, why are you out of uniform?' translated the interpreter for the glaring Gestapo officer.

'I am an Australian Army officer, and I escaped from Oflag VI-B on 30 August. This *is* my uniform – it was damaged in the camp and I altered it when making repairs.'

'You *are* a British spy', repeated the Gestapo man. 'What is your mission in Germany?'

'I have no "mission". I am an escaped prisoner of war.'

'You have come to do what – collect information, commit acts of sabotage against the Reich? What were you doing in the area where you were arrested?'

'I was passing through it on my way out of Germany.'

'How did you get maps and a compass?'

'I made them myself.'

'Impossible! You lie, Herr Crawford! You had better start telling me the truth or things will go badly for you. You are a prisoner of state security and you *will* answer my questions.' The Gestapo officer lit a cigarette with a silver lighter and leaned back in his chair. 'When and how did you enter Germany?' he asked in a conversational tone.

'Look, mate, as I've told you repeatedly, I'm an Australian prisoner of war. I entered Germany as a prisoner of war in 1941 after being captured on Crete. I escaped from Oflag VI-B on 30 August. You have my name, rank and number and you have seen my identity tags. Check with the camp.'[10]

'You are no longer classed as a prisoner of war, Herr Crawford', announced the Gestapo man imperiously. 'You were apprehended in a restricted military area. The penalty for spying in the Reich is death!'[11] The officer banged the flat of his hand on the table-top to make his point. 'You should consider that fact! I can have you taken from here to a special camp for enemies of the state!'

'As I've told you, and will keep telling you until I'm blue in the face, I am an escaped Australian Army officer', declared Crawford in a low voice. 'I know my rights under the Geneva Convention and one of them is a duty to escape from enemy captivity. I haven't done anything illegal.' The Gestapo man ignored him and changed tack, making some notes on the paper in front of him.

'Herr Crawford, we wish for you to make a written statement.'

'My name is Crawford, Alexander. I am a captain in the Australian Army. My army number is ...'

'Yes, yes, we know all that. You *will* make a written statement.'

'My name is Crawford, Alexander, Captain ...' repeated Crawford slowly, leaning back in his chair and crossing his arms defiantly.

'You are not cooperating with us, Herr Crawford. You are in a lot of trouble and you must cooperate to save yourself', said the German. He pointed his index finger at Crawford and barked: 'The Geneva Convention does not protect spies.'

'You have my Army and POW numbers. Go and check these with Oflag VI-B', said Crawford angrily. 'Everything I've said to you is easily verifiable.'[12]

Crawford stuck firmly to this line and the two German officers eventually gave up after another half hour of fruitless questioning. Gathering up their papers, they stormed out of the room and Crawford was escorted back to his cell.

An hour later his cell door was flung open and in stepped another German security officer accompanied by a large and mean-looking Alsatian dog. The officer started shouting questions at Crawford in German. Crawford just looked blank. 'I don't speak German', he said, spreading his hands before him. The security officer mumbled something under his breath and then ordered the dog to watch the prisoner while he left the cell for a few moments.

When the German came back to Crawford's cell an unexpected sight greeted him – his ferocious Alsatian had its head in Crawford's lap and was nuzzling quietly up to the Australian prisoner.

'*Schweinehund*!' screamed the German, kicking the dog viciously in the ribs. '*Nutzlos verdammtes Tier*!' He dragged the 'useless fucking animal' out of the cell by its collar.[13]

Later in the day the young Army lieutenant who had acted as a translator for the Gestapo visited Crawford. He politely asked him if he would sign a statement. Doug glanced at the sheet of typewritten paper.

'Sorry, cobber, but I don't read German. I won't sign something I can't understand.'

'But this is exactly what you said', the German replied in a somewhat surprised tone. 'I am a school teacher – at least I was – and I can promise you that this is an exact translation of your every word.'

Crawford still looked unsure.

'Sign this, and you will be returned to Warburg', said the German, holding out the paper and a pen. 'Your men are moving soon to a new camp, and you must join them. The espionage charges against you have been dropped – you have my word on this.'

Crawford believed him. His wide-eyed innocence and apparent honesty seemed genuine enough. Crawford scanned the statement again.

'Very well, I'll sign it, but with one proviso. I wish to write at the end that I do not understand German at all.'

'Agreed',[14] replied the German in a relieved tone and Crawford took the pen from his outstretched hand.

*

Tomes and Corfield made it successfully to a point just south of Celle, a town on the bank of the River Aller, a tributary of the Weser. Celle is the southern gateway to the great Lüneburg Heath, 25 miles north-east of Hannover and 75 miles south of Hamburg. The problem once again was the large number of people walking around, as well as lights and possibly an aerodrome. At dawn on 10 September, the two evaders found themselves in an area of bungalows and cottages, with many cyclists passing by on local roads on their way to work. The British officers couldn't find a decent hide, so they made do behind a few saplings just 100 yards from a house. It was a massive mistake. Although they covered their hide with some cut branches, it wasn't long before they were spotted.

At midday Tomes and Corfield heard Germans shouting nearby and a dog barking. Peering out from behind their hide they were confronted by a German civilian in shirtsleeves armed with a double-barrelled shotgun. The gun was levelled at them menacingly, while a small terrier at the man's feet barked constantly at the strangers.

'*Kommen von dort*!' commanded the German several times, indicating with his shotgun that the two Britons should come out into the open.

'*Sie sind Russen*?' asked the German, thinking that the two bedraggled and unshaven British officers must be Soviet POWs.

'*Nein, nein*', said Tomes, who spoke several languages with varying degrees of fluency. '*Wir sind kroatischen Freiwilligen Eisenbahner*', he continued, declaring them to be Croatian volunteer railway workers. '*Wir gehen nach Celle zu Fuss*',[15] Tomes went on, claiming that they were walking to Celle. This information cut no ice with the German, who ordered them to accompany him for a mile to another house, where they were put in the backyard and watched through a window while the German consulted with a friend.

A local Polish woman was called. A large crowd of locals had by now gathered. Tomes spoke Serbo-Croat to the Pole, while she questioned them in her own language, which Tomes also understood to some degree.

The Polish woman asked where their papers were. Tomes replied that they had lost them.[16] It was a weak excuse and the Germans knew it. The pair were marched to an inn and placed under the authority of the local worthies while the police were called. Tomes and Corfield could have run for it, but it was daytime and the locals would undoubtedly have shot at them.

Put aboard a truck, the two evaders were driven to Celle police station. The police already had a list of escaped POWs from Warburg, and in a few minutes had matched up names, descriptions and photographs with the two exhausted and grubby men standing before them. Tomes and Corfield spent the rest of the day and night in separate cells while the Germans organised transport and an escort to take them back to Warburg.[17] It was a crushing blow – so much planning, so much effort, so much discomfort, and all for nothing. Soon they were riding a train back to Warburg along the very same line that they had walked beside for days. They hardly spoke, just sat glumly looking out of the window at the lush countryside as it slipped by.

CHAPTER SEVENTEEN

Three Blind Mice

*The stalwart trio who achieved their objective, owed much
to our gallant friends in the Underground movement ... The
courage, singleness of purpose, tenacity and endurance of
those constantly engaged in this hazardous work, should
live as an inspiration to all communities and people.*

Major Tom Stallard, Durham Light Infantry

'What does it say?' whispered Albert Arkwright to Henry Coombe-Tennant. The two men crouched beside a small road in misty darkness peering up at a sign mounted atop a white post. A little further away Rupert Fuller waited, taking a bearing with his tiny compass.

'I'm not sure', said Coombe-Tennant, 'but I can tell you one thing ... it's not written in German!'

'You mean ...' gasped Arkwright.

'Yes, by Jove, I think we're in Holland!' exclaimed Coombe-Tennant, grinning broadly and slapping his comrade across the back.

'We need to be absolutely sure before we start whooping for joy', said Arkwright, a shiver of excitement passing down his spine. 'Come on, let's find a canal and take a bearing.'[1] The three men kept going due west along the quiet country road. They felt that they had crossed the Dutch frontier, but there remained a niggling doubt – they had to have confirmation. If they came to a canal running east to west, according to their maps they would definitely be in the Netherlands. The trio picked up the pace, an almost childlike sense of discovery overtaking them.

The final stretch to the border had been especially challenging. On 10 September Arkwright's group had marched through the town of Lengerich without incident and continued until fairly late in the morning of the 11th, lying up near the town for the day. Lengerich lies at the northern tip of the Teutoburg Forest and just over nine miles south-west of Osnabrück. In the evening the three evaders pushed west and struck a canal that ran north-west. They walked along the towpath to Hörstel-Riesenbeck. The path was deserted and it was a moonless night. They continued along the canal until 13 September when they stumbled into another military area with searchlights, anti-aircraft guns and night fighters overhead.[2] They were a night's march from the Dutch frontier.

*

Many other Olympia evaders had fallen into German hands. Brooke Oldman was captured on 12 September at Lüneburg in northern Germany, twenty miles south-east of Hamburg, having made excellent progress since reluctantly leaving the wounded Lieutenant Hunt at the country railway station.[3] Tom Stallard and Dick Page's luck ran out on the German–Dutch frontier on 13 September. They were close to the town of Gronau in Westfalen, just six miles by rail to the Dutch town of Enschede over the border in Overijssel province.[4] Stallard and Page were seen by civilians out for an evening walk and reported to the local police. The same evening, Martin Gilliat and Phil Pardoe also fell into German hands, captured close to Hamburg. Gilliat, Pardoe and Oldman had managed to trek an impressive 200 miles from Warburg in sixteen exhausting nights.[5] Around the same time, Brockie Mytton and Noel Hyde had been recaptured close to the city of Aachen on the Belgian frontier.[6]

For Stallard, recapture was a very bitter pill. He had created, planned and led Operation Olympia, getting 32 men over the wire.

It was his second successful escape from the camp. To be caught within sight of Holland was deeply disappointing for him, probably more so than the other Olympia evaders. If any man at Warburg had burned with an all-consuming desire to be free, it had been Tom Stallard. Now he was back 'in the bag'. The Germans knew that he was a major figure in the world of POW escaping, and he could expect some harsh treatment. 'Once again Tom was denied that extra stroke of luck or act of Providence, call it what you will, which alone could guide a prisoner all the way home from the heart of an occupied continent',[7] wrote his friend Major Arkwright many years afterwards.

*

Arkwright and his comrades began their approach to the Dutch frontier on 14 September. They were the last free Olympia evaders. They allowed themselves a night to cover the distance and place themselves into a suitable jumping-off position from which to attempt to cross. What little information they possessed about the frontier was vague and contradictory.

They arrived at their jumping-off point in the early hours of 15 September. Sleep was impossible; they were all too excited and nervous. Most of the day was spent studying the diagram of the frontier that they had put together back at Warburg. In 1941 two fellow officers had managed to escape from a hospital just over the German side of the frontier. Both men had tried to cross into Holland. One reported that the border was completely unmarked and open and the Germans had picked him up one day inside Holland. The other officer had reported that the border was a well protected barrier of barbed wire fences and sentry patrols – not dissimilar to the perimeter fences at Oflag VI-B.[8] The only thing Arkwright's group knew for certain was that the frontier was marshy and very treacherous.

Once darkness had fallen on 15 September the three evaders set off. They walked three to four miles, crossing a small river, a railway line and a road, arriving close to the border around midnight. The ground sloped gently away from the road into a marsh. Arkwright's group descended carefully, as the terrain was hard going, visibility was poor and there was no moon. A light mist had come up, further obscuring their path. The weather and light conditions concealed them from any German patrols, but it also made walking extremely difficult. Stumbling and tripping over humps and holes, Arkwright plunged into a small morass up to his waist. He wearily clambered out, but before he could warn Coombe-Tennant, who was walking behind him, he too fell into the stinking wet ooze.

Looking at their watches, the party realised that they had plenty of time. They were making a lot of noise as they tried to negotiate the marsh in the dark, enough to alert any German sentries posted along the frontier, so they decided instead to backtrack to the road and try to find a drier alternative route west.

After heading north and then north-west they struck a track running almost due west. It probably led across the marsh, but it might also lead to a German sentry post. Throwing caution to the wind, the three evaders decided to risk it. Moving almost silently, they quickly covered a quarter of a mile, leaving the marsh behind them. When the path turned south they left it and struck across heathland.[9]

They kept walking, encountering paths that headed west but not seeing any water features. Arriving at another heath and some pine trees, some rather ghostly narrow lanes ran between the woods. There were no barbed wire barriers or guards. After three or four miles they stopped.

Next came green grass, fields and hedges with small country houses dotted about. It was then that Arkwright and Coombe-Tennant spotted the signpost beside the road. Hardly daring to believe their eyes, they decided to push on until they hit a canal that their maps told them was just inside Holland. On and on they went, turning north-west and following a bridle path. Suddenly a canal loomed out of the gloom in front of them. Fuller whipped out his compass and swiftly took a bearing. It ran east to west – it was confirmation – they *were* in Holland. They shook hands, but the euphoria was short-lived. Holland was an occupied country full of German troops, and although they hoped that the locals would be friendly, there were plenty of quislings and collaborators among them. They would have to exercise extreme caution in attempting to make contact with the Dutch. It had taken them seventeen nights to reach Holland, but they didn't want to do anything foolish now they were there.

*

Arkwright, Coombe-Tennant and Fuller had made it out of Germany. Twenty-nine others had been recaptured, and they now found themselves sent to new camps. Oflag VI-B was closed down completely on 12 September when the large party that was headed for Oflag VII-B at Eichstätt departed. All of the Olympia escapees were given two weeks' solitary confinement as punishment, sweating it out in wooden isolation cells in the cooler, existing on a diet of bread and water until released back into the general camp population. Almost to a man, these brave and resourceful soldiers immediately began making new plans for escape, and once again Tom Stallard would be at the forefront.

*

Arkwright's group followed the towpath beside the canal, passing under a bridge across which a whole fleet of Dutch cyclists passed on their way to work in Germany. Now began a desperate hunt for somewhere to hide, as it was rapidly getting light. They settled on a hedgerow a few feet thick and only a hundred yards from a farmhouse.

Sheltering inside the hedgerow, the evaders tried to decide

what to do. Their whole plan since leaving Warburg had been to get out of Germany – they had given little thought to what to do if they succeeded. They had left the camp with food for eighteen nights and they had been on the road for seventeen. They needed help, but it was impossible just to walk up to the nearest house, bang on the front door and demand food and shelter.[10] Although they felt sure that most Dutch would willingly help them, they could not expect civilians to risk their lives doing so. The Gestapo routinely imprisoned in concentration camps anyone they caught harbouring or assisting escaped Allied POWs or downed airmen. 'And yet something told us that help would come',[11] said Arkwright. They wouldn't ask for it, or do anything to compromise their Dutch allies. Instead, the trio opted to remain passive and to wait and see what happened. As it turned out, this course of action soon paid off.

The three escapees lay in the hedge and tried to sleep. It started to rain and a frigid wind blew up. They huddled together, cold, wet and rather miserable. In the afternoon a small boy came down the hedgerow leading a pony. He immediately saw the Britons, but rather than being afraid the boy simply greeted them, and they returned the greeting. Arkwright and his companions guessed correctly that the boy understood they were allies and needed help.

That evening two men approached Arkwright's group. The Britons were unafraid, for if these men were collaborators they would not have waited until nightfall to approach. In the darkness the five men tried to communicate using English, French and German, and the farmer settled on German. When Coombe-Tennant told him that they were escaped British POWs he was taken aback. The farmer, J.H. Eppink, a tall, slim, blond-haired man in his early forties, had assumed that they were French, as he said that around 60 a week crossed the frontier in his district.[12]

Eppink went away and later whistled to them; whereupon the other Dutchman indicated that the Britons should follow him. They met up near the farm, named 'Boddenkuiper', were shown into the stables, and then climbed a ladder to the hayloft above. The loft was to be their home for the next nine days while Eppink contacted the Dutch Underground. Eppink's wife brought the exhausted Britons bread, butter and warm milk.[13] That first night Arkwright, Coombe-Tennant and Fuller dug into the hay and had their first comfortable night's rest since 29 August.[14]

For Eppink and his family, the sudden arrival of three British POWs was not treated lightly. They were all in grave danger, and the first thing that Eppink had to do was find some assistance in dealing with the situation. Everyone knew that the Gestapo was extremely crafty, and they often tried to infiltrate Underground organisations, one method being to introduce fake evaders. Arkwright's group was not going anywhere until the Underground was sure of their identities. One or even two escaped British POWs was plausible, though extremely rare, but three unheard of.

The next morning Arkwright's group was awakened by sunlight pouring into the loft through small glass tiles set into the roof. For several minutes they hardly stirred, just watching dust motes as they twirled and danced in the sunbeams. They had realised that they were no longer masters of their own destiny and were now completely dependent on others. All the stress and tension of the previous seventeen nights spent creeping like hunted animals across the darkened German countryside came out of them. They were relaxed.

About 7.00am a cheerful Eppink appeared at the trapdoor to the loft. He brought them milk, bread and cold bacon and as the Britons ate ravenously he spoke a little in broken French, which Coombe-Tennant understood. He told them that he had been a soldier and was taken prisoner in 1940 and held for three or four months before returning to his farm.[15]

On 18 September a visitor arrived. He was introduced as a local veterinary surgeon, and Arkwright's group referred to him thereafter as 'the Doctor'. He was a member of the Dutch Underground movement. Small, slightly rotund, and with thick brown hair, the Doctor seemed quite embarrassed by the task that he had been set. Speaking excellent English, he had come to check the Britons' *bona fides*, to make sure they were who they claimed to be. They offered their prisoner of war identity discs that had been issued to them at their first camp, Oflag VII-C at Laufen. Of course, the Gestapo could easily fabricate these. Next, Fuller extracted a small notebook from his pocket and took out a photograph of his wife and child and gave it to the Doctor. On the reverse of the photograph was the stamp of the company that took it, including their English address and telephone number. Arkwright showed the Doctor his windcheater, originally sent to him at Oflag VI-B by his wife, and which he had managed to obtain from storage shortly before the escape. The labels all showed its English manufacture. Finally, each man gave the doctor his British Army identity number. None of this 'evidence' was cast-iron, and the Germans could easily fake it, so the Doctor also questioned them about their escape and the time they had spent on the run inside Germany, making notes as they spoke. Before he left, the Doctor handed them a roll of English illustrated newspapers and some cigarettes and enquired as to their comfort.[16]

*

Arkwright's group had become, to use the Dutch parlance, *Onderduikers* or 'people in hiding'. By the time they received shelter from Eppink, the Dutch resistance movement was well established and used to sheltering many different types of evaders. In many regards, the Netherlands was actually one of the least attractive nations for escaped prisoners of war. It was small and had the densest population in Europe, which meant that it was extremely difficult to conceal illegal activity from the occupiers and their collaborators. From the beginning of the German occupation in 1940, the Nazis had treated the Dutch differently from the other occupied nations, classing them as fellow Aryans. There was widespread collaboration in Holland, and thousands of young Dutchmen joined the Waffen-SS and other German military formations. But there were plenty of others who bravely resisted.

The Underground consisted of many little groups – some social democrats, some Catholics and some Communists – all working independently of one another and engaged in different types of resistance. Typical activities were cutting telephone wires, distributing anti-German leaflets and tearing down Nazi posters. Others forged ration cards or money, collected intelligence for the Allies or published underground newspapers. Any person caught engaging in these activities was sent to a concentration camp. After 1944, they were usually shot.

The most popular resistance activity in Holland was hiding people from the Nazis. Many Dutch risked their lives helping Jews, and when the Germans raided the Old Jewish Quarter in Amsterdam in February 1941, the Communist Party of the Netherlands called a general strike. Holland ground to a halt, marking a major act of defiance against the Germans. Many Jews were hidden from the round-ups, most famously Anne Frank and her family.

The first Britons to become *Onderduikers* were soldiers who failed to make it to the evacuation beaches at Dunkirk in May 1940 – many found shelter with sympathetic families in Dutch Flanders. Thousands of French soldiers who escaped from German captivity made their way to Holland and were hidden or passed along to Belgium and France. Eppink had naturally assumed that Arkwright's group represented more French evaders. Later, as the air war against Germany grew in intensity, the Dutch collected and hid British and American bomber pilots and crewmen. Altogether, over 4,000 Allied soldiers became *Onderduikers*.

*

Arkwright's team, resting in Eppink's hayloft, began to meet the other members of the farmer's family. Every morning at 7.00 one of Eppink's two attractive daughters, aged seventeen and twenty, would tap on the trapdoor and call 'Hullo'. Coombe-Tennant, the group's spokesman by virtue of his language skills, would rouse himself from the hay and let the girl up. Arkwright and Fuller, both married men with children, ribbed the bachelor Coombe-Tennant after observing his embarrassed attempts to make conversation with the girls. Arkwright thought Coombe-Tennant to be a quiet and shy young man with no interest in the opposite sex. Breakfast usually consisted of a saucepan of hot milk, slices of white or wholemeal bread with butter, and sometimes cold bacon, cheese or honey and an occasional boiled egg.[17] Compared to their fare on the road, it was a veritable feast.

Eppink provided the Britons with washing, shaving and toilet facilities in the stable below the loft. They were not permitted to leave the stables, but they were being well taken care of. Eppink's daughters washed their clothes and mended their socks and underwear.[18]

On 17 September Arkwright's party was visited by 'Jan', a member of the Dutch Underground. Jan was in a group that already had extensive experience in moving escaped French POWs through Holland and into Belgium.[19] The whole process was well rehearsed. However, Arkwright and his companions were the first Britons the group had encountered, and they faced some challenges. Firstly there was the language barrier. A Frenchman would blend into Belgium, but only Coombe-Tennant spoke French. England was much further away than Belgium or France, and the chances of getting the three Britons home were extremely remote. But Jan soon impressed them with his drive, enthusiasm and determination. They came to believe that in Jan's steady hands the remote chance was a little bit more attainable.

Jan was a mining engineer by trade and had been born in the Dutch East Indies. In his late thirties, Jan had, like Eppink, helped defend Holland from the German invasion in 1940. As a reserve lieutenant he had not been sent to a prisoner of war camp, but instead the Germans had appointed him an inspector of several factories in the city of Oldenzaal, close to the German border in Overijssel province. Jan lived in a handsome brick house in the village of Rossum, just outside Oldenzaal. He had visited England before the war and spoke the language fluently.[20]

Jan told the Britons that he thought he could move them through Holland to Belgium without too much difficulty, and he would try to contact a similar organisation in Belgium. In a week they would move to his house, but for the time being it was too dangerous. In a blasé manner, Jan told them that he and his house were currently under Gestapo surveillance and he wanted things to go quiet again before making the move.[21] Arkwright and the others were shocked to hear this, and a little worried that Jan didn't seem particularly bothered by this revelation, but they decided that it was none of their concern – and judging by the man's character, he obviously knew what he was doing.

Arkwright's group continued to rest and rebuild their strength. The gargantuan helpings at mealtimes soon restored their spirits and increased their weight. Lunch, the main meal of the day, usually consisted of pork with a huge mound of potatoes and other vegetables, followed by stewed fruit, pears or rhubarb. 'By the time we had finished we were generally gasping and comatose and fit for nothing for the next hour or so but to lie quietly and allow the digestive juices to do their work',[22] said Arkwright.

*

After nine days hidden in the hayloft the Dutch decided to move the group to Rossum. Civilian clothes were provided for the trip, and the three men tried to make themselves as smart as possible.[23] The Doctor took them in his car in the dead of night. As a local veterinary surgeon, he was allowed a limited ration of petrol, but he was forbidden to carry passengers. The journey to Jan's house was ten miles, and the Britons travelled the whole way with their hearts in their mouths. Partly it was the fear of recapture, but partly also the Doctor's crazed driving as he thrashed his little black car along country tracks beside a canal, the vehicle bouncing wildly in the deep cart ruts. It was the first time Arkwright, Fuller and Coombe-Tennant had been in a car for two years.[24]

On arrival at Jan's house, the redoubtable resistance fighter came out to greet the evaders with his two dogs at his heels. The Britons were introduced to Jan's Swedish wife, whom they addressed as 'Madame' for the duration of their stay. Jan had a small daughter, a housemaid and another man living with them called 'the Soldier'. This curious fellow fascinated the Britons. He looked hard-bitten and ruthless and worked in a factory nearby. A veteran of the Spanish Civil War, the Soldier had lost his Dutch citizenship after fighting against Franco.[25]

The days were passed eating, sleeping, reading and playing cards as Jan continued his efforts to make contact with an escape line in Belgium. When it was mentioned that Coombe-Tennant was an accomplished pianist, an old piano was dragged out of storage and the young officer spent hours playing Beethoven, dance music and jazz. Arkwright took up knitting, making socks for Jan and his young daughter. Fuller mostly slept, Arkwright commenting 'that he had the easy conscience of a righteous man'.[26]

Always uppermost in the British evaders' minds was getting back to England, and most importantly beginning the next leg of their journey. Jan brought disappointing news. Travel by sea was impossible and he was experiencing difficulty in contacting the escape line in Belgium. But he would not stop trying.

One night the whole household was woken by Frida, Jan's sheepdog, barking at the approach of strangers to the house. Arkwright went to the upstairs landing and stood listening while Jan went to investigate. He expected the door to be broken down at any moment by the Gestapo. Instead, the nocturnal visitors were two escaped French POWs who had been given Jan's address as a refuge. He bedded them down and appeared unfazed by the imposition.

The Frenchmen were determined to get home and Jan decided to keep them at his house to act as guides for Arkwright's group should he fail to contact the Belgians. The two groups were not permitted to meet, and Jan told the French that the Britons were three important secret agents. A few nights later three more French POWs arrived, and Jan's house was overflowing with evaders.

After two weeks at Jan's, Arkwright and his companions desperately wanted to get moving again. They knew the terrible danger in which they placed Jan and his family by remaining.[27] They were impatient to be moving towards England, but also deeply grateful to Jan and his family for the incredible care that they had received. And then good news arrived. Jan had managed to make contact with someone in Belgium who could help – a man known only as 'Den Blauen' or 'the Blue One'. It was the first link to an extraordinary escape organisation created and run by an attractive young Belgian woman. Its name was Comet Line.

CHAPTER EIGHTEEN

Comet Line

*Dédée became a symbol of courage and defiance
during her extraordinary career. Her lively charm
and energy won over the most faint-hearted.*

Major Airey Neave, MI9

The parlour door was flung open with a crash, causing Arkwright, Coombe-Tennant and Fuller to start from their comfortable armchairs in alarm. The young Belgian woman who had guided them to the café in Liège stood in the doorway, out of breath and with an expression of deep alarm on her pretty face.

'The Gestapo', she gasped. 'The Gestapo has arrested the Chief!' 'The Chief' was the local organiser of anti-German resistance and the person responsible for smuggling Allied evaders through the city.

'My God!' exclaimed Fuller. 'What happened?' The three Britons had arrived a few hours before and been fed by the café proprietor and his wife. They had been relaxing in the private upstairs sitting room after their lunch, reading newspapers and smoking.

'The Gestapo arrested him, his wife and their little daughter and have taken them to the German headquarters for questioning', said the young woman, ashen-faced. 'The *Boche* may soon know about this café. They may even be watching this place already.'

Arkwright's group looked at one another. They knew that these people who were helping them so freely were risking their lives, and that the British officers were the biggest piece of incriminating evidence if the Germans burst in.

'We should leave, mademoiselle', said Coombe-Tennant forcefully. 'Before anything happens.'

'*Non, monsieur*! You don't know the city. The *Boche* will pick you up in half an hour.' The young woman clutched her handbag strap tightly. 'You must go down to the bar. Pretend you are ordinary customers. If the Gestapo come, they will probably not pay attention to you but look instead for people hiding.'[1] Pulling on their coats and caps, the trio was escorted downstairs and soon found themselves sitting around a wooden table in silence, sipping at glasses of cold beer and trying not to look terrified. Behind the bar, the café owner's wife cleaned glasses and appeared to be on the verge of a nervous breakdown. She constantly scanned the street outside the windows, waiting for the black cars that would signal the arrival of the dreaded Gestapo, dressed in black leather coats and grey fedora hats.

*

Three weeks earlier, on 23 September 1942, Arkwright's group had crossed over from Holland into Belgium. Jan and his friend P.J. Goorhuis, a tall, serious and darkly handsome Underground helper, had set off with the three Britons and two of the French POWs in tow. The plan had been to arrive at 4.00pm at a little village close to the frontier. Jan and Goorhuis would lead them to a bridle path that led to a quiet sector of the border where there should not be any guards, and then they would be on their own. Jan and Goorhuis would not go beyond the frontier, and locating 'the Blue One' would be the evaders' dangerous task.

The British officers carried a tracing of Jan's map of the Belgian border and were given a month's supply of tobacco and cigarette papers. They dared not engage locals in conversation at train stations, and could occupy themselves slowly rolling cigarettes instead. Madame equipped them with three days' worth of sandwiches.

After a sleepless night, on the Monday morning they had breakfasted with the household and then made to leave. 'We can never thank you, Madame', said Arkwright with feeling, his comrades echoing this sentiment. Madame laughed: 'You will come back and thank us after the war',[2] she said, embracing each of them in turn.

At 6.00am the evaders left. The air was cold and bit into their cheeks, but the sharpness of the morning made them feel elated and in high spirits. They were finally moving again. They walked three miles to the station at Oldenzaal in three groups. Few people were about, and they joined a loose group of men and women. The station waiting room was full and the glare of the electric lamps harsh and unforgiving – Arkwright and his companions felt conspicuous and split up, standing or sitting in different parts of the room attempting to feign nonchalance. Arkwright noticed that the two Frenchmen carried off the air of indifference much better than the tense Englishmen.[3] While they waited, Jan sidled up to each man and quietly passed him a ticket.

The train arrived amid much steam and noise and they boarded with the other commuters. The found seats and feigned sleep to avoid conversation with their Dutch neighbours. Arkwright was amused when he noticed one of his fellow travellers reading an English book – it seemed almost like an act of rebellion against the Germans. Four hours later, the train stopped at Utrecht, a city of 165,000 people. For the first time Arkwright and his friends saw Nazi collaborators – Dutchmen wearing blue uniforms, strutting around the station attempting to look superior. Arkwright thought their bombast actually hid their uneasiness among their own people.

After an hour's wait at Utrecht the evaders switched to another train. This time all seven of them had a compartment to themselves, so they could converse freely. The ticket collector stepped into their compartment, glancing at each of them in turn as he clipped their tickets. As he left, pulling the sliding wooden door across, he gave them a slow wink.[4]

Arriving at Weert, a small town near Maastricht, they were only a couple of miles from the frontier. Following Jan and Goorhuis at a discreet distance, the fugitives were led towards the border. Suddenly, Jan and Goorhuis stopped on the path and stood to one side, allowing the five evaders to pass by them. As they did so, no one stopped to shake hands or to say goodbye – it would have been too dangerous. Instead, the five evaders walked straight past the two Dutchmen, quietly mumbling 'thank you' as they went.

Following the path, Fuller taking a bearing from his homemade compass, the group paused for a smoke in a thick belt of trees. It was 5.00pm and there were two hours of daylight remaining. They knew that the Blue One's house was three miles beyond the frontier. The plan was to send one of the Frenchmen forward to make contact with him.

Steering via compass, they trudged on through derelict land, crossing small streams. Then a small river appeared, blocking their route. There was no bridge – was this the frontier? Following a path alongside the river they suddenly saw a uniformed official coming towards them on the opposite side. The evaders had no idea whether he was Dutch or Belgian, but he paid them no attention. Then they came to a footbridge upon which a man was fishing. One of the Frenchmen asked the fisherman whether he had had any luck. After a short conversation the Frenchmen confirmed that the man was a Belgian – they had crossed the frontier.[5] Arkwright and his companions were both overjoyed and relieved.

Walking past ploughed fields and fenced meadows, they struck out across open country towards the Blue One's village. A ploughman had stopped his team of horses and was staring at them. He raised his hand and signalled. One of the French soldiers strode over and conversed with the Belgian for ten minutes. He returned with a warning – German military vehicles regularly used the main road ahead. The ploughman had immediately guessed that the group was a party of evaders, and had asked whether they were English. Jan had warned them earlier that the Belgians would not help Britons, as it was too difficult and dangerous. The Frenchman had been noncommittal in his reply. The farmer offered to help them. But could he be trusted? The word 'quisling' constantly came to mind, a well-founded paranoia. The Frenchman said he believed that the man was genuine so they decided to take the risk.

The farmer went off to telephone friends who he said would help them. When he returned he told the evaders that all was well. He was also delighted when he discovered that Arkwright's group was British.[6] The farmer spoke good English, which was another surprise. He told them that they would have to hide in a thick hedgerow until dark, and then he could smuggle them into his house.

Lying in the hedgerow chatting, the evaders were surprised to discover that the friends whom the farmer had called were a Belgian woman and her seventeen-year-old daughter. The two women came out to the fields to greet them and were on excellent form, tremendously excited to meet the escapees. The mother, Madame Groenen, was a smart and businesslike young lady, and both she and her daughter spoke fluent English. They took great delight in showing Arkwright's group RAF badges and other mementoes that they had been given by appreciative Allied aircrew they had hidden. For their part, Arkwright and his friends shared the women's excitement so much that 'we soon found ourselves soaring in the clouds'.[7] Through a chance encounter, they had made contact with the fabled Comet Line.

*

The saga of Comet Line had begun with the appearance at the British Consulate in Bilbao, Spain in August 1941 of a 25-year-old Belgian woman, two other Belgians, and a British soldier. The Consul's eyes had grown ever wider as the young woman, Andrée De Jongh, known to all as Dédée, recounted how she and her father had begun hiding Allied soldiers in 1940, shortly after Belgium surrendered, and how she had then taken it upon herself to deliver this British soldier, Private James Cromar, in person to consular officials in neutral Spain. In order to do this she had smuggled Cromar from Brussels all the way through occupied France and collaborationist Vichy France, and then climbed over the Pyrenees led by a tough Basque guide.[8]

Dédée was an attractive personality with a compelling, feminine face, her auburn hair brushed back from her forehead. Although physically slight, her eyes and mouth hinted at a stubborn and determined streak. Her father had nicknamed her 'Little Cyclone', an extremely apt description. Dédée had originally trained as a nurse and was inspired to help Allied soldiers by the tragic story of Edith Cavell, the British nurse executed by the Germans in Brussels during the First World War.

In Bilbao, Dédée told the Consul that she needed proper funding. With money, she and her schoolmaster father Frédéric intended to create an escape line of safe houses between Brussels and the Franco-Spanish frontier. It cost her 6,000 Belgian francs to move each man from the Belgian capital to St Jean de Luz on the Spanish border, and 1,400 pesetas for the mountain guides.[9]

Contact was swiftly established with MI9, the Whitehall outfit that assisted escaping British POWs. Other escape lines already existed, but traitors and quislings had heavily compromised them. Dédée's fresh new line, codenamed 'Comet', would remain completely under her control. All its operatives were Belgian and the chances of German infiltration minimised. MI9 agreed to provide the funding, but contact between London and Dédée was irregular and difficult as she refused a radio operator. Nevertheless, Comet Line soon began to produce results. Dédée made sure that only trained soldiers and airmen were sent down the line to Spain, and she used a series of mostly young female operatives who could blend in with ordinary society to help move the men south. Soon, dozens of men were returning to England, all of them full of praise for the 'Postman', as Dédée was codenamed by MI9, the extraordinary heroine whose name evoked misty-eyed appreciation and gratitude from the tough servicemen she had helped.[10] More than one had fallen a little in love with this amazing woman, and they all worried about the terrible risks that she and her organisation were taking to help the Allied war effort.

*

After a meal with the farmer, Arkwright's group and the two Frenchmen were taken to the large house of Dr Michel Groenen in Tongerlo, escorted surreptitiously inside by Comet Line operative Madame Groenen, whom they had met earlier by the hedgerow. Dr Groenen had expressly forbidden his wife from bringing evaders to the property for fear of the consequences for their family, which included five children, but Madame Groenen evidently gained a thrill from flouting her husband's wishes as well as aiding the Allied cause. Removing their boots, the escapers spent an awkward hour recounting their experiences since leaving Warburg to the mistress of the house, before being hidden in a disused coach house next door.

During the next day the evaders were hidden inside the main house's attic. Eventually, Madame Groenen confessed all to her husband, who, contrary to the impression given by his wife, was not a tyrant but an extremely charming and courteous 65-year-old medical doctor, tall, slim and with a slight stoop. Dr Groenen, who was an expert in TB, spoke no English, but he was a passionate hunter and was thrilled when he discovered that he owned a book about shooting over dogs written by one of Major Arkwright's close relatives.[11]

The next move was to the house of an older lady, five miles by bicycle. The two Frenchmen decided to strike off without Arkwright's group. Perhaps being in a country that spoke their language gave them a false sense of confidence. Such negligence was a terrible blunder – both men were recaptured within days. The three British officers, meanwhile, cycled through the chill night air accompanied by two young Comet Line operatives. They rode almost parallel to the Dutch border, east then a little south, heading for Maeseyck in the north-eastern corner of Belgium.

When they arrived at the older lady's house one of their guides carelessly drew his Browning pistol from his pocket and handed it to their hostess, Madame de la Salle, making a laughing comment that he hadn't had to use it. The Britons were surprised to discover that their young guides were armed and were prepared to shoot to kill if necessary to protect the evaders.

Their guide for the next part of the journey was a young woman who took them to her father's modest home. The next morning at 5.00, after a virtually sleepless night, Arkwright's group, following a hasty breakfast and several cups of strong black coffee, walked to the local tram terminus. They would be travelling twenty miles into the city of Liège, led by the girl.

The first part of the journey passed without incident, but as they waited to change lines on the outskirts of Liège they spied large numbers of Belgian police heading for the waiting crowd. A truck pulled up and out jumped a dozen policemen, dressed in dark blue high-necked tunics with red facings, jackboots and blue caps. They ordered everyone to stand still and began to scan the faces in the crowd carefully, hands resting on brown leather holsters. Arkwright, Coombe-Tennant and Fuller froze, nervously pulling on hand-rolled cigarettes or pretending to read newspapers. The police pressed through the crowd towards the Britons. Two came level with Coombe-Tennant. Their hard blue eyes swept over his face. Coombe-Tennant smiled weakly. The gendarmes brushed past him on each side. The three Britons, nervous sweat trickling down their backs, stood rooted to the spot, hardly believing their luck. None of them had generated even a flicker of interest from the police. Only later did Arkwright discover that the police had been clamping down on black marketeers, not looking for escaped POWs.

Once in central Liège, Arkwright's group alighted from the tram and followed the young woman at a discreet distance. They passed many German soldiers on leave, taking a vicarious delight in going undetected among their enemies. It seemed like half the city was in field-grey. There were Germans sitting in groups at pavement cafés, drinking coffee while white-aproned waiters bustled around them. Others walked with pretty young Belgian women in colourful summer dresses and hats, heedless of the looks of disdain from other Belgians.

After a short walk the Belgian girl led Arkwright and his friends into a red-fronted café and handed them over to the proprietor, who came forward and greeted them in French. A harassed-looking middle-aged man with a bad comb-over, he took the Britons upstairs to his private apartment, fed them breakfast and told them to relax. Everything was going to be all right. They took him at his word.

Later that morning the evaders had a surprise visitor – an Englishwoman. She was married to a local confectioner and was active within the Comet Line. When she heard about three Englishmen in Liège she demanded to meet them. Arkwright thought that the middle-aged Englishwoman was in a pitiable state of nerves.[12] The Gestapo kept intermittent tabs on her, but she had thus far avoided internment. The British officers were delighted to see her, but also shocked by her anxiety of mind, so much so that Coombe-Tennant asked her whether she would like to come with them and try to get back to England. She demurred, claiming that she could not leave her Belgian husband, business and friends, but her isolation and almost pathetic excitement in meeting three of her countrymen touched them deeply.

It was on the same afternoon, after meeting the Englishwoman, and while they were relaxing after lunch, that the young woman returned with news of the Gestapo raid on the chief of resistance operations in Liège.

The young woman told Arkwright and the others that her husband had gone to try to find out what had happened and whether the Gestapo had discovered anything about the café. Shortly after, the three evaders were ushered downstairs to the bar and given beers while the Underground decided what to do with them. They sat in awkward silence, unable to converse because of the other customers. Edith Piaf was playing on the radio behind the bar and the customers kept up a lively conversation all around them, the room smoky and cheerful.

The decision was soon made to move Arkwright's group to another location on the outskirts of Liège. Led again by the brave young woman, the evaders entered another small café and posed once more as customers. Once the other genuine customers had left, the three British officers were shown into the kitchen. The young woman told them that she was waiting for a telephone call from the people who would shelter them that night.

In the event, the saviours turned out to be two middle-aged and very respectable ladies dressed head-to-toe in black. It was a short walk from the café to their semi-detached house. When Arkwright's group entered through the kitchen door they discovered another, older woman bathing a child, an orphan whom the ladies had adopted. It took Arkwright and the others some time to work out the relationships, but one woman, Madame Courenne, was married, the other was her spinster sister, and the third woman her mother-in-law.

The three escapees settled around the kitchen table while the ladies busied themselves preparing dinner. The smell of potatoes frying in a pan on the stove was reassuring and familiar and they chatted amiably with the gentle women, struck again by the incongruity of their appearances and their dangerous roles within Comet Line.

The kitchen door opened and in stepped a man introduced to the evaders as the Chief. He was well built and wearing a workman's flat cap and a neckerchief. The Gestapo had just released him after ransacking his home looking for evidence. None was found, though they had kept his wife and child for further questioning. The nervous café owner from earlier and Monsieur Courenne accompanied him. All three men looked worried. They played a dangerous game of cat-and-mouse with the Gestapo and the price of a single mistake would be the utter destruction of themselves and their families. All this risk to help escaped Allied POWs and downed airmen. There was a strong feeling in the small kitchen that evening that a serious disaster had been narrowly averted.[13] The German cat had been fooled once again.

Gradually the aura of gloom passed as the evaders relaxed in the house. The day after the close brush with calamity, Arkwright's group were each treated to a proper bath, their first since capture in 1940. Madame Courenne and the other women, Jeanne and Matilde, washed and repaired their clothes. Two pleasant days passed reading and relaxing.[14]

A mysterious man visited the house to provide them with false identity cards. They were each photographed and were almost childishly pleased with the finished articles. The evaders were described as artisans living in different towns near the Franco-Belgian frontier, and their worn and slightly shabby clothing conformed perfectly to this cover story.

*

On a Sunday in early October, they had just finished their lunch when one of the ladies came into the dining room to tell them to get ready to leave immediately. She told them that a man whom they had helped some weeks before, purporting to be a Belgian pilot trying to get to England, had turned out to be a Nazi agent. He had just completed the line and had placed all the information he could about safe houses and helpers in the hands of the Gestapo. The Germans could already be on their way. The Belgian ladies hastily packed up their house as best they could, not knowing if they would ever return, locked the front door and took the escapers by tram to the station, where they all boarded a train to Brussels.

The three-hour journey to Brussels passed without incident, Arkwright and his companions once more feigning sleep to avoid conversation with fellow passengers. The Belgian capital was the headquarters of the Military Administration in Belgium and northern France under the command of General Alexander, Baron von Falkenhausen. Tens of thousands of Wehrmacht and SS troops garrisoned the city and it was also the main Gestapo HQ for the area.

Arriving after dark, the evaders followed the two sisters through blackened streets. After several creaking and chilly tram trips they eventually arrived at a large block of flats. The husband and wife who opened the door clearly were not expecting them but quickly recovered from their shock. The two ladies, looking tired and strained, bade the evaders farewell.

Arkwright, Coombe-Tennant and Fuller spent the night concealed in an attic room. Brussels had impressed them all, and Arkwright noted that 'there was an atmosphere of dignity and peace about Brussels which made itself noticeable'.[15]

The next morning, before it was fully light, they were taken to a large nearby church, where they sat waiting on a hard wooden pew at the back. A choir occasionally started up, and many people came in and out of the church, this being the time for morning prayers. Eventually their host from the night before came in accompanied by a smartly dressed younger man. Arkwright's group rose and followed the pair outside.

They walked through the centre of Brussels during the morning rush hour and eventually ended up in a quiet residential neighbourhood of substantial detached houses. Entering one, a lady came to greet them, and the younger man quietly left. Madame was possessed of the curious serenity that Arkwright and his companions had noticed everywhere in Brussels. She made them comfortable in her large sitting room, and after lunch she and a spinster sister who lived with her started to improve the evaders' appearances. They were to be transformed from working men into gentlemen.

The two older women first cut their hair, giving them all short back and sides. Then hot water was fetched and they washed their faces and shaved. The doorbell rang and an older man came into the house accompanied by a young lady who spoke perfect English. The old man laid out several suitcases and bags on the living room floor and opened them. Inside was a treasure trove of clothing, from suits and shirts to hats and shoes, all of it brand new. Each evader was redressed in a shirt, tie and snappy suit. They handed over the boots they had been issued at Oflag VI-B in return for handsome brown brogues. The boots would be sold on the black market. Each man was also given a small attaché case containing a washing and shaving kit, soap, towels and a pair of navy blue serge trousers and shirts of the same colour. Arkwright and his companions handed over their identity cards and the young girl quickly left with them while the evaders tried on clothes.

When the girl returned she gave each of them a new identity card, a forgery but perfect in every way, and a permit signed by a German officer giving them permission to cross over into France for the purpose of transacting private business of an urgent nature. Finally, they were each given 100 Belgian francs and a small leather notecase to carry their identity documents in.[16]

The psychological effect of the evaders' new costumes was immediate. They knew that they looked the part and with their impeccable documents it should be a straightforward matter to pass into France. They felt confident and relaxed.

Madame and her sister took Arkwright's group to the main station in Brussels, where they were met by three men who would act as their guides into France. The guides explained that each evader would pair off with one guide. They must not stand or sit near their fellow escapers. They should also not appear to be travelling with their guides, just keep an eye on them and follow their lead. Arkwright and his friends were then each given a first-class railway ticket to Lille in northern France.

Boarding the plush Pullman carriage, the evaders and their guides found seats. They read newspapers or gazed out at the rolling countryside that sped by the windows. Just before the French frontier at Baisieux a uniformed German border official appeared in the carriage. To the horror of Arkwright and his companions, he began walking slowly down the coach, randomly asking passengers what their business was and why they were travelling to France. Arkwright watched from his seat transfixed as the German slowly approached. He knew that his own French was sufficient to answer a few questions, and Coombe-Tennant was fluent, but Captain Fuller could hardly speak a word. The German continued to approach them, Arkwright gripping his folded newspaper tightly in his lap, his heart racing. Suddenly, the German stopped beside Fuller, who stared up at him blankly.

'*Pourquoi allez-vous en France?*'[17] the German said in thickly-accented French.[18] Listening intently a few seats away, Arkwright knew that the answer, which all three had committed to memory, was that one had affairs of a pressing nature in that country. Silence descended upon the coach like a pall. For several seconds the protagonists were caught in frozen tableaux, the German staring down at Fuller, one hand resting on a seatback, the other clutching a notebook. Fuller's blue eyes looked back at the German, his hands folded calmly in his lap, his face as blank as that of a mystified child. And all around them the other passengers sat stiff-backed and silent, their eyes and ears fixed on the strange little scene unfolding before them, the only noise the rumble of the train's wheels on the track.

The silence was broken by the German's harsh voice repeating his question. Still Fuller stared into the official's annoyed face, a puzzled frown knitting his eyebrows as the alien words flowed over him.[19] He fought down a fit of panic like a bursting grenade, his mind frozen. Stage fright. He had 'dried', forgotten his lines. Arkwright and Coombe-Tennant had heard the German's question and they knew the answer, but they could only sit and watch, helpless to intervene on their friend's behalf.

Both Arkwright and Coombe-Tennant knew, with a sick, dread certainty that roiled in their guts, that Rupert Fuller was only seconds away from certain exposure and recapture.

CHAPTER NINETEEN

The Last Frontier

We accepted that we could be arrested. It was our job. We didn't say 'if we get arrested,' we said 'when we get arrested.'

Dédée De Jongh

R upert Fuller, a puzzled frown still fixed firmly to his face, sat silently staring at the German border official as the train headed for the Franco-Belgian frontier at Baisieux. The silence in the first-class carriage was palpable as everyone waited for Fuller to answer the German's question. Further back, Major Arkwright and Captain Coombe-Tennant had to fight the strong desire to rise from their seats, walk over to the German and give him the answer that he demanded. Would this be how the adventure ended, sitting in a railway carriage in south-west Belgium? The three Comet Line guides were pale and sweating. Exposure was now a very real possibility. They could almost feel the Gestapo thumbscrews tightening.

Fuller's next-door neighbour, a Belgian merchant, was unable to bear the suspense any longer and announced to the carriage in general: '*Vous avez, bien sur, quelques affaires à régler, monsieur?*' ('You have, of course, some business to attend to?')

Fuller seemed to be jolted out of his reverie by the Belgian's sudden interjection and replied '*Oui*'.

But Fuller's strange behaviour had by now fully awakened the German's interest.

'*Quel est votre nom?*' said the German, asking for Fuller's name. Fuller again said nothing.

'*Quel est votre entreprise*?' asked the official, demanding to know Fuller's business. Fuller stared at him, then a dim light came into his eyes and he offered another monosyllabic reply: '*Affaires*.'

'*Pourquoi allez-vous en France*?' said the German more loudly, repeating his earlier question. After what seemed an interminable pause, Fuller spoke: '*Pourquoi pas*?' ('Why not?') Several of the other passengers giggled quietly at this answer, perhaps assuming that Fuller was deliberately aggravating the officious German.

'*Pouvez-vous parler français*?' said the German, demanding to know whether Fuller even spoke French.

'*Oui*', replied Fuller casually. The German sighed deeply and announced that on arrival at the frontier Fuller would have to wait for further questioning, pocketing his fake identity documents.[1] Fuller looked nonplussed as the German continued his way down the coach, passing by Arkwright. He came level with Coombe-Tennant and questioned him – fortunately his answers in first-rate French provoked no comment from the German, who eventually disappeared through the door at the end of the carriage, slamming it shut behind him with grim finality.

When the train slowly pulled into the little frontier town of Baisieux the passengers all disembarked on the Belgian side before passing through a customs shed and emerging on the French side of the platform. The empty train was shunted forward to meet them. Fuller and his companions hoped that the German had forgotten about his strange encounter in the coach, but he was waiting for Fuller when he alighted and he marched the Briton straight off for interrogation.

For Arkwright and Coombe-Tennant it was an indescribably awful scene – their comrade who had been at their side since vaulting the fence at Warburg was hauled off, probably for good. Both men were convinced that Fuller would be swiftly exposed by the Germans and arrested. They shuffled forward in the line towards the customs control, deeply depressed.

A French customs officer took Fuller into a small room inside the station. Shortly, a German military policeman entered and started shouting at Fuller in French and German. The evader played, as he put it, the 'idiot boy' and said nothing.[2] The German changed tack and gave Fuller a cigarette and started to question him in French about his identity documents. Fuller answered in a rambling and indecipherable mutter. The Frenchman then asked him whether he suffered from nerves and if he was ill. Fuller, understanding a little, decided to play along. He collapsed moaning onto the table, holding his head in his hands.

'*Quelle est votre adresse?*' said the German. The British officer gave a muffled and unintelligible reply. He jumped to his feet and started pacing around the room looking at the notices on the walls and occasionally repeating the address that he had memorised from the false identity papers. The German and the Frenchman agreed that this was the address on the papers they held in their hands. The German then asked Fuller if he was married, and what was his wife's name. Again, because Fuller had taken the time to memorise his identity papers, he was able to provide the correct answer. The German thought that Fuller was just feeble-minded and was losing interest.

Fuller walked up to the German and tapped the gorget emblazoned with a Nazi eagle that he wore around his neck on a chain, the symbol of a military policeman, saying in bad French: '*Qu'est-ce que c'est que ça?*'[3] ('What is that?') The German roared with laughter and handed Fuller back his papers. '*Hier raus!*' he said, smiling, '*Raus!*' The Frenchman swiftly opened the door and led Fuller back to the train.

In the meantime, Arkwright and Coombe-Tennant had passed through customs without difficulty, merely having to open their attaché cases and present their papers for inspection to the elderly officials. They quickly found their seats again on the train and sat silently, worrying about Fuller but also concerned about their own situation. Aside from their fear that Fuller would be exposed and recaptured, it had also occurred to them that if the Germans caught one British POW on the train they might decide that where there was one there were probably others. After all, prisoners normally travelled in pairs – it was almost standard practice. A detailed examination of the passengers might soon reveal fake documentation or poor language abilities. Arkwright's French was only conversational at best, and his accent obvious to any questioning French policeman. The three Comet Line guides were also deeply concerned lest this method of smuggling evaders across the frontier be compromised.[4] All five on the train were a bundle of nerves and trying desperately to conceal their inner turmoil from their fellow passengers.

The train gave a few hard, squeaky jerks, the wheels spinning, and then slowly started to move along the platform. The steam whistle gave two cheerful toots, then suddenly the door at the end of the carriage was flung open and a French border guard roughly bundled Rupert Fuller inside. Fuller walked up the carriage past Arkwright, dropping him a sly wink as he passed. Finding his seat, Fuller stood and opened the window and peered out. Pulling out a white handkerchief from his coat pocket, the grinning Fuller vigorously waved at the French border official and the German military policeman who were standing on the platform watching the train pull away. They both slowly raised their hands in uncertain response as the train gathered speed out of the station. To Arkwright and Coombe-Tennant, Fuller's actions looked like pure bravado; but, concerned that the German might not have fallen for his 'idiot boy' act, he was actually checking to see whether anyone had boarded the train after him. After all, the German was no fool, and sending someone to tail him might have revealed whom he was travelling with. Fuller saw no one enter the train after him, and satisfied that all was well he ceased his waving and took his seat. Further down the carriage one of the guides was heard to whisper, 'He has saved himself'[5] to his companion. Fuller then proceeded to slouch down in his seat and fall fast asleep with his head resting on the window and his mouth wide open.

*

The train soon lumbered into the industrial city of Lille. The evaders and their guides would change to the Paris train, but there would be a wait of several hours. The guides decided to make certain that Fuller was not being followed. The three Britons, accompanied by two of the guides, spent half an hour wandering around the busy streets of Lille. Following a discreet distance behind was the third guide. He reported no tail. Arkwright and his companions knew Lille well, for during the winter of 1939 and the spring of 1940 their regiments had been billeted nearby as part of the British Expeditionary Force, and once a fortnight the officers had come into the city for haircuts, shopping and a good meal.[6]

After an excellent lunch the evaders and their guides boarded the crowded Paris train. Although they all had first-class tickets, they had to stand the whole way in the corridor. In Paris Dédée De Jongh and her father Frédéric met them when their train arrived at the Gare du Nord. Dédée had relocated to Paris along with her father after she had aroused some interest from the Gestapo in Brussels, leaving Comet Line operations there in the hands of her close friend 'Nemo', the codename of Baron Jean Greindl.[7]

The head of Comet Line's Paris area operations was another aristocrat, Count Jacques Legrelle, aka 'Jérôme'. Dédée and her young friend Jean-François Nothomb (aka 'Franco') acted as guides to take evaders from the French capital into Spain, while Frédéric De Jongh was in charge of arranging the forging of identity papers and travel documents and booking train tickets.

Major Arkwright had little idea of Dédée's pre-eminent role in Comet Line when he first met her. 'She was quiet and unobtrusive',[8] he recalled, and it was easy to see why she was underestimated

– after all, who could believe that this shy young woman from a respectable Brussels household was the mastermind of a notorious escape line that was hunted by the Gestapo and the German Army's security police? But it was her very unobtrusiveness that was her greatest asset in the deadly game she played so well.

Dédée took Arkwright's group and the guides through the busy Paris Metro to an unassuming block of flats. This was Comet Line's main base.

That evening, before the guides left for Brussels to collect the next batch of evaders, a large and raucous dinner party was held in the flat, where the wine flowed freely and Arkwright and his companions relaxed and got to know some of the Comet Line operatives a little better. Dédée continued to fascinate the Britons. 'She was unusual in many ways', said Arkwright, 'though she could speak English extremely well she never did so except when it was absolutely necessary. Nor would one have supposed on making her acquaintance that she had a brain as sharp as a needle and quite outstanding organisational ability.'[9] Dédée gave the impression of being a quite insignificant, almost incidental, member of the party.

The next day Arkwright's group was transformed into French citizens. Their Belgian identity documents were replaced and each was given a dark blue beret, then the fashion for many men, to wear outside in order to blend in with the Parisians. By now, all three Britons were well versed in looking inconspicuous – they knew how to behave in the street and on public transport, how to occupy themselves normally in any given situation to avoid conversation – and they trusted their guides implicitly.

After a comfortable lunch in the flat, the group carried their luggage and a large parcel of provisions to the Gare Montparnasse so they could catch a train south. Accompanying them were Dédée, Jean-François, another Comet Line operative and an escaped Russian POW they nicknamed 'Stalin'. The Russian, an air gunner who had been shot down on a raid over eastern Germany, had escaped from a terrible camp outside Berlin. The Germans had treated their Soviet prisoners with the same degree of callousness and bestiality that the Britons had witnessed at the labour camp attached to Oflag VI-B. 'Stalin' had realised that he had to escape or perish of starvation or physical abuse. He had absconded only three days previously and train-hopped through Germany to the French frontier, where the Resistance had fortuitously picked him up and handed him over to Dédée. It was decided to smuggle 'Stalin' to England, as getting him back to the Soviet Union was logistically impossible.

Everyone relaxed on the journey south – the rhythm of the train was 'something wildly exhilarating'[10] as it carried them closer and closer to their goal. Paris was almost halfway across German-occupied Europe from Warburg, and there was a feeling among Arkwright's group that the most difficult phase of their evasion had been completed.

It was an overnight journey, and dawn found them a few miles outside Bordeaux on the Atlantic coast. At this time, only northern France was under direct German occupation, the south remaining under Vichy collaborationist control. But because of the importance of their 'West Wall' defences and U-boat bases, the Germans did occupy the entire length of France's Atlantic coast. In every village that the evaders' train chugged through, German soldiers were seen on guard or lounging around on station platforms.

As they went ever southwards the country changed. The air grew soft and balmy, the sun warm. The harvest had been gathered in and the fields had a dead look about them. But the gardens of the little houses that the train passed were full of vines and plump melons growing on trelliswork or on the sides of the buildings. The landscape was pretty and inviting and served to raise the escapers' morale.

At 11.00am on 17 October the train arrived at its final destination, the end of the line: the small seaside town of St-Jean-de-Luz. Sitting on the edge of the Bay of Biscay at the western end of the

Pyrenees, it consisted of lots of grand seventeenth- and eighteenth-century houses built by ship-owners and wealthy Basque merchants.

Waiting for them on the platform was a formidable Belgian woman who ran Comet Line operations in the south of France, Elvire De Greef. Known by her codename 'Tante Go' (after her dog), De Greef greeted them all warmly. She was not quite middle-aged, a slight woman with grey eyes and a round, high cheek-boned face.[11] She and her family had tried to flee to England in 1940 but had been overtaken by the German advance. She had settled in St-Jean-de-Luz and become heavily involved in smuggling and other black market activities. This work was in addition to her more important work as an organiser for Comet Line. De Greef knew all the smugglers and undercover agents in the bistros of the provincial city of Bayonne and in St-Jean-de-Luz, while her husband Fernand worked as a translator at the German *Kommandantur* in the nearby town of Anglet. Fernand had access to official stamps and supplied his wife with blank identity cards and special passes for the occupied coastal zone. De Greef's son Freddy acted as a courier for his parents, while their eighteen-year-old daughter Janine escorted evaders from St-Jean station to safe houses in the town.[12]

At the station when Arkwright's group alighted was another member of Comet Line, a dark-complexioned, well-built Basque peasant called Henri. They left the station in small groups, Arkwright and Fuller going with Elvire De Greef. Instead of taking the two officers straight to the safe house, De Greef led them down to the seafront. Both Britons sucked in their breath at the sight – the morning sunshine dancing off the flickering green water, little fishing boats bobbing in the harbour against a backdrop of grand Spanish-style houses and waterside cafés. Arkwright and Fuller were a riot of emotions as they breathed deeply the salty air, gulls wheeling overhead and waves slapping against the seawall. Across the watery expanse lay England and home – it was almost unbearable. Waves of homesickness assailed them, mingled with sudden panic that some misfortune might yet scupper their chances of reaching home. De Greef, perhaps sensing their emotions, clapped them on the back and pointed south to where a line of craggy hills rose in the distance. She said only one word – 'Spain'.[13] Arkwright and Fuller snapped out of their reverie.

'Well, I'll be damned', muttered Fuller in awe.

They had known they were close to the frontier, of course, but to be able to see Spain from where they stood was simply incredible. They had left Oflag VI-B two months before – now they were finally within sight of a neutral country. Cross those hills that appeared almost blue in the distant haze, and they would be home free. They seemed so close that a man might simply walk there in an afternoon, but hidden dangers lay in the hills and all was not as simple as it first appeared. Crossing this particular frontier would require an entirely new set of skills.

*

A buxom Frenchwoman who acted as cook and housekeeper met the evaders at the safe house. She and Henri constantly joked with each other and their guests. After a dinner of rabbit stew, the Britons and the Comet Line personnel tried on different types of mountain shoes. The shoes were canvas with soles of coarse, woven grass, ideal for gripping on slippery rocks. They reminded Arkwright of native hunting shoes he had used in the Himalayas in India before the war, but with the addition of the canvas uppers. Then the Frenchwoman ordered them to bed. She knew that they would need all their energy for the following night, for they were to cross the Pyrenees and enter Franco's Spain.

The following day the group had an unexpected visitor. A tired-looking and rather bedraggled man hammered on the door and asked for some food. He was clearly familiar to the Frenchwoman and Dédée and was quickly ushered inside. His codename was 'B', but Arkwright and his companions were astonished to discover that this Comet Line operative was an Englishman. In 1939 Albert Johnson had been employed as secretary and chauffeur in Brussels to Count Henri de Baillet-Latour, President of the International Olympic Committee. When war had broken out, Johnson had decided to return to England and enlist, but an official at the British Embassy had foolishly dissuaded him. When Belgium and France were overrun in 1940 Johnson had fled to southern France, settling in Anglet near the Spanish frontier. He had joined Comet Line and made many trips across the Pyrenees.

Johnson, who was known locally as 'Albert Jonion', fascinated Arkwright. Johnson told him that he could have escaped back to England on numerous occasions but had decided that his work for Dédée and Comet Line was more vital to the war effort than his enlisting. He was a quiet, pale Londoner in his late thirties with sensitive brown eyes and was a man of the greatest endurance and loyalty.[14]

*

The next night the evaders and their guides left the safe house and walked four miles out of St-Jean-de-Luz to an isolated farm. The rest of their night march to freedom would encompass a journey of around twenty miles. This did not sound like much, but Arkwright's group had done very little walking in the six weeks since they had crossed the Dutch frontier and they were considerably less fit than when they had 'boy scouted' across Germany.

No fences or any other barriers blocked the frontier. Instead, the River Bidassoa marked the line between France and Spain. The Germans had numerous patrols on the French side and the Spanish border police controlled the other side. Both would have to be carefully avoided. The terrain was mountainous, with many almost sheer rock faces and plunging valleys, the area interspersed with old Basque smugglers' paths and sheep tracks.

After a supper of eggs, fresh sardines and homemade cheese

at the farm, the evaders met their guide. He was a grizzled and wiry-looking Basque mountain man, smuggler and salmon poacher named Jean. What impressed Arkwright about Jean was not so much his tough, robust looks but his odour. Jean stank, and Arkwright realised that he would have no problem following the guide through the mountains, even in pitch darkness, as long as Jean kept upwind of him. Jean lived by his wits and the sweat of his brow, having no settled occupation.[15] But he looked strong and clearly knew the mountains like the back of his hand. The Pyrenees were so difficult to cross that even Dédée, who had already made the journey twenty times before, did not feel comfortable conducting a party across on her own.

As soon as it was dark, the party left the farmhouse and formed into a single file with Jean leading. Behind the aromatic Basque trailed Dédée, followed by François, 'Stalin', Fuller, Coombe-Tennant and Arkwright. Each had a stout ash walking stick.

They began to climb the first small mountain, about 1,000 feet high. There was a full moon, its light bathing the hills in a silvery glow. As the group approached the summit they paused to catch their breath and stared back for a last glimpse of France. Arkwright and his companions felt exalted, as though they could climb for ever. Cresting the summit, they stopped and peered down into the deep valley before them. Moonlight reflected off the River Bidassoa. Jean crouched and scanned the valley and the mountains beyond for some time, his keen eyes looking for German or Spanish patrols. Nothing. He grunted and signalled with his hand for them to follow as he started down the scree slope towards the river far below, as sure-footed as the mountain sheep that occasionally started away from the group as they clambered noisily down.

A mist had started to rise from the river and was slowly creeping up the valley sides, providing the evasion party with a natural smokescreen from any hostile eyes. Members of the party constantly slipped or stumbled on the rocks, unused to the terrain, causing noise that brought reproachful looks from Jean and Dédée.

When he arrived at the riverbank, Jean did not hesitate but slipped into the water like a basking seal leaving a rock.[16] The rest followed him in single file. The water was freezing cold, knee-deep and running fast. Several of the party had difficulty keeping their balance, but everyone got across without a dunking.

Almost without pausing, the evaders and their guides flung themselves at the almost vertical face of a railway embankment before them, crossed it and then struggled up another difficult rock face to a road. They lay gasping for breath on the narrow level surface while Jean's eyes scanned constantly for trouble. The valley was as silent as the grave. The only sounds were their deep breathing and the river rushing over rocks hundreds of feet below.

Dédée tapped Arkwright lightly on the shoulder. 'Welcome to Spain', she said, her face sweaty and her attractive eyes beaming with triumphant light. Arkwright and his companions struggled to their feet, feeling light-headed. 'You are free men', said Dédée, rising with them. Arkwright, Coombe-Tennant and Fuller grinned wildly at her words, hearing them but hardly daring to believe them. Although a hard climb through several miles of rugged mountains remained before they would reach complete safety away from the frontier, they were, at this moment, standing on neutral Spanish soil. The Germans had no power over them any longer.

For a moment the three men stood shoulder-to-shoulder and stared back in the direction they had come. They said nothing, words seeming superfluous at their moment of triumph. The mist had filled the valley below and they could see nothing. It was as if a grey curtain had been pulled across Nazi-occupied Europe.

Grasping their walking sticks firmly, Albert Arkwright, Henry Coombe-Tennant and Rupert Fuller turned their backs on the past and began to climb steadily towards freedom and home.

Epilogue

Albert Arkwright

Awarded the Military Cross for his successful escape from Warburg, after the war Arkwright became a farmer in Midlothian, Scotland. He published an exciting account of Operation Olympia entitled *Return Journey* in 1948. Arkwright died in 1990, aged 83.

Rex Baxter

Returning to Australia in August 1945 after his release from Colditz, Baxter was reunited with his wife Kathleen. He worked in the publicity department of the Vacuum Oil Company until he retired in 1989. Rex Baxter passed away after a short illness in Melbourne in 1991.

Jack Champ

Imprisoned in Colditz with many other Wire Job escapers, Champ arrived in Australia in June 1945. A week later he married his fiancée of five years and started a family. His wife died in 1954 and Champ later remarried. He worked for the Ford Motor Company in its accounts department. The author of several short stories, he was also a keen yachtsman in Geelong, where he lived until his death in 1998 aged 85.

Henry Coombe-Tennant

For his successful escape from Oflag VI-B Coombe-Tennant received the Military Cross and promotion to Major. Later in the war the French honoured him with the prestigious Croix de Guerre. He left the Army in 1947 and joined MI6, where he worked under the infamous traitor and KGB agent Kim Philby. Coombe-Tennant never married and later converted to Roman Catholicism. He became an Augustinian monk, taking the name Dom Joseph Coombe-Tennant. He died in a monastery in 1989 aged 76.

Fred Corfield

After his release from captivity in 1945, Corfield was awarded a Mention in Despatches and became a barrister in London. In 1955 he was elected a Conservative MP and served as Minister of Housing in 1963. In the early 1970s Corfield was Aviation Supply Minister and then Minister for Aerospace, but was sacked from the Heath government after being made the scapegoat for the collapse of Rolls-Royce. Knighted in 1972, Corfield became a QC and then sat as a judge until 1987. Sir Frederick Corfield died in August 2005, aged 90.

Doug Crawford

Repatriated to Australia in April 1945, he was greeted off the gangplank by his wife and four-year-old daughter, whom he met for the first time. Crawford stayed in the Army until 1983, rising to the rank of Lieutenant Colonel. Thereafter he worked as a commercial fisherman and then as a wine consultant in Brisbane. He retired to Norman Park, Queensland.

Johnnie Cousens

Cousens was promoted to Major while still a POW. In April 1945, when his camp was being evacuated west away from the advancing Red Army, American fighter planes strafed the column of prisoners that he was in. Cousens was severely wounded, losing his left leg. In 1947 he was promoted to Lieutenant Colonel and received the MBE for his extraordinary contribution to Operation Olympia and other escape attempts. Leaving the Army in 1961, he became

Administration Officer at the Light Infantry Depot in Shrewsbury, 1962–66. Cousens died in July 1975 aged 69.

Rupert Fuller

After the war Fuller rose to the rank of Lieutenant Colonel. He was awarded the Military Cross in 1945 for his successful escape and evasion from Oflag VI-B. Fuller went back to the Continent and revisited many of the places that featured in his escape. He met many of the Dutch, Belgian and French civilians who had helped him, Arkwright and Coombe-Tennant and was able to personally thank them.

Martin Gilliat

Sent to Colditz Castle, Gilliat was held in such high regard by the other prisoners that they elected him their Adjutant. Awarded a Mention in Despatches for his wartime escape attempts and made an MBE in 1946, Gilliat went on to have a glittering career that took him all over the world. In 1947 he arrived in India as Lord Mountbatten's Deputy Military Secretary, surviving an assassination attempt in Delhi when his car was ambushed and he was wounded in the neck. In 1948–51 he served as Comptroller to the Commissioner General for the UK in South-East Asia and then went to Australia as Military Secretary to the Governor-General, the famous victor in the Burma campaign, Field Marshal Sir William Slim. Created a Companion of the Royal Victorian Order in 1954, two years later Gilliat became Private Secretary and Equerry to HM Queen Elizabeth, The Queen Mother. He held this post for 37 years, sharing all facets of the Queen Mother's life. Knighted in 1962, Gilliat also served as Vice Lieutenant of Hertfordshire between 1971 and 1986. Passionate about horse racing and the theatre, Gilliat was reticent about his wartime exploits and never discussed them. Sir Martin Gilliat died of cancer in May 1993 aged 80.

Jock Hamilton-Baillie

'HB' never stopped trying to escape and in June 1943 was engineer on the famous Eichstätt Tunnel Job, during which he and 62 other officers managed to escape. All were subsequently recaptured and HB was among several men who were sent to Colditz. Released in April 1945, HB was awarded the Military Cross for his vital roles in the Warburg Wire Job and Eichstätt Tunnel. When Colditz was liberated, HB pocketed the castle's keys – 50 years later when he was visiting the former POW camp, his tour guide had misplaced the key to a particular door. HB reached into his coat pocket and pulled out the original set of keys he had pinched in 1945 and unlocked the door, much to the guide's astonishment.

HB went up to Cambridge and also married in 1947. In 1950 he was Brigade Major of 44 Parachute Brigade before taking command of 5 Field Squadron, Royal Engineers in Germany in 1953. He was present at atomic bomb tests in Australia, and was Chief Instructor at the Army Apprentices College, Chepstow. Promoted to Brigadier, HB ended his Army career as Director, Engineering Services and an ADC to Queen Elizabeth II. After retirement HB worked for ten years as a full-time lecturer at the Royal Military College of Science, Shrivenham, and also tirelessly raised money for the Red Cross, the organisation he believed had saved his life in 1945. HB died in April 2003, aged 84.

Noel Hyde

Noel Hyde was Mentioned in Despatches in 1947 for his wartime escape attempts. He stayed in the RAF, becoming Group Captain (Intelligence) for the US 2nd Tactical Air Force, the Americans investing him with the Legion of Merit in 1950. In 1953 Hyde was appointed Commanding Officer of RAF Binbrook, for which he received a CBE, and in 1956 Commandant of the Central Flying School. His final active command was in 1960 as Commandant of the RAF Staff College in Andover. He retired in 1962 and died in September 1987, aged 76.

Andrée 'Dédée' De Jongh

Comet Line delivered 400 Allied soldiers and airmen to neutral Spain, and Dédée personally took 116 men over the Pyrenees. Betrayed to the Gestapo in the French Basque country in January 1943 on her 33rd journey to freedom, Dédée was brutally tortured by the Germans. The Gestapo refused to believe that this slight young woman was the fearless leader of Comet Line and allowed her to live. Imprisoned initially at Fresnes in Paris, she was later sent to Ravensbrück and Mauthausen concentration camps, and was liberated from the latter by Allied troops in April 1945. Her father Frédéric was arrested by the Gestapo on 7 June 1943 and executed on 28 March 1944. A school in Brussels has been named in his honour.

Dédée was widely honoured for her wartime work, receiving the US Medal of Freedom, the George Medal from Britain, and the Légion d'Honneur from France. Belgium created her a Chevalier of the Order of Léopold and awarded her the Croix de Guerre with palm. She was also made an honorary Lieutenant Colonel in the Belgian Army.

Dédée moved to the Belgian Congo, then Cameroon, Ethiopia and finally Senegal, working as a nurse in leper hospitals. She retired to Brussels, where she was created a Countess in the Belgian nobility in 1985. 'Little Cyclone' died in 2007 aged 90.

Robert Melsome

Melsome was able to continue sending secret messages to the War Office in London until April 1945, dangerous work that was highly commended by his superiors. Awarded an MBE in 1946, Melsome decided to stay in the Army and was promoted several times up to Brigadier in 1957. He also returned to cricket, playing for the Nigerian national side against Gold Coast in 1948. Melsome retired from the Army in 1961 and died in November 1991 aged 85.

Jean-François Nothomb

When the Gestapo arrested Dédée in January 1943, Nothomb succeeded her as leader of Comet Line. He was arrested by the Gestapo on 18 January 1944 and survived several concentration camps before being liberated in April 1945. Britain awarded him the Distinguished Service Order for his incredible exploits in getting Allied servicemen into Spain.

Oflag VI-B

After all the British and Commonwealth officers were transferred out in September 1942 the Germans moved in 1,077 Polish officers from Romania and a further 1,500 Poles from camps in Germany. The Polish finished a tunnel that had originally been started by Jock Hamilton-Baillie and on 20 September 1943 47 escaped from the camp. The Germans recaptured twenty within four days, and these Polish officers were returned to Warburg before being transferred to Buchenwald concentration camp and executed. A further seventeen Polish evaders were captured over the following days and they were taken to the Gestapo prison in Dortmund and murdered. Ten Polish officers managed to remain free, some returning to their homeland and the remainder making it to Allied lines.

On 27 September 1944, RAF bombers attacking the nearby railway junction at Nörde accidentally bombed Oflag VI-B, killing 90 Polish prisoners. A memorial was erected on the site of the old camp in 1985 to commemorate the total of 128 POWs who perished from Oflag VI-B, including the British Lieutenant Dupree. The US Army liberated the camp on 3 April 1945.

Phil Pardoe

Awarded a Mention in Despatches for his role in Operation Olympia and for escaping through the Eichstätt Tunnel in May 1943 (during which he made it to the Danube River before being recaptured), Pardoe was sent to Colditz. He was liberated in May 1945 and returned to civilian life.

Tom Stallard

As punishment for Olympia and other escapes, Stallard was sent to Colditz Castle, where he continued to play a vital role in escape attempts, latterly serving as head of the 'X' Committee. After his release in 1945 Stallard received the Distinguished Service Order he had been awarded in 1940 during the Dunkirk rearguard action, and he was given an MBE for his extraordinary contribution to organising escapes from German captivity. At the investiture ceremony at Buckingham Palace King George VI was surprised that Stallard had only two medal ribbons above his left breast pocket – prisoners of war missed out on campaign stars and received only the 1939–45 Star and the War Medal. 'Here I am', said the King, 'about to bestow this decoration and appointment to this Order upon one of my officers with no campaign stars. Here lies a story and I will hear it now.' The investiture was held up accordingly while Stallard regaled the King with the stories of Dunkirk and Operation Olympia.

Stallard left the Army a Lieutenant Colonel in 1948 and became a wine trade salesman and company director in Bournemouth. He died in a rest home in Bognor Regis in April 1983 aged 78.

Dick Tomes

Tomes was awarded the MBE in 1945 and stayed in the Army. In 1955–56 he served in Cyprus during a very difficult time in the nation's history, serving as Senior Staff Officer to the Governor. Lieutenant Colonel Tomes was awarded an OBE in 1956 for his highly praised service.

David Walker

Although he managed to escape from German POW camps three times, Walker was recaptured on each occasion. He was sent to

Colditz with the other repeat offenders. Awarded an MBE in 1945, Walker went to India where he worked for the Viceroy, Earl Wavell, until leaving the Army in 1947. Emigrating to Canada in 1948, Walker became a successful author, writing twenty novels and over 100 short stories, several of which were made into films. His writing brought him the prestigious Governor General's Award for Fiction in 1952 and 1953 and an honorary doctorate of letters from the University of New Brunswick. Walker was very active in community affairs, chairing several committees, and was made a Member of the Order of Canada in 1987. Stallard's second-in-command on Operation Olympia died in 1992, aged 81.

Some of the others ...

Lieutenant Dennis Bartlett, Royal Tank Regiment, escaped through the Eichstätt Tunnel with many other former Warburg Wire Job artists. He was on the run for three days. Recaptured, Bartlett was sent to Colditz and served on the Escape Committee. He already had the Military Cross from before capture but was awarded a Mention in Despatches for his escape activities.

Captain Pat Campbell-Preston managed to remain free for four days after escaping down the Eichstätt Tunnel. Sent to Colditz, he was awarded the MBE in 1945.

Captain Brockie Mytton, 15th/19th King's Royal Hussars, escaped from an Oflag with four companions in spring 1944. Recaptured, he served on the Escape Committee at Oflag VIII-F. He was also awarded the MBE in 1945.

Lieutenant Brooke Oldman, King's Own Yorkshire Light Infantry, escaped from prison in autumn 1944 as part of a bogus fatigue party. He and a companion were recaptured by Hitler Youths three days later on their way to France and held by the Gestapo for six weeks. Oldman received the Military Cross after the war.

Maps

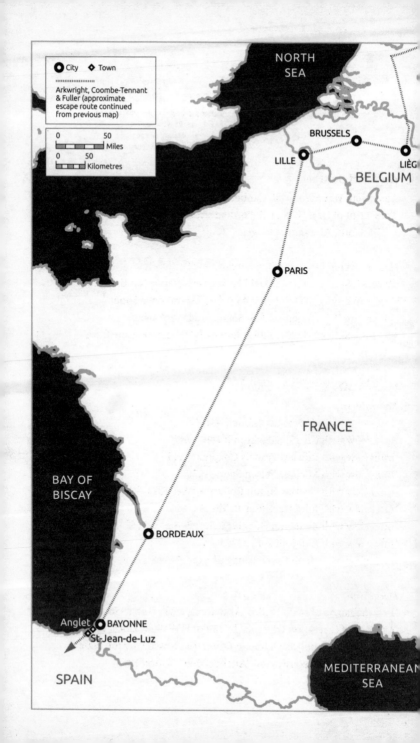

Bibliography

Archival Sources
Australian War Memorial, Canberra
Transcript of Oral History Recording: Accession No. S00579,
  'Crawford, Alexander Douglas "Doug"'

Harriet Irving Library, University of New Brunswick
MG L35, Series 2, File 7: David H. Walker: 'Report on Escape
  from Warburg, 8 October 1945'; 'Correspondence about
  Warburg Wire Escape, 1945–53'
MG L35, Series 2, Box 1, File 2: David H. Walker: 'Escape from
  Warburg'

Imperial War Museum, London
Recordings:
'Interview with Robert Eric Loder, 4827'
'Interview with Charles Leighton Irwin, 4847'
'Interview with Edward Francis Chapman, 11194'
'Interview with Michael Sefton Scott, 11203'
'Interview with Charles Hilton Roderick Gee, 13717'
'Interview with John Hamilton-Baillie, 14781'
'Interview with Benjamin Dennis Skelton Ginn, 21750'
'Interview with Ken Johnson, 23825'
'Interview with Hugh Bruce Ismay Cheape, 31948'

Documents:
'Private Papers of Major A.S.B. Arkwright, MC', Docs. 956
'Account of Operation Olympia' by Major E.W. Few, Docs. 1065
'Appendix – Operation Olympia: Order for Crossing by the Four
  Teams Simultaneously, and "Anchor Men"', Docs. 1065

'Account of the Electronic Devices used in Operation Olympia, the Escape from Oflag VI-B, Warburg in 1942' by Major K.A. Searle, Docs. 1154

'Private Papers of Capt. G.P. Bowring, MC, TD', Docs. 11856

'Private Papers of Colonel L.T. Tomes, OBE', Docs. 12734

Hamish Forbes, 'Letter to his Children Telling of His Experiences in the Second World War, 1939–1945', Private Papers of Maj. Sir Hamish Forbes, MBE, MC, Bt., Docs. 16193

The National Archives (Public Record Office), Kew

'HEIN, G F aka STEVENS, P Date of birth: 15.02.1919', HO 405/20069

'Oflag VI-B', TS26/233

'Oflag VI-B Dössel/Warburg', WO208/3290

'Account of Escape from Oflag VI-B (Dössel/Warburg)' by Captain R.J. Fuller *et al.*, WO208/3290

'Oflag VI-B', WO224/73

'Account of Escape of Capt. A.H.S. Coombe-Tennant, Welsh Guards, Maj. A.S.B. Arkwright, The Royal Scots Fusiliers, Capt. R.J. Fuller, The Royal Sussex Regiment', WO373/62

'Capt. Ronald William Leah', WO373/64

'Lt. Brooke Deare Oldman', WO373/64

'Lt. Philip Pardoe', WO373/64

'Lt. Dennis Edward Allan Bartlett, MC', WO373/100

'Capt. George Patrick Campbell-Preston', WO373/100

'Capt. Frederick Vernon Corfield', WO373/100

'Capt. Brochwel Robert Mytton', WO373/100

'Maj. Thomas Stallard, DSO', WO373/100

'Capt. Martin John Gilliat', WO373/103

'Capt. David Harry Walker', WO373/103

'Lt. Col. John Warwick Tomes, MBE', WO373/164

Author's private correspondence with Operation Olympia descendants

Major Michael Bond

Colonel Richard Cousens, OBE

Ben Hamilton-Baillie

Kenneth Jacob

Published Sources

Arkwright, A.S.B., *Return Journey* (London: Seeley, Service & Co. Ltd., 1948)

Brickhill, Paul, *Reach for the Sky: The Story of Douglas Bader, Hero of the Battle of Britain* (London: Phoenix, 2012)

Brickhill, Paul, *The Great Escape* (London: Phoenix, 2012)

Champ, Jack and Colin Burgess, *The Diggers of Colditz* (Kenthurst, NSW: Kangaroo Press, 1997)

Chancellor, Henry, *Colditz: The Definitive History* (London: Coronet Books, 2002)

Crawley, Aiden, *Escape from Germany, 1939–45 – Methods of Escape used by RAF Airmen in World War II* (London: The Stationery Office, 2001)

Doyle, Peter, *Prisoner of War in Germany* (Shire Publications Ltd., 2008)

Gilbert, Adrian, *POW: Allied Prisoners in Europe, 1939–45* (London: John Murray, 2007)

Gillies, Midge, *Barbed Wire University: The Real Lives of Allied Prisoners of War in the Second World War* (London: Aurum Press, 2012)

Hardy, Freya, *Great Escapes of World War II: Tom Dick and Harry to Stalag to Colditz* (R.W. Press, Kindle eBook, 2012)

Kaplan, Philip and Jack Currie, *Behind the Wire: Allied Prisoners of War in Hitler's Germany* (Barnsley: Pen & Sword Books, 2012)

Longden, Sean, *Dunkirk: The Men They Left Behind* (London: Constable, 2009)

MacKenzie, S.P., *The Colditz Myth: British and Commonwealth Prisoners of War in Nazi Germany* (Oxford: Oxford University Press, 2006)

McGregor, Malcolm, *Officers of the Durham Light Infantry, 1758–1958* (Durham: The Rifles Office)

Neave, Airey, *Saturday at MI9* (Barnsley: Pen & Sword Books, 2010)

Neave, Airey, *They Have Their Exits* (Barnsley: Pen & Sword
  Books, 2013)
Nichol, John and Tony Rennell, *The Last Escape: The Untold Story
  of Allied Prisoners of War in Germany 1944–45* (London: Penguin
  Books, 2003)
Nichol, John and Tony Rennell, *Home Run: Escape from Nazi
  Europe* (London: Penguin Books, 2008)
Reid, P.R., *Colditz: The Full Story* (London: Pan, 2009)
Sebag-Montefiore, Hugh, *Dunkirk: Fight to the Last Man* (London:
  Penguin Books, 2007)
Stevens, Marc H., *Escape, Evasion and Revenge* (Barnsley: Pen &
  Sword Military, 2011)
Wood, J.E.R. (ed.), *Detour: The Story of Oflag IV-C* (London:
  Falcon Press, 1946)

Journal and Newspaper Articles

'Portrait of a Prisoner of War', Durham Light Infantry *Regimental
  Journal*, June 1966
'Olympia' by Lt. Colonel T. Stallard, DSO, MBE, *Silver Bugle*,
  Spring 1971
'Obituary – Lt. Col. Sir Martin Gilliat', *The Independent*, 1 June 1993
'Obituary – Air Commodore "Dim" Strong', *Daily Telegraph*,
  7 September 2011

Online Sources

'Diary of Lieutenant Reg Wood, Middlesex Regiment', 8 August
  1942, www.pegasusarchive.org
'The Prisoner Story', Royal Monmouthshire Royal Engineers
  (Militia) Museum, www.monmouthcastlemuseum.org.uk

Notes

Prologue
1. Jack Champ and Colin Burgess, *The Diggers of Colditz* (Kenthurst, NSW: Kangaroo Press, 1997), p. 58.
2. Ibid, p. 58.
3. Transcript of Oral History Recording: Accession No. S00579, 'Crawford, Alexander Douglas "Doug"', 8 May 1989, Australian War Memorial, Canberra.

Chapter 1: Barbed Wire Horizon
1. 'Portrait of a Prisoner of War', Durham Light Infantry *Regiment Journal*, June 1966, p. 138.
2. A.S.B. Arkwright, *Return Journey* (London: Seeley, Service & Co. Ltd., 1948), p. 17.
3. 'Portrait of a Prisoner of War', Durham Light Infantry *Regiment Journal*, June 1966, p. 138.
4. Ben Hamilton-Baillie to author, private correspondence, 18 July 2013.
5. Jack Champ and Colin Burgess, *The Diggers of Colditz* (Kenthurst, NSW: Kangaroo Press, 1997), p. 35.
6. Ibid, p. 38.
7. Ibid, p. 41.
8. Ibid, p. 42.
9. Ibid, p. 42.
10. 'Oflag VI-B Dössel/Warburg', WO208/3290, The National Archives (Public Record Office), Kew.
11. Ibid.
12. Ibid.
13. 'Interview with John Hamilton-Baillie', 14781, Reel 2, Imperial War Museum, London.
14. 'Account of the Electronic Devices used in Operation Olympia,

the Escape from Oflag VI-B, Warburg in 1942' by Major K.A. Searle, Docs. 1154, Imperial War Museum, London.

15. A.S.B. Arkwright, *Return Journey* (London: Seeley, Service & Co. Ltd., 1948), p. 22.

16. Hamish Forbes, 'Letter to his Children Telling of His Experiences in the Second World War, 1939–1945', Private Papers of Major Sir Hamish Forbes, MBE, MC, Bt., Docs. 16193, Imperial War Museum, London.

17. Ibid.

18. 'Private Papers of Major A.S.B. Arkwright, MC', Docs. 956, Imperial War Museum, London.

19. Obituary – Air Commodore 'Dim' Strong, *Daily Telegraph*, 7 September 2011.

20. 'Interview with John Hamilton-Baillie', 14781, Reel 2, Imperial War Museum, London.

21. 'Interview with Charles Leighton Irwin', 4847, Reel 2, Imperial War Museum, London.

22. 'Interview with John Hamilton-Baillie', 14781, Reel 2, Imperial War Museum, London.

23. A.S.B. Arkwright, *Return Journey* (London: Seeley, Service & Co. Ltd., 1948), p. 13.

Chapter 2: Trial and Error

1. 'Sketch Map of Oflag VI-B Warburg', 'Account of the Electronic Devices used in Operation Olympia', Docs. 1154, Imperial War Museum, London.

2. 'Account of Operation Olympia' by Major E.W. Few, Docs. 1065, Imperial War Museum, London.

3. Marc H. Stevens, *Escape, Evasion and Revenge* (Barnsley: Pen & Sword Military, 2011), p. 151.

4. Ibid, p. 154.

5. 'HEIN, G F aka STEVENS, P Date of birth: 15.02.1919', HO 405/20069, The National Archives (Public Record Office), Kew.

6. 'Diary of Lieutenant Reg Wood, Middlesex Regiment', 1 January 1942, www.pegasusarchive.org, accessed 10 May 2013.

7. Jack Champ and Colin Burgess, *The Diggers of Colditz* (Kenthurst, NSW: Kangaroo Press, 1997), p. 35.

8. 'Diary of Lieutenant Reg Wood, Middlesex Regiment', 17 March 1942, www.pegasusarchive.org, accessed 10 May 2013.

9. 'Portrait of a Prisoner of War', Durham Light Infantry *Regiment Journal*, June 1966, p. 139.

10. Ibid, p. 140.

11. Ibid, p. 140.

12. 'Diary of Lieutenant Reg Wood, Middlesex Regiment', 10 April 1942, www.pegasusarchive.org, accessed 10 May 2013.

13. Ibid, 17 April 1942.

14. 'Account of Operation Olympia' by Major E.W. Few, Docs. 1065, Imperial War Museum, London.

15. 'Private Papers of Major A.S.B. Arkwright, MC', Docs. 956, Imperial War Museum, London.

16. 'Diary of Lieutenant Reg Wood, Middlesex Regiment', 26 May 1942, www.pegasusarchive.org, accessed 10 May 2013.

17. Transcript of Oral History Recording: Accession No. S00579, 'Crawford, Alexander Douglas "Doug"', Australian War Memorial, Canberra.

Chapter 3: The Wire

1. 'Private Papers of Major A.S.B. Arkwright, MC', Docs. 956, Imperial War Museum, London.

2. 'Portrait of a Prisoner of War', Durham Light Infantry *Regiment Journal*, June 1966, p. 139.

3. Ben Hamilton-Baillie to author, private correspondence, 18 July 2013.

4. A.S.B. Arkwright, *Return Journey* (London: Seeley, Service & Co. Ltd., 1948), p. 18.

5. Ibid, p. 19.

6. Ibid, p. 20.

7. Ibid, p. 20.

8. 'Interview with John Hamilton-Baillie', 14781, Reel 2, Imperial War Museum, London.

9. 'Private Papers of Major A.S.B. Arkwright, MC', Docs. 956, Imperial War Museum, London.

10. Ben Hamilton-Baillie to author, private correspondence, 18 July 2013.

11. A.S.B. Arkwright, *Return Journey* (London: Seeley, Service & Co. Ltd., 1948), p. 27.

12. 'Interview with John Hamilton-Baillie', 14781, Reel 2, Imperial War Museum, London.

13. Ibid.

14. Ibid.

15. Ben Hamilton-Baillie to author, private correspondence, 18 July 2013.

16. 'Interview with John Hamilton-Baillie', 14781, Reel 2, Imperial War Museum, London.

17. Ibid.

18. Malcolm McGregor, *Officers of the Durham Light Infantry, 1758–1958* (The Rifles Office, Durham).

19. Group photo 1st Battalion officers, Belfast, 1929, D/DLI 2/1/278 (105), Durham Record Office.

Chapter 4: Short Circuit

1. 'Account of the Electronic Devices used in Operation Olympia, the Escape from Oflag VI-B, Warburg in 1942' by Major K.A. Searle, Docs. 1154, Imperial War Museum, London.

2. 'Private Papers of Major A.S.B. Arkwright, MC', Docs. 956, Imperial War Museum, London.

3. 'Account of the Electronic Devices used in Operation Olympia, the Escape from Oflag VI-B, Warburg in 1942' by Major K.A. Searle, Docs. 1154, Imperial War Museum, London.

4. Ibid.

5. Ibid.

6. Ibid.

7. 'Account of Operation Olympia' by Major E.W. Few, Docs. 1065, Imperial War Museum, London.

8. 'Account of the Electronic Devices used in Operation Olympia, the Escape from Oflag VI-B, Warburg in 1942' by Major K.A. Searle, Docs. 1154, Imperial War Museum, London.

Chapter 5: Diversions

1. 'Interview with Charles Leighton Irwin', 4847, Reel 3, Imperial War Museum, London.

2. 'Private Papers of Capt. G.P. Bowring, MC, TD', Docs. 11856, Imperial War Museum, London.

3. Hamish Forbes, 'Letter to his Children Telling of His Experiences in the Second World War, 1939–1945', Private Papers of Major Sir Hamish Forbes, MBE, MC, Bt., Docs. 16193, Imperial War Museum, London.

4. 'British Air Ace Describes His Last Trip Over France' by Group Captain Douglas Bader, North American Newspaper Alliance, 3 December 1945.

5. Ibid.

6. 'The Prisoner Story', Royal Monmouthshire Royal Engineers (Militia) Museum, www.monmouthcastlemuseum.org.uk, accessed 17 July 2013.

7. A.S.B. Arkwright, *Return Journey* (London: Seeley, Service & Co. Ltd., 1948), p. 21.

8. Ibid, p. 21.

9. 'British Air Ace Describes His Last Trip Over France' by Group Captain Douglas Bader, North American Newspaper Alliance, 3 December 1945.

10. 'Interview with Charles Leighton Irwin', 4847, Reel 2, Imperial War Museum, London.

11. 'British Air Ace Describes His Last Trip Over France' by Group Captain Douglas Bader, North American Newspaper Alliance, 3 December 1945.

12. 'Private Papers of Capt. G.P. Bowring, MC, TD', Docs. 11856, Imperial War Museum, London.

13. Ibid.

14. Ibid.

15. Ibid.

16. 'Olympia' by Lt. Col. T. Stallard, DSO, MBE, *Silver Bugle*, Spring 1971, p. 24.

17. A.S.B. Arkwright, *Return Journey* (London: Seeley, Service & Co. Ltd., 1948), p. 25.

18. Ibid, p. 25.

19. Ibid, p. 25.

20. 'Account of Operation Olympia' by Major E.W. Few, Docs. 1065, Imperial War Museum, London.

21. 'Private Papers of Major A.S.B. Arkwright, MC', Docs. 956, Imperial War Museum, London.

22. A.S.B. Arkwright, *Return Journey* (London: Seeley, Service & Co. Ltd., 1948), p. 26.

23. Ibid, p. 26.

24. Ibid, p. 26.

25. 'Private Papers of Major A.S.B. Arkwright, MC', Docs. 956, Imperial War Museum, London.

26. 'Diary of Lieutenant Reg Wood, Middlesex Regiment', 31 May 1942, www.pegasusarchive.org, accessed 10 May 2013.

Chapter 6: 'Big X'

1. Ben Hamilton-Baillie to author, private correspondence, 18 July 2013.

2. 'Oflag VI-B Dössel/Warburg', WO208/3290, The National Archives (Public Record Office), Kew.

3. Ibid.

4. Ibid.

5. Ibid.

6. Ibid.

7. Ibid.

8. 'Portrait of a Prisoner of War', Durham Light Infantry *Regiment Journal*, June 1966, p. 138.

9. A.S.B. Arkwright, *Return Journey* (London: Seeley, Service & Co. Ltd., 1948), p. 31.

10. Ibid, p. 31.

11. 'Interview with John Hamilton-Baillie', 14781, Reel 2, Imperial War Museum, London.

Chapter 7: Operation Timber

1. 'Account of Operation Olympia' by Major E.W. Few, Docs. 1065, Imperial War Museum, London.

2. 'Diary of Lieutenant Reg Wood, Middlesex Regiment', 4 March 1942, www.pegasusarchive.org, accessed 13 May 2013.

3. Ibid, 31 March 1942.

4. Ibid, 17 April 1942.

5. Ibid, 26 May 1942.

6. 'Account of Operation Olympia' by Major E.W. Few, Docs. 1065, Imperial War Museum, London.

7. A.S.B. Arkwright, *Return Journey* (London: Seeley, Service & Co. Ltd., 1948), p. 32.

8. 'Account of Operation Olympia' by Major E.W. Few, Docs. 1065, Imperial War Museum, London.

9. A.S.B. Arkwright, *Return Journey* (London: Seeley, Service & Co. Ltd., 1948), p. 34.

10. 'Account of Escape from Oflag VI-B (Dössel/Warburg)' by Captain R.J. Fuller *et al.*, WO208/3290, The National Archives (Public Record Office), Kew.

11. A.S.B. Arkwright, *Return Journey* (London: Seeley, Service & Co. Ltd., 1948), p. 32.

12. 'Private Papers of Major A.S.B. Arkwright, MC', Docs. 956, Imperial War Museum, London.

13. Jack Champ and Colin Burgess, *The Diggers of Colditz* (Kenthurst, NSW: Kangaroo Press, 1997), p. 60.

Chapter 8: Practice Makes Perfect

1. 'Private Papers of Major A.S.B. Arkwright, MC', Docs. 956, Imperial War Museum, London.

2. 'Account of Escape from Oflag VI-B (Dössel/Warburg)' by Captain R.J. Fuller *et al.*, WO208/3290, The National Archives (Public Record Office), Kew.

3. 'Private Papers of Major A.S.B. Arkwright, MC', Docs. 956, Imperial War Museum, London.

4. A.S.B. Arkwright, *Return Journey* (London: Seeley, Service & Co. Ltd., 1948), p. 35.

5. Jack Champ and Colin Burgess, *The Diggers of Colditz* (Kenthurst, NSW: Kangaroo Press, 1997), p. 36.

6. Ibid, p. 36.

7. Ibid, p. 37.

8. Ibid, p. 37.

9. Ibid, p. 38.

10. Ibid, p. 38.

11. 'Account of Operation Olympia' by Major E.W. Few, Docs. 1065, Imperial War Museum, London.

12. Obituary – Lt. Col. Sir Martin Gilliat, *The Independent*, 1 June 1993.
13. 'Private Papers of Colonel L.T. Tomes, OBE', Docs. 12734, Imperial War Museum, London.
14. Jack Champ and Colin Burgess, *The Diggers of Colditz* (Kenthurst, NSW: Kangaroo Press), 1997, p. 39.
15. Ibid, p. 39.
16. Ibid, p. 39.
17. A.S.B. Arkwright, *Return Journey* (London: Seeley, Service & Co. Ltd., 1948), p. 36.
18. Ibid, p. 46.
19. 'Account of Escape from Oflag VI-B (Dössel/Warburg), by Captain R.J. Fuller *et al.*, WO208/3290, The National Archives (Public Record Office), Kew.
20. 'Appendix – Operation Olympia: Order for Crossing by the Four Teams Simultaneously, and "Anchor Men"', Docs. 1065, Imperial War Museum, London.
21. Jack Champ and Colin Burgess, *The Diggers of Colditz* (Kenthurst, NSW: Kangaroo Press), 1997, p. 41.
22. Ibid, p. 41.
23. Ibid, pp. 43–4.
24. Ibid, p. 44.
25. A.S.B. Arkwright, *Return Journey* (London: Seeley, Service & Co. Ltd., 1948), p. 46.
26. Ibid, p. 49.
27. 'Private Papers of Captain G.P. Bowring', Docs. 11856, Imperial War Museum, London.
28. Jack Champ and Colin Burgess, *The Diggers of Colditz* (Kenthurst, NSW: Kangaroo Press), 1997, p. 44.
29. A.S.B. Arkwright, *Return Journey* (London: Seeley, Service & Co. Ltd., 1948), p. 50.
30. 'Private Papers of Colonel L.T. Tomes, OBE', Docs. 12734, Imperial War Museum, London.

Chapter 9: The Road Less Travelled

1. A.S.B. Arkwright, *Return Journey* (London: Seeley, Service & Co. Ltd., 1948), p. 42.
2. Ibid, p. 40.

3. Ibid, p. 41.
4. Transcript of Oral History Recording: Accession No. S00579, 'Crawford, Alexander Douglas "Doug"', 8 May 1989, Australian War Memorial, Canberra.
5. A.S.B. Arkwright, *Return Journey* (London: Seeley, Service & Co. Ltd., 1948), p. 41.
6. Ibid, p. 41.
7. Ibid, pp. 45–6.
8. Aiden Crawley, *Escape from Germany, 1939–45 – Methods of Escape used by RAF Airmen in World War II* (London: The Stationery Office, 2001), p. 84.
9. Ibid, p. 85.
10. Ibid, p. 86.
11. Ibid, p. 87.
12. Ibid, pp. 88–9.
13. A.S.B. Arkwright, *Return Journey* (London: Seeley, Service & Co. Ltd., 1948), p. 38.
14. Ibid, p. 38.
15. Ibid, p. 46.
16. Transcript of Oral History Recording: Accession No. S00579, 'Crawford, Alexander Douglas "Doug"', 8 May 1989, Australian War Memorial, Canberra.
17. Jack Champ and Colin Burgess, *The Diggers of Colditz* (Kenthurst, NSW: Kangaroo Press, 1997), p. 59.
18. Ibid, p. 59.
19. A.S.B. Arkwright, *Return Journey* (London: Seeley, Service & Co. Ltd., 1948), p. 44.
20. Ibid, p. 38.
21. Ibid, p. 39.
22. Transcript of Oral History Recording: Accession No. S00579, 'Crawford, Alexander Douglas "Doug"', 8 May 1989, Australian War Memorial, Canberra.
23. A.S.B. Arkwright, *Return Journey* (London: Seeley, Service & Co. Ltd., 1948), p. 39.
24. 'Private Papers of Major A.S.B. Arkwright, MC', Docs. 956, Imperial War Museum, London.
25. Jack Champ and Colin Burgess, *The Diggers of Colditz* (Kenthurst, NSW: Kangaroo Press, 1997), p. 59.

Chapter 10: Pack Up Your Troubles

1. Jack Champ and Colin Burgess, *The Diggers of Colditz* (Kenthurst, NSW: Kangaroo Press, 1997), p. 60.
2. Ibid, p. 61.
3. 'Diary of Lieutenant Reg Wood, Middlesex Regiment', 8 August 1942, www.pegasusarchive.org, accessed 7 August 2013.
4. 'Private Papers of Major A.S.B. Arkwright, MC', Docs. 956, Imperial War Museum, London.
5. 'Account of the Electronic Devices used in Operation Olympia, the Escape from Oflag VI-B, Warburg in 1942' by Major K.A. Searle, Docs. 1154, Imperial War Museum, London.
6. Ibid.
7. Ibid.
8. Aiden Crawley, *Escape from Germany, 1939–45 – Methods of Escape used by RAF Airmen in World War II* (London: The Stationery Office, 2001), p. 91.
9. Jack Champ and Colin Burgess, *The Diggers of Colditz* (Kenthurst, NSW: Kangaroo Press, 1997), p. 60.
10. 'Appendix – Operation Olympia: Order for Crossing by the Four Teams Simultaneously, and "Anchor Men"', Docs. 1065, Imperial War Museum, London.
11. A.S.B. Arkwright, *Return Journey* (London: Seeley, Service & Co. Ltd., 1948), p. 58.
12. Jack Champ and Colin Burgess, *The Diggers of Colditz* (Kenthurst, NSW: Kangaroo Press, 1997), p. 60.
13. Ibid, pp. 60–61.
14. Ibid, p. 61.
15. 'Olympia' by Lt. Col. T. Stallard, DSO, MBE, *Silver Bugle*, Spring 1971, p. 24.
16. Jack Champ and Colin Burgess, *The Diggers of Colditz* (Kenthurst, NSW: Kangaroo Press, 1997), p. 61.

Chapter 11: Fifteen Yards to Freedom

1. 'Private Papers of Major A.S.B. Arkwright, MC', Docs. 956, Imperial War Museum, London.
2. A.S.B. Arkwright, *Return Journey* (London: Seeley, Service & Co. Ltd., 1948), p. 61.

3. 'The Wire' by David Walker, in J.E.R. Wood (ed.), *Detour: The Story of Oflag IV-C* (London: Falcon Press, 1946), p. 61.

4. A.S.B. Arkwright, *Return Journey* (London: Seeley, Service & Co. Ltd., 1948), p. 62.

5. 'Interview with John Hamilton-Baillie', 14781, Reel 2, Imperial War Museum, London.

6. Jack Champ and Colin Burgess, *The Diggers of Colditz* (Kenthurst, NSW: Kangaroo Press, 1997), p. 61.

7. Ibid, p. 62.

8. Ibid, p. 62.

9. Ibid, p. 63.

10. A.S.B. Arkwright, *Return Journey* (London: Seeley, Service & Co. Ltd., 1948), p. 64.

11. 'Interview with John Hamilton-Baillie', 14781, Reel 2, Imperial War Museum, London.

12. 'Olympia' by Lt. Col. T. Stallard, DSO, MBE, *Silver Bugle*, Spring 1971.

13. 'The Wire' by David Walker, in J.E.R. Wood (ed.), *Detour: The Story of Oflag IV-C* (London: Falcon Press, 1946), p. 61.

14. A.S.B. Arkwright, *Return Journey* (London: Seeley, Service & Co. Ltd., 1948), p. 63.

15. 'Private Papers of Major A.S.B. Arkwright, MC', Docs. 956, Imperial War Museum, London.

16. Jack Champ and Colin Burgess, *The Diggers of Colditz* (Kenthurst, NSW: Kangaroo Press, 1997), p. 63.

17. 'The Wire' by David Walker, in J.E.R. Wood (ed.), *Detour: The Story of Oflag IV-C* (London: Falcon Press, 1946), p. 61.

18. 'Account of the Electronic Devices used in Operation Olympia, the Escape from Oflag VI-B, Warburg in 1942' by Major K.A. Searle, Docs. 1154, Imperial War Museum, London.

19. Ibid.

20. Jack Champ and Colin Burgess, *The Diggers of Colditz* (Kenthurst, NSW: Kangaroo Press, 1997), p. 63.

21. Ibid, p. 64.

22. A.S.B. Arkwright, *Return Journey* (London: Seeley, Service & Co. Ltd., 1948), pp. 66–7.

23. Jack Champ and Colin Burgess, *The Diggers of Colditz* (Kenthurst, NSW: Kangaroo Press, 1997), p. 64.

24. 'The Wire' by David Walker, in J.E.R. Wood (ed.), *Detour: The Story of Oflag IV-C* (London: Falcon Press, 1946), p. 61.
25. Ibid, p. 61.
26. Ibid, p. 61.

Chapter 12: Zero Night
1. 'Account of the Electronic Devices used in Operation Olympia, the Escape from Oflag VI-B, Warburg in 1942' by Major K.A. Searle, Docs. 1154, Imperial War Museum, London.
2. Transcript of Oral History Recording: Accession No. S00579, 'Crawford, Alexander Douglas "Doug"', 8 May 1989, Australian War Memorial, Canberra.
3. 'The Wire' by David Walker, in J.E.R. Wood (ed.), *Detour: The Story of Oflag IV-C* (London: Falcon Press, 1946), p. 62.
4. Ibid, p. 62.
5. A.S.B. Arkwright, *Return Journey* (London: Seeley, Service & Co. Ltd., 1948), p. 67.
6. 'Private Papers of Colonel L.T. Tomes, OBE', Docs. 12734, Imperial War Museum, London.
7. 'Account of Escape from Oflag VI-B (Dössel/Warburg)' by Captain R.J. Fuller *et al.*, WO208/3290, The National Archives (Public Record Office), Kew.
8. A.S.B. Arkwright, *Return Journey* (London: Seeley, Service & Co. Ltd., 1948), p. 67.
9. 'The Wire' by David Walker, in J.E.R. Wood (ed.), *Detour: The Story of Oflag IV-C* (London: Falcon Press, 1946), p. 61.
10. Jack Champ and Colin Burgess, *The Diggers of Colditz* (Kenthurst, NSW: Kangaroo Press, 1997), p. 159.
11. 'The Wire' by David Walker, in J.E.R. Wood (ed.), *Detour: The Story of Oflag IV-C* (London: Falcon Press, 1946), p. 62.
12. Ibid, p.62.
13. Ibid, p. 62.
14. Transcript of Oral History Recording: Accession No. S00579, 'Crawford, Alexander Douglas "Doug"', 8 May 1989, Australian War Memorial, Canberra.
15. A.S.B. Arkwright, *Return Journey* (London: Seeley, Service & Co. Ltd., 1948), p. 67.
16. Ibid, p. 67.

17. Transcript of Oral History Recording: Accession No. S00579, 'Crawford, Alexander Douglas "Doug"', 8 May 1989, Australian War Memorial, Canberra.
18. Jack Champ and Colin Burgess, *The Diggers of Colditz* (Kenthurst, NSW: Kangaroo Press, 1997), p. 65.
19. 'Private Papers of Colonel L.T. Tomes, OBE', Docs. 12734, Imperial War Museum, London.
20. 'The Wire' by David Walker, in J.E.R. Wood (ed.), *Detour: The Story of Oflag IV-C* (London: Falcon Press, 1946), p. 62.
21. 'The Wire' by David Walker, in J.E.R. Wood (ed.), *Detour: The Story of Oflag IV-C* (London: Falcon Press, 1946), p. 62.
22. 'Account of Operation Olympia' by Major E.W. Few, Docs. 1065, Imperial War Museum, London.
23. 'The Wire' by David Walker, in J.E.R. Wood (ed.), *Detour: The Story of Oflag IV-C* (London: Falcon Press, 1946), p. 62.
24. 'Account of the Electronic Devices used in Operation Olympia, the Escape from Oflag VI-B, Warburg in 1942' by Major K.A. Searle, Docs. 1154, Imperial War Museum, London.
25. Ibid.
26. 'The Wire' by David Walker, in J.E.R. Wood (ed.), *Detour: The Story of Oflag IV-C* (London: Falcon Press, 1946), p. 62.
27. Ibid, p. 62.
28. Ibid, p. 62.
29. A.S.B. Arkwright, *Return Journey* (London: Seeley, Service & Co. Ltd., 1948), p. 68.
30. Jack Champ and Colin Burgess, *The Diggers of Colditz* (Kenthurst, NSW: Kangaroo Press, 1997), p. 65.
31. 'Account of Operation Olympia' by Major E.W. Few, Docs. 1065, Imperial War Museum, London.
32. 'Private Papers of Colonel L.T. Tomes, OBE', Docs. 12734, Imperial War Museum, London.
33. 'Account of Operation Olympia' by Major E.W. Few, Docs. 1065, Imperial War Museum, London.
34. A.S.B. Arkwright, *Return Journey* (London: Seeley, Service & Co. Ltd., 1948), p. 68.
35. Jack Champ and Colin Burgess, *The Diggers of Colditz* (Kenthurst, NSW: Kangaroo Press, 1997), p. 66.

36. 'Private Papers of Colonel L.T. Tomes, OBE', Docs. 12734, Imperial War Museum, London.

37. A.S.B. Arkwright, *Return Journey* (London: Seeley, Service & Co. Ltd., 1948), p. 68.

38. 'The Military Cross', WO373/62, The National Archives (Public Record Office), Kew.

39. 'Lt. Brooke Deare Oldman', WO373/64, The National Archives (Public Record Office), Kew

40. Ibid.

41. 'Private Papers of Colonel L.T. Tomes, OBE', Docs. 12734, Imperial War Museum, London.

42. Transcript of Oral History Recording: Accession No. S00579, 'Crawford, Alexander Douglas "Doug"', 8 May 1989, Australian War Memorial, Canberra.

43. 'Private Papers of Major A.S.B. Arkwright, MC', Docs. 956, Imperial War Museum, London.

Chapter 13: 'Another British Evacuation'

1. 'Interview with John Hamilton-Baillie', 14781, Imperial War Museum, London.

2. 'Account of the Electronic Devices used in Operation Olympia, the Escape from Oflag VI-B, Warburg in 1942' by Major K.A. Searle, Docs. 1154, Imperial War Museum, London.

3. Ibid.

4. Jack Champ and Colin Burgess, *The Diggers of Colditz* (Kenthurst, NSW: Kangaroo Press, 1997), p. 67.

5. Ibid, p. 67.

6. Ibid, p. 67.

7. Ibid, p. 67.

8. Ibid, p. 68.

9. 'Account of the Electronic Devices used in Operation Olympia, the Escape from Oflag VI-B, Warburg' in 1942 by Major K.A. Searle, Docs. 1154, Imperial War Museum, London.

10. Ibid.

11. 'Private Papers of Capt. G.P. Bowring, MC, TD', Docs. 11856, Imperial War Museum, London.

12. Ibid.

Chapter 14: A Walk in the Woods

1. 'Private Papers of Colonel L.T. Tomes, OBE', Docs. 12734, Imperial War Museum, London.
2. Ibid.
3. Transcript of Oral History Recording: Accession No. S00579, 'Crawford, Alexander Douglas "Doug"', 8 May 1989, Australian War Memorial, Canberra.
4. 'The Military Cross', WO373/62, The National Archives (Public Record Office), Kew.
5. A.S.B. Arkwright, *Return Journey* (London: Seeley, Service & Co. Ltd., 1948), p. 71.
6. Ibid, pp. 71–2.
7. 'Private Papers of Colonel L.T. Tomes, OBE', Docs. 12734, Imperial War Museum, London.
8. A.S.B. Arkwright, *Return Journey* (London: Seeley, Service & Co. Ltd., 1948), p. 74.
9. Ibid, p. 75.
10. Ibid, p. 75.
11. 'Account of Escape from Oflag VI-B (Dössel/Warburg)' by Captain R.J. Fuller *et al.*, WO208/3290, The National Archives (Public Record Office), Kew.
12. 'Private Papers of Colonel L.T. Tomes, OBE', Docs. 12734, Imperial War Museum, London.
13. Ibid.
14. 'The Military Cross', WO373/62, The National Archives (Public Record Office), Kew.
15. A.S.B. Arkwright, *Return Journey* (London: Seeley, Service & Co. Ltd., 1948), pp. 84–5.
16. 'Account of Escape from Oflag VI-B (Dössel/Warburg)' by Captain R.J. Fuller *et al.*, WO208/3290, The National Archives (Public Record Office), Kew.
17. Transcript of Oral History Recording: Accession No. S00579, 'Crawford, Alexander Douglas "Doug"', 8 May 1989, Australian War Memorial, Canberra.
18. Jack Champ and Colin Burgess, *The Diggers of Colditz* (Kenthurst, NSW: Kangaroo Press, 1997), p. 69.

Chapter 15: '*Hände hoch!*'

1. Transcript of Oral History Recording: Accession No. S00579, 'Crawford, Alexander Douglas "Doug"', 8 May 1989, Australian War Memorial, Canberra.
2. 'Account of Escape from Oflag VI-B (Dössel/Warburg)' by Captain R.J. Fuller *et al.*, WO208/3290, The National Archives (Public Record Office), Kew.
3. A.S.B. Arkwright, *Return Journey* (London: Seeley, Service & Co. Ltd., 1948), p. 86.
4. 'Private Papers of Colonel L.T. Tomes, OBE', Docs. 12734, Imperial War Museum, London.
5. Ibid.
6. Ibid.
7. Ibid.
8. A.S.B. Arkwright, *Return Journey* (London: Seeley, Service & Co. Ltd., 1948), p. 87.
9. 'Private Papers of Colonel L.T. Tomes, OBE', Docs. 12734, Imperial War Museum, London.
10. A.S.B. Arkwright, *Return Journey* (London: Seeley, Service & Co. Ltd., 1948), p. 87.
11. Ibid, p. 88.
12. 'Account of Escape of Capt. A.H.S. Coombe-Tennant, Welsh Guards, Maj. A.S.B. Arkwright, The Royal Scots Fusiliers, Capt. R.J. Fuller, The Royal Sussex Regiment', WO373/62, The National Archives (Public Record Office), Kew.
13. Ibid.
14. Transcript of Oral History Recording: Accession No. S00579, 'Crawford, Alexander Douglas "Doug"', 8 May 1989, Australian War Memorial, Canberra.
15. Jack Champ and Colin Burgess, *The Diggers of Colditz* (Kenthurst, NSW: Kangaroo Press, 1997), p. 70.

Chapter 16: The Bitter Road

1. 'Account of Escape of Capt. A.H.S. Coombe-Tennant, Welsh Guards, Maj. A.S.B. Arkwright, The Royal Scots Fusiliers, Capt. R.J. Fuller, The Royal Sussex Regiment', WO373/62, The National Archives (Public Record Office), Kew.

2. 'Private Papers of Colonel L.T. Tomes, OBE', Docs. 12734, Imperial War Museum, London

3. Ibid.

4. 'Capt. Ronald William Leah', WO373/64, The National Archives (Public Record Office), Kew.

5. 'Account of Operation Olympia' by Major E.W. Few, Docs. 1065, Imperial War Museum, London.

6. Transcript of Oral History Recording: Accession No. S00579, 'Crawford, Alexander Douglas "Doug"', 8 May 1989, Australian War Memorial, Canberra.

7. 'Private Papers of Colonel L.T. Tomes, OBE', Docs. 12734, Imperial War Museum, London.

8. A.S.B. Arkwright, *Return Journey* (London: Seeley, Service & Co. Ltd., 1948), p. 91.

9. Ibid, p. 91.

10. Transcript of Oral History Recording: Accession No. S00579, 'Crawford, Alexander Douglas "Doug"', 8 May 1989, Australian War Memorial, Canberra.

11. Jack Champ and Colin Burgess, *The Diggers of Colditz* (Kenthurst, NSW: Kangaroo Press, 1997), p. 71.

12. Ibid, p. 71.

13. Ibid, p. 71.

14. Ibid, pp. 71–2.

15. 'Private Papers of Colonel L.T. Tomes, OBE', Docs. 12734, Imperial War Museum, London.

16. Ibid.

17. Ibid.

Chapter 17: Three Blind Mice

1. A.S.B. Arkwright, *Return Journey* (London: Seeley, Service & Co. Ltd., 1948), p. 96.

2. 'Account of Escape of Capt. A.H.S. Coombe-Tennant, Welsh Guards, Maj. A.S.B. Arkwright, The Royal Scots Fusiliers, Capt. R.J. Fuller, The Royal Sussex Regiment', WO373/62, The National Archives (Public Record Office), Kew.

3. 'Lt. Brooke Deare Oldman', WO373/64, The National Archives (Public Record Office), Kew.

4. 'Maj. Thomas Stallard, DSO', WO373/100, The National Archives (Public Record Office), Kew.

5. 'Capt. Martin John Gilliat', WO373/103, The National Archives (Public Record Office), Kew.

6. 'Capt. Brochwel Robert Mytton', WO373/100, The National Archives (Public Record Office), Kew.

7. 'Portrait of a Prisoner of War', Durham Light Infantry *Regimental Journal*, June 1966.

8. A.S.B. Arkwright, *Return Journey* (London: Seeley, Service & Co. Ltd., 1948), p. 92.

9. Ibid, p. 95.

10. Ibid, p. 97.

11. Ibid, p. 97.

12. 'Account of Escape of Capt. A.H.S. Coombe-Tennant, Welsh Guards, Maj. A.S.B. Arkwright, The Royal Scots Fusiliers, Capt. R.J. Fuller, The Royal Sussex Regiment', WO373/62, The National Archives (Public Record Office), Kew.

13. A.S.B. Arkwright, *Return Journey* (London: Seeley, Service & Co. Ltd., 1948), p. 97.

14. 'Account of Escape of Capt. A.H.S. Coombe-Tennant, Welsh Guards, Maj. A.S.B. Arkwright, The Royal Scots Fusiliers, Capt. R.J. Fuller, The Royal Sussex Regiment', WO373/62, The National Archives (Public Record Office), Kew.

15. Ibid.

16. A.S.B. Arkwright, *Return Journey* (London: Seeley, Service & Co. Ltd., 1948), p. 106.

17. Ibid, p. 106.

18. Ibid, p. 109.

19. 'Account of Escape of Capt. A.H.S. Coombe-Tennant, Welsh Guards, Maj. A.S.B. Arkwright, The Royal Scots Fusiliers, Capt. R.J. Fuller, The Royal Sussex Regiment', WO373/62, The National Archives (Public Record Office), Kew.

20. A.S.B. Arkwright, *Return Journey* (London: Seeley, Service & Co. Ltd., 1948), p. 110.

21. Ibid, p. 112.

22. Ibid, p. 113.

23. 'Account of Escape of Capt. A.H.S. Coombe-Tennant, Welsh Guards, Maj. A.S.B. Arkwright, The Royal Scots Fusiliers,

Capt. R.J. Fuller, The Royal Sussex Regiment', WO373/62,
The National Archives (Public Record Office), Kew.

24. A.S.B. Arkwright, *Return Journey* (London: Seeley, Service &
Co. Ltd., 1948), p. 115.

25. Ibid, p. 117.

26. Ibid, p. 121.

27. Ibid, p. 123.

Chapter 18: Comet Line

1. A.S.B. Arkwright, *Return Journey* (London: Seeley, Service &
Co. Ltd., 1948), p. 165.

2. Ibid, p. 128.

3. Ibid, p. 130.

4. Ibid, p. 134.

5. 'Private Papers of Major A.S.B. Arkwright, MC', Docs. 956,
Imperial War Museum, London.

6. A.S.B. Arkwright, *Return Journey* (London: Seeley, Service &
Co. Ltd., 1948), p. 141.

7. Ibid, p. 144.

8. Airey Neave, *Saturday at MI9* (Barnsley: Pen & Sword Books,
2010), p. 128.

9. Ibid, p. 129.

10. Ibid, p. 129.

11. A.S.B. Arkwright, *Return Journey* (London: Seeley, Service &
Co. Ltd., 1948), p. 151.

12. Ibid, p. 163.

13. Ibid, p. 171.

14. Ibid, p. 171.

15. Ibid, p. 175.

16. 'Private Papers of Major A.S.B. Arkwright, MC', Docs. 956,
Imperial War Museum, London.

17. A.S.B. Arkwright, *Return Journey* (London: Seeley, Service &
Co. Ltd., 1948), p. 182.

18. 'Account of Escape of Capt. A.H.S. Coombe-Tennant, Welsh
Guards, Maj. A.S.B. Arkwright, The Royal Scots Fusiliers,
Capt. R.J. Fuller, The Royal Sussex Regiment', WO373/62,
The National Archives (Public Record Office), Kew.

19. Ibid.

Chapter 19: The Last Frontier

1. A.S.B. Arkwright, *Return Journey* (London: Seeley, Service & Co. Ltd., 1948), p. 183.
2. 'Account of Escape of Capt. A.H.S. Coombe-Tennant, Welsh Guards, Maj. A.S.B. Arkwright, The Royal Scots Fusiliers, Capt. R.J. Fuller', The Royal Sussex Regiment, WO373/62, The National Archives (Public Record Office), Kew.
3. Ibid.
4. A.S.B. Arkwright, *Return Journey* (London: Seeley, Service & Co. Ltd., 1948), p. 183.
5. Account of Escape of Capt. A.H.S. Coombe-Tennant, Welsh Guards, Maj. A.S.B. Arkwright, The Royal Scots Fusiliers, Capt. R.J. Fuller, The Royal Sussex Regiment, WO373/62, The National Archives (Public Record Office), Kew.
6. A.S.B. Arkwright, *Return Journey* (London: Seeley, Service & Co. Ltd., 1948), p. 188.
7. John Nichol and Tony Rennell, *Home Run: Escape from Nazi Europe* (London: Penguin, 2007), p. 470.
8. A.S.B. Arkwright, *Return Journey* (London: Seeley, Service & Co. Ltd., 1948), p. 192.
9. Ibid, p. 192.
10. Ibid, p. 194.
11. Airey Neave, *Saturday at MI9* (Barnsley: Pen & Sword Books, 2010), p. 138.
12. Ibid, pp. 137–8.
13. A.S.B. Arkwright, *Return Journey* (London: Seeley, Service & Co. Ltd., 1948), p. 197.
14. Airey Neave, *Saturday at MI9* (Barnsley: Pen & Sword Books, 2010), p. 139.
15. A.S.B. Arkwright, *Return Journey* (London: Seeley, Service & Co. Ltd., 1948), p. 202.
16. Ibid, p. 205.

Index

51st Highland Division 4, 5, 37, 38

207 Squadron 97

Aachen 203, 214

air raids 22, 27, 66

  aircrew losses in 72

Altenbeken 180, 183

Amsterdam 221

anchor men 96, 100, 152

Anglet 252

Appell parade 56–8

Arkwright, Albert

  background 2

  backpack 119

  Belgium 227, 230–41, 243–6

  clothing 119–21

  and diversions 59–60, 62–7, 102–3

  and escape plans 30–2, 35–6, 39–41

  escape route 117

  and food for journey 108–9

  France 247–54

  German freedom

    30 Aug–1 Sep 174–6, 178–80, 182–4

    2–4 Sep 187–8, 191, 194–6

    5 Sep onwards 199–200, 203, 205

  Holland 213–14, 215–25, 228–30

  later life 255

  and perimeter lights control 43

  Spain 254

  and timber raid 81, 87

  and training programme 92–3, 96, 99, 104

  on Zero Day 134, 138–40, 143, 145

  on Zero Night 148–51, 154–5, 158–9, 161–2

backpacks 119

Bader, Douglas 24, 26, 57, 59–60

Baillet-Latour, Henri de 252

Baisieux 240, 243–6

Bartlett, Dennis 149, 203, 262

Baxter, Rex

  after recapture 165–7

  escape route 117

  escape attempts 5

  later life 255

  and training programme 94–5, 98–100

  on Zero Day 138, 140, 143

  on Zero Night 149–51, 154–6

Bayonne 250

BBC broadcasts 72
Belgium 227, 230–41, 243–6
Bessel-Browne, Ian 76, 78
Beverungen 188–9
Bidassoa, River 252, 253–4
Bielefeld 199–200
Bilbao 231–2
'The Blue One' 225, 230
bluff 19–21
Bornholm 205
Borwick, Michael 133, 136
Bowring, G.P. 60–1, 169
Brinkord, Oberst 102, 124–5,
    163–5, 168
Brockway, Pilot Officer 72
Bruce, Dominic 20, 26
Brussels 238–40, 247, 251
Buchan, John (Lord
    Tweedsmuir) 38
Burgdorf 206
Butsbach 114

Calais 97
'Camp Police' 141
Campbell-Preston, Pat
  as code-letter writer 76
  later life 262
  recapture 182, 184
  on Zero Night 147, 151–4,
    157, 160
Cavell, Edith 232
Celle 206, 210–11
Champ, Jack
  after recapture 165–7
  clothing 121
  escape attempts 5
  escape route 117
  later life 255

  and training programme
    94–5, 98–100
  vision of ensnarement 123
  on Zero Day 138, 140, 143–4
  on Zero Night 149, 151, 154–6
Charlemagne, Emperor 189
'The Chief' 227, 236–7
children, German 176–7, 199
chocolate, discovery of 107–8
Christie, Hector 56
'The Circuit' 43, 104
climbing apparatuses 36–41,
    75–7, 137–8
clothing, escapers' 119–21
cobbler's hut 45–54, 126–7, 142,
    147, 153, 167–8
Colditz 255, 257, 258, 261, 262
Cologne 66
Comet Line 225, 231–41, 243–
    54, 259, 260
compasses 119
Coombe-Tennant, Henry
    (Arkwright's group)
  Belgium 227, 230–41, 243–6
  and escape preparations 35–6,
    100, 127
  France 247–54
  German freedom
    30 Aug–1 Sep 174–6,
      178–80, 182–4
    2–4 Sep 187–8, 191,
      194–6
    5 Sep onwards 199–200,
      203, 205
  Holland 213–14, 215–25,
    228–30
  later life 255–6
  Spain 254

on Zero Night 151, 154–5,
158–9, 161–2
Corfield, Fred
escape route 118
German freedom
30 Aug–1 Sep 171–2,
177–8, 180–1
2–4 Sep 188–90, 191–4
5 Sep onwards 200–1,
203–5, 206, 210
later life 256
recapture 210–11
on Zero Night 151, 155, 157–
8, 159–60
Courenne, Madame 236–7
Cousens, Johnnie
background 41
as 'Controller' 131
and diversions 41–2, 58, 61–3,
65–6, 79, 103
later life 256–7
and perimeter lights control
127
on Zero Day 140–1
on Zero Night 147, 148, 152
Crawford, Doug
after recapture 199, 204,
205–9
escape attempts xvii–xix, 5, 32
escape route 118
German freedom 173, 184–5
later life 256
recapture 187, 196–8
tailoring 120
and training programme 99
on Zero Day 138–9, 144
on Zero Night 147, 149–52,
156–7, 160–1

Crawford, Rae 173
Crete 4, 207
Cromar, James 232
Cruickshank, George 39, 93, 133,
136

De Greef see Greef
De Jongh see Jongh
Dédée see Jongh, Andrée De
'Deep Field' 15–16, 35, 77, 131,
153, 156–7
Dining Hut No. 2 81, 83–8
diphtheria 10
'The Doctor' 219–20, 223–4
Döhren, Georg von 184
Doren 205
Dössel 110
Dunkirk 2, 168, 221, 261
Dupree, John 136–8
Dutch Underground 213, 219–
24, 228

Eden, H.C.H. 11, 12, 69
Eichstätt 124, 127, 217, 258, 260,
262
Elizabeth, Queen, The Queen
Mother 257
Elze 200–1
Enschede 190, 214
Eppink, J.H. 218–22
Escape Committee 69–70
and bluff 19–20
and Few 'escape' 25
final go-ahead 137
importance 75
and perimeter lights control
46–8, 51–2, 54
provisional go-ahead 75–8

Escape Committee *(continued)*
  and training programme 99
  and wire plan 35–42
escape materials, smuggling of
  73–4
escape routes 109–11, 117–19
Eschershausen 193–4, 200

Falkenhausen, Alexander, Baron
  von 238
'ferrets' 82–3
Few, Maurice 1, 11, 25–6
Filmer, C.H. 21
fire-lighting 178–9
food, hoarding 108
Forbes, Hamish 13, 56
forgery 74–5
Fortune, Victor 5, 12, 70
France 247–54
Frank, Anne 221
French POWs 225, 228–34
Fuller, Rupert (Arkwright's
  group)
  Belgium 227, 230–41, 243–6
  clothing 119–21
  and crossing fences 35–6
  and diversions 62–7, 102–3
  escape route 117
  and food for journey 108–9
  France 247–54
  German freedom
    30 Aug–1 Sep 174–6,
     178–80, 182–4
    2–4 Sep 187–8, 191, 194–6
    5 Sep onwards 199–200,
     203, 205
  Holland 213–14, 215–25,
    228–30

later life 257
Spain 254
substitute for 134
and training programme
  92–3, 99, 104
on Zero Day 134, 138, 140
on Zero Night 149, 151, 154–
  5, 158–9, 161–2

Geelong 143
Geneva Convention 208
George VI, King 261
Gestapo 198, 206–9, 218–20, 223
  in Belgium 227–8, 235–8
Gilliat, Martin
  background 97
  German freedom
    30 Aug–1 Sep 173
    2–4 Sep 190
    5 Sep onwards 203
  later life 257
  recapture 214
  and training programme 97–8
  on Zero Night 157
Gilroy, C.B. 73
Ginn, Skelly 32
Glemnitz, Hermann 59
'Goons' 100
Goorhuis, P.J. 228–30
Graham, Bert 47–8
grapnels 96, 102–3, 148
Great Escape 74
Greef, Elvire De ('Tante Go')
  250–1
Greef, Fernand De 250
Greef, Freddy De 250
Greef, Janine De 250
Greindl, Jean ('Nemo') 247

Grimm, Brothers 185
Groenen, Madame 231, 233
Groenen, Michel 233
Gronau in Westfalen 190, 214
guardroom 163–9

Hager, Leutnant 11–12, 55–60,
    66
Halle 200
Hamburg 173
Hamelin 189
Hamilton-Baillie, Jock
    background 37
    climbing apparatuses 36–41,
        75–7, 137–8
    'Deep Field' observation 35
    and escape attempts 4, 11–13,
        15–16, 26, 111
    and Hut 13 tunnel 135–8
    later life 258
    and timber raid 82–5
    and training programme 92
    war injuries 97
Hand, Jack
    escape route 118
    on Zero Day 138–9
    on Zero Night 147, 150, 152,
        156–7
Hannover 203
Henri (St-Jean-de-Luz) 250–1
Herbert Johnson Ltd 120
Hohenwepel 158
Holland 213–25
Holzminden 193
Hopetoun, Charlie, Earl of 56–7
Hörstel-Riesenbeck 214
Howard, Mark 140
Höxter 118, 189–90

Hunt, Lieutenant 155, 159–60,
    190–1, 201–3
Hut 13 133, 135–8
Hut 20 130, 141–5, 147–8
Hut 21 130, 141–5, 147–8
Hut 27 138–9, 140–1
Hut 28 138–9, 140–1
Hyde, Noel 97, 203, 214, 258–9

intelligence 70–2
Irwin, Charles 55, 60

'Jan' 222–5, 228–30
Jean (Basque) 253–4
Jeanne (Liège) 237
Johnson, Albert ('B') 251–2
Johnston, Johnnie 137, 150
Jongh, Andrée De (Dédée) 231–
    3, 243, 247–8, 251–4, 259
Jongh, Frédéric De 232, 247, 259

Karlsrühe 115
Kassel 8, 110, 117, 185
    jail 204
Kayll, J.R. 72, 156, 167
Kennedy, 'Bush' 18, 21
Kennedy, G.W. 12, 57–8, 70, 83,
    124, 137
Kiel 97
Kommandantur 71

ladders see climbing apparatuses
Landesschützen Bataillon 255
    58–9
Laufen 3, 4, 220
Leah, Ronald 173, 201
Legrelle, Jacques ('Jérôme') 247
Lehrte 205

Lengerich 214
Leyden, Private 174
Liège 227, 234–5
Lille 240, 247
Lübeck 4, 19
Lüneburg 214

Macleod, 'Jumbo' 32–3, 35, 145
'Madame' 224, 228–9
Maeseyck 234
maps 73, 118–19
Massey, Lionel 61
Matilde (Liège) 237
McDonnell, James 22–4, 176
Melsome, Robert ('I') 47, 70–3,
      78, 169
   background 70–1
   debriefing of RAF escapers
      116–17
   later life 259
MI6 255–6
MI9 71–3, 118, 232
Morrice, Squadron Leader 32
Morris, Flight Lieutenant 156,
      167
Moulson, Ron
   after escape 165, 167–8
   and perimeter lights control
      48–54, 126, 142–3, 147, 153
Mountbatten, Lord 257
Münster 27, 117, 160, 184, 201
music 92
music room 92
Mytton, Brockie 56, 203, 214, 262

Nagold 115
nails 88–9
Neave, Airey 227

Nothomb, Jean-François
      ('Franco') 247, 253, 260

occupied nations, as escape route
      111
Oflag VI-B
   arrival 2–9
   conditions 10–11
   dissolution 124, 217
   guards 58–9
   jurisdiction 184
   later history 260
   surroundings 110
Oflag VII-B 124, 130, 217
Oflag VII-C 3, 220
Oflag VIII-F 262
Oflag IX-A 12
Oflag IX-A/H 160
Oldenzaal 223
Oldman, Brooke 155, 159–60,
      191, 201–3, 214, 262
Onderduikers 220, 221
Operation Olympia, provisional
      dates set 101–2
Osnabrück 117, 214
'other ranks' prisoners 45

Paderborn 8, 162
Page, Dick
   escape with Stallard and
      McDonnell 22–4
   German freedom
      30 Aug–1 Sep 176–7, 179
      2–4 Sep 190
      5 Sep onwards 203
   recapture 214
   and training programme 100
   on Zero Night 154, 157, 158

Palmer, 'Prince' 18, 20
parcels, escape materials in 73–4
Pardoe, Phil
    and diversions 56–7
    German freedom
        30 Aug–1 Sep 173
        2–4 Sep 190
        5 Sep onwards 203
    later life 260–1
    recapture 214
    on Zero Night 157
Paris 247–9
Philby, Kim 256
Piaf, Edith 236
prison camp papers 74–5
punishments 125
Pyrenees 251–4

'Q' Department 73, 118, 120, 174

Rademacher, Hauptmann 7,
    82–3
    and escapers 164–9
    and music room 92–3, 101
    and punishments 125
    searches 7, 66, 82, 168–9
    on Zero Day 139–40
Radford, W. 72
radio 72, 169
RAF escapers
    experiences 111–16
    lessons from 116–17
Red Cross parcels, string from
    88–9
Reichswald 184
Rommel, Erwin 37
rope 88–9
Ross (Team 2) 145

Rossum 223
Rotenburg an der Fulda 124
Royal Army Ordnance Corps
    (RAOC) 43–4
Rügen 205
Russell, Steve
    and climbing apparatus 39
    and training programme 93,
        96, 99
    on Zero Day 139, 144
    on Zero Night 147, 150
Russian camp 60–1
Russian POW ('Stalin') 248–9,
    253

Saint-Valery-en-Caux 37
Salle, Madame de la 234
Salonika 4
scaling apparatuses 36–41, 75–7,
    137–8
Schwaney 180, 182
scrounging 21
Searle, Ken
    after escape 163, 165, 167–8
    and perimeter lights control
        43–54, 126–7, 142–3, 147,
        153
Slim, William 257
'The Soldier' 224
Somerset, Nigel 70
Spain 231–2, 251–4
Spangenburg 160
sports 91, 103–4
St-Jean-de-Luz 232, 249–52
Stalag Luft III 14, 74
Stallard, Tom
    after recapture 217
    background 2–3

Stallard, Tom *(continued)*
  briefing 130–1
  and diversions 65–6, 79
  Escape Committee
    discussions 75–8
  and escape date choice
    125–31
  escape with Page and
    McDonnell 22–4
  and escape travel planning
    116–19
  German freedom
    30 Aug–1 Sep 176–7, 179
    2–4 Sep 190
    5 Sep onwards 203
  later life 261
  presentation of plan 29–42
  recapture 214–15
  substitute for 134
  and timber raid 82–9
  and training programme 91,
    93–5, 98–100, 103–5
  on Underground movement
    213
  on Zero Day 134–5, 137–8,
    140, 144
  on Zero Night 152–5, 157,
    158
Stevens, Peter 19–21, 75
Stralsund 205
Strong, 'Dim' 14
Stürtzkopf, Oberst 6–7, 8, 24,
    58, 102
  and sports 91, 103–4
substitutes 125–6, 134
'suicide jobs' 75
Sweden, as escape destination
    111

Swinburn, H.R. 10, 71, 81
Switzerland, as escape
    destination 110–11
Syngem 72

'tail-end Charlies' *see* anchor men
tailors 120
Team 1
  composition 128
  on Zero Night 148–51, 155
Team 2
  composition 128
  on Zero Night 147–50
Team 3
  composition 128
  on Zero Night 149–52, 155–6
Team 4
  composition 128–9
  on Zero Night 147–52,
    156–7
'Toasters' 11
Tomes, Dick
  escape route 118
  German freedom
    30 Aug–1 Sep 171–2,
    177–8, 180–1
    2–4 Sep 188–90, 191–4
    5 Sep onwards 200–1,
    203–5, 206, 210
  later life 261
  recapture 210–11
  and training programme 97,
    104
  on Warburg camp 17
  on Zero Night 148, 151, 155,
    157–8, 159–60
Tongerlo 233
training programme 91–104

Trelleborg 205
tunnels
    discovery 82–3
    early attempts 13–15
    tragedy 133, 135–8
Tunstall, Peter 20

Utrecht 229

Walenn, Gilbert 'Tim' 74
Walker, David
    background 38
    and briefing 130, 131
    later life 261–2
    recapture 182, 184
    on Stallard 69
    and timber raid 84
    and training programme 78,
        91, 93, 96, 98, 100–1
    on Zero Day 135, 144–5
    on Zero Night 147–8, 149–54,
        157, 160
Warburg 110, 117
    see also Oflag VI-B

water containers 174–5
Wavell, Earl 262
Weert 229–30
Wehrkreis VI 184
Weldon, Frank 137
Weser, River 188–9
Wildberg 115
Wilhelms 185
Willebadessen 174, 175
wire job, plan 29–42
Wylie, Ken ('Big X') 12, 25,
        46–8, 51, 65–70, 75–8
    and training programme 99

'X' Committee see Escape
    Committee
'X' Organisation 69–70

Young, Ken 61
Young, R.M. 100, 149, 201

Zero Day 129–30, 133–45
Zero Hour 138, 141–2
Zero Night 147–62